Praise for *The Path to a Meaningful Purpose* by Luis A. Marrero

"*The Path to a Meaningful Purpose* is a much needed solution to the broader social disillusionment and disengagement epidemic, including in the work environment. The combination of thorough research and extension of compassion provides direction for people who long for a better understanding of themselves and to have a life full of meaning and purpose. I look forward to learning more from Luis and to be inspired by his premise that achieving our potential is not a pipedream but can be a practical reality." — Betsy Jordyn, Founder of The Consultant's Institute and CEO of Accelera Consulting Group, Orlando, Florida

"This book will prove to be a seminal contribution in the coming personal-fulfillment movement. Luis Marrero has created a powerful way to give wings to the purpose alignment challenge that will increasingly mark the internet age. Here comes everybody." — Dave Guerra, author of Superperformance, and The Superperforming CEO: Liberating the Promise Within. Houston, Texas

"I've worked side by side with Luis Marrero for several years and witnessed his passion and process for meaningful purpose. His book brings multiple disciplines together to create the fundamental approach to find one's true potential and singular purpose. Luis lives what he teaches."— Andra Brooks, Ph.D., Managing Director, Nsight 2 Success, Austin, Texas

"*The Path to a Meaningful Purpose* is a refreshing new look at the meaning of our identities, meaning of life and our human condition. Mr. Marrero looks in a grand new way at the nature of identity and the way we set our goals. Eventually this affects our status and state in society. *The Path to a Meaningful Purpose* is a must read for those interested in setting goals and understanding identity." — Paul Homsy MD, MPH, Psychiatrist, Copperfield Psychiatry, Houston, Texas

The Path
to a Meaningful Purpose

Psychological Foundations
of Logoteleology

Luis A. Marrero, MA, RODP

iUniverse LLC
Bloomington

THE PATH TO A MEANINGFUL PURPOSE
PSYCHOLOGICAL FOUNDATIONS OF LOGOTELEOLOGY

iUniverse books may be ordered through booksellers or by contacting:

iUniverse LLC
1663 Liberty Drive
Bloomington, IN 47403
www.iuniverse.com
1-800-Authors (1-800-288-4677)

ISBN: 978-1-4759-8639-6 (sc)
ISBN: 978-1-4759-8641-9 (hc)
ISBN: 978-1-4759-8640-2 (ebk)

Library of Congress Control Number: 2013909447

Printed in the United States of America

iUniverse rev. date: 08/02/2013

This book is dedicated to my parents, Roberto and Virginia Marrero.

Contents

List of Illustrations

Preface

For more than twenty years I have been a student of psychology on a quest to discover what makes us human and to what meaningful end. I have been particularly interested in learning about the role of purpose, motivation, and meaning in an identity and how each of these influences decision making and choice selection. I am intrigued by how we become who we are, and why our paths take a particular course. Some paths lead to a life of success and realization, some where people get by, while others end in tragic and ruinous conditions.

To understand the reasons behind such starkly different outcomes, an obvious foundational starting point for me was to study the works of Viktor Frankl's logotherapy. I was also heavily influenced by Alfred Adler's Individual Psychology and his view on meaning. Loyola University at Chicago's Joseph Rychlack's formulation on the fundamental teleological view of human beings, where he discusses concepts such as intention, purpose, and free will, was instrumental in deepening my understanding of self-directed mental operations. I was also aided by psychiatrist Dale Mathers's work on the role of meaning and purpose in analytical psychology, and University of Rochester's Edward L. Deci and Richard M. Ryan on self-determination theory. These and other resources allowed me to conceptualize a scheme where I could explain how meanings influence motivation and eventually purpose. Dr. Carol Dweck's work on self-theories was particularly helpful in my understanding of the role of motivation on behavior. With my new understanding owed to these and other researchers and authors, a clearer concept of meaningful purpose evolved. I call this concept logoteleology (lōgō—tel-ee-**ol**-*uh*-jee), or the science of meaningful purpose.

While influenced by the above-mentioned schools of thought, I like to think of logoteleology as primarily offshoots of **existential analysis** or **logotherapy,** and **teleology**. While logoteleology draws from established and sound psychological concepts and practices, it is also unique and different in a number of ways. For instance, logoteleology distinguishes and treats *purpose, motivation,* and *meaning* as three separate but interactive mental functions. I must also state that my approach through this book is not to disprove and challenge others' theories as wrong; rather, my goal and resolve is to offer a framework that is valuable, relevant, and meaningful.

This volume presents the psychological foundations of logoteleology. Its mantra is *to enable people to succeed in their higher purpose.* It is scholarly work. It also assumes the reader is versed in basic psychology. However, it is my hope that the definitions and writing style make the reading understandable to those with limited knowledge in psychology. I have added definitions throughout the book to assist in the understanding and interpretation of concepts.

This first volume is particularly important to me because I feel responsible for how the content can influence behavior in others. It is my desire that readers of future books know that logoteleology can be trusted because it is well researched, and it is a carefully thought-out method. My goal is to present practical solutions based on good science, not clever opinions and hearsay. I am not interested in theory for its own sake. Theories without solutions are meaningless. I am a pragmatist who cares to find and propose answers to real-world problems at every level.

Thus, in this volume, the heavy reliance on research is deliberate. Future books will rely on the findings reported on this introductory work and as a result will have fewer quotes and citations. It is my wish that future readers, who might want to know on what basis I make claims and recommendations, will find answers in this first volume and its updated versions. Once the psychological foundations are explained, future books in the planned anthology will deal with specific subjects, such as its broader and practical application to individual and group development, the improvement of organization performance and leadership, and others.

I also make clear throughout the volume where concepts are works in progress, and have encouraged further research and testing to ensure validity and usefulness. It is my hope that others will also build on this foundational work.

Basic Propositions

An aspirational theory demands operating propositions or axioms. These fundamental principles or propositions are shared here and explained throughout the book. Specifically, logoteleology proposes that:

1. *People strive for meaning.* I agree with Frankl "that man's main concern is not to seek pleasure or to avoid pain but rather to find a meaning to his life."[1] Nor do I disagree with Adler's Individual Psychology's basic proposition that humans strive "from a minus situation towards a plus situation, from a feeling of inferiority towards superiority, perfection, totality" or with what Frankl described as the pursuit of power. I believe that since a child can be forced into a premature and forced decision regarding his or her identity and style of life, the potential autonomous path of a life with meaning is thwarted and distorted into unauthentic and subconscious scripts. Logoteleology proposes that as an adult, the individual is tasked with finding, creating, or inventing meaning in order to regain autonomy and control over his or her life.

2. *All meaning-fulfillment is social, transcendental, or other-directed and required for social and psychological adjustment.* I believe all

1 Viktor Frankl, *Psychotherapy and Existentialism*, (New York: Pocket Books, 1967), 38

meaningful actions and healthy mental states are accomplished through dealings that benefit others. Being meaningful, in simple terms, comes from being outwardly oriented versus inwardly oriented.

3. *Telos (Purpose or Ends), Thelos (Will), and Logo (Meaning or Reason) are three distinct mental functions in a psychological system called identity.* As separate and distinct functions each can be individually and collectively studied, diagnosed, and helped.

4. *Meanings precede purpose.* The role of purpose is to fulfill meanings.

5. *Will responds to and is energized by the degree of meaningfulness of an outcome.*

6. *Humans are teleological or purpose-driven.* "We are goal-authors and goal-directors."[2] Much of our behavior is directional and goal fulfilling. Who we are and what we have accomplished in life are the outcomes of our intentions.

7. *Individuals are generally not aware of their own teleology.* Many people are not aware that a lot of behavior is goal driven and directional, nor are they cognizant of how their hidden scripted drives or introjects influence their behavior. This proposition is consistent with that of Alfred Adler. "Adler's goal concept is characterized particularly by the fact that the individual is largely unaware of his goal, that it is a hidden or unconscious goal, a goal which the individual does not understand. It is the true nature of the individual's hidden goal which constitutes, according to Adler, the essential content of the unconscious."[3]

8. *Maladjustment is characterized by two features: the absence of*

---

2 Bogdan, Radu J., *Grounds for Cognition* (Hillsdale, New Jersey: Lawrence Erlbaum Associates, Inc, 1994), 123.

3 Ansbacher, Heinz L. and Ansbacher, Rowena R., ed, *The Individual Psychology of Alfred Adler* (Basic Books; First Edition, First Printing edition, 1956), 89.

a clear life purpose and/or a defining meaning. Adjustment is defined as having a clear life purpose that achieves something meaningful. I believe that the confidence resulting from a meaningful purpose is at the heart of successful living.

9. *Creating meaningful purpose requires conscious decision making and choice.* Selecting a meaningful life purpose is an intentional act rather than a scripted (introjected) decision made in early childhood. Authentic purpose formation is self-selected versus imposed by subconscious, archaic, ineffective, and thus many times unwanted introjects.

10. *The individual's meanings—conscious or not—influences every psychological process.* I agree with Adler's Individual Psychology that it is important "to understand that mysterious creative power of life which expresses itself in the desire to develop, to strive, to achieve, and even to compensate for defeats in one direction by striving for success in another. This power is *teleological,* it expresses itself in the striving after a goal, and, in this striving, every bodily and psychological movement is made to cooperate."[4]

11. *In the absence of an intentional purpose, subconscious scripted drives influence behavior.* We are the end we pursue. We cannot avoid but to strive toward an end. Adler stated, "A person would not know what to do with himself were he not oriented toward some goal. We cannot think, feel, will, or act without the perception of some goal."[5]

12. *There is a tension between the authentic, consciously intended purpose and the unauthentic, scripted subconscious purpose.* Conscious intentions can and are challenged by hidden and more powerful purposes. Logoteleology helps individuals discover these hidden inner purposes, understand the meaning

4 Ibid., 92.
5 Ibid., 96.

they pursue, and replace the archaic and obstructive meaning with a healthier alternative.

13. *There are answers to life's challenges through meaningful purpose.* I optimistically believe answers to individual and social problems exist; and where absent, solutions can be found and even invented. Moreover, I believe life calls each person to answer those questions posed by life.

14. *We have three authentic tasks to fulfill in life: to allow, to cooperate, and to transcend.* Meaningful behavior includes caring for others, fostering peace and peace of mind, encouraging the state of happiness, nurturing creative and interesting situations, and generating prosperity.

It is my sincere hope that this first volume of a planned anthology will deepen understanding and provide answers to our most fundamental existential questions. More importantly, it is my desire that the concepts covered here have a transformational impact on the reader, as they have proven to do so in preliminary exposure and trials.

Luis A. Marrero, MA, RODP
Houston, Texas

Acknowledgments

Cultivate the habit of being grateful for every good thing that comes to you, and to give thanks continuously. And because all things have contributed to your advancement, you should include all things in your gratitude.—Ralph Waldo Emerson

This book would not have been possible without the assistance, feedback, and encouragement of dear friends, colleagues, and family. I am indebted to Cathy D'Eramo, Nahir Rivera, Dan Persuitte, Jonathan D. Marrero, Christian C. Marrero, Christopher L. Marrero, Ariana Stern Luna, Dave Guerra, Betsy Jordyn, Dr. Andra Brooks, Jennifer Walker, Tomas Morell, and Dr. Paul T. Homsey for providing invaluable insight and recommendations for improving the content of this book. However, I take full responsibility for errors and omissions.

I thank my wife, Nahir Marrero, for her support and patience these past few years, particularly for allowing me to invest weeknights and weekends researching and writing this book.

I am profoundly grateful to Khalil Rivera for his artwork on the cover and some of the graphics of this book.

I am as well thankful to clients and students from whom I learned so much as I tested and improved the theories and models discussed in this book. I too want to recognize Karen West, my YSC, Ltd. partner, who back in 2009 believed in me and in the potential contribution of logoteleology.

I look forward to making new friends and being part of a growing community dedicated to improving our world through meaningful purpose.

Chapter 1: What Brought Us Together?

You are probably reading this book because we share a common interest in answering four questions:

- Who am I?
- What matters in life?
- Why am I here?
- How do I go about fulfilling my life's purpose?

For me, these are more than philosophical or metaphysical questions. These questions and their answers, I believe, are at the core of people's quality of life and their very real and practical *now and in this moment* needs and wants. They impact people's state of happiness, their peace of mind, their capacity to relate well with others, the degree to which life is experienced as challenging and interesting, and whether or not they are prosperous. These questions surfaced many years ago when I faced unexpected personal and professional challenges—all hitting me at the same time—and I was restlessly trying to make sense of what was happening. I was blessed in many ways, yet there was something wrong and I knew it. Upon facing such challenges I suddenly encountered feelings of emptiness and frustration, and I was hungry for answers, for a way out.

This brings me to the beginning of my story, which starts with a search for answers in a bookstore.

A Café Mocha and No Whipped Cream

As stated in the acknowledgments, my interest in purpose and meaning started in the 1980s. Yet while my interest on the subject started a few decades ago, the catalyst that began my research for this book happened on a winter's day in the late 1990s. It started in one of those large Barnes and Noble bookstores with a Starbucks coffee shop on site.

After ordering my usual café mocha—"and no whipped cream, please"—to warm me up (it was an unusually chilly day), I walked to the section where one finds psychology, self-help, and management books. These were the ideal spots to find answers to my concerns. And since books had always been good, faithful, and supportive helpers, I went to find answers from some of these dear friends. Little did I know at the moment I was about to have a profound experience that would forever change my life.

Browsing through the psychology aisle, I came across Viktor Frankl's *Man's Search for Meaning.*

Have it at home. Read it a while ago. Good read too! I thought.

I was led by my fondness for Frankl's works to pick the book up and satisfy my curiosity to explore what answers he would offer. I flipped through the pages and came upon a quote that hit me like a ton of bricks. The line that impressed me so intensely was, "Life ultimately means taking the responsibility to find the right answers to its problems and to fulfill the tasks which it constantly sets for each individual."

> "Life ultimately means taking the responsibility to find the right answers to its problems and to fulfill the tasks which it constantly sets for each individual."
>
> Viktor Frankl

I reread the quote a number of times, thought about its meaning, and then raised my eyes, looked around me, scanned the many aisles of books in this very large bookstore, and experienced an epiphany. For the first time in my life I saw books, bookstores, and libraries in a new light. "The answers *are* here!" I told myself.

I repeated, "The answers *are* here! They have been here all along!"

Books had always offered answers to me. They are the place where you go to find answers, such as "Where do butterflies come from?" But reading Frankl's quote, the word "answers" brought a new and far-reaching significance and implication. What I concluded from Frankl's quote was that the fundamental problems faced by me and the rest of humankind have answers. The answers are in our midst, bound in books, professional and technical journals, electronic databases, and in the wisdom and experience of people around us. *Mankind, I concluded, does not suffer from a lack of answers. Rather, it suffers despite the answers being available.* That conclusion became the central thesis for my eventual investigation and personal quest.

Mankind, I concluded, does not suffer from a lack of answers. Rather, it suffers despite the answers being available.

So I took Frankl's quote as a personal challenge: to take the responsibility to find the right answers to my problems, and once found, to implement the solutions to improve my life. If the answers are in my midst, then let me find and act on them. To do so, and as a learning opportunity, I would play two roles: first, to be my own guinea pig, taking responsibility for solving my problems, and second, to act as the scientist who would observe and learn from "the guinea pig's" experience while solving the problem.

With the belief that answers do exist, and as the subject of my own experiment, my task as subject and observer was to follow a scientific and action research method[6]:

1. Identify and prioritize areas to improve upon
2. Seek answers
3. Take action on the answers
4. Observe and learn from the results
5. Repeat successful practices
6. If not successful, go back to step two
7. If successful practices can be improved, go back to step one

In the process of learning, applying, and improving myself, *purpose, will,* and *meaning* surfaced as central themes in my search for answers. Over time I developed a theory on meaningful purpose, or **logoteleology,** which I will share in this first book. Logoteleology is in the business of reducing meaningless actions and promoting meaningful deeds.

Shortly after my epiphany at the Barnes and Nobles bookstore, as a personal quest I promised myself to write a book with my findings in order to help others who might share my need. Once into my research, it became clear that I would have to write more than one book. I thereafter committed to write an anthology, starting with the foundational volume in your hands. The goal of the first book would be to develop a psychological framework on meaningful purpose where I and others could subsequently test hypotheses. Future versions and additional books would report findings and present new theories and models to broaden understanding and offer solutions. Books, besides imparting knowledge, can also serve as wonderful mirrors to build self-awareness,

6 Kurk Lewin, "Action Research and Minority Problems." *Journal of Social Issues* 2, no. 4 (1946): 34–36. Action research is "a comparative research on the conditions and effects of various forms of social action and research leading to social action" that uses "a spiral of steps, each of which is composed of a circle of planning, action, and fact-finding about the results of the action."

self-knowledge, strengthen one's conscience, and make life better. I plan to build a compendium of mirrors.

> Logoteleology is the science of Meaningful Purpose.

The first problem to tackle was to answer this question: "If answers do exist, what prevents people from learning and putting them into practice?"

The second problem to solve is more preventive in nature. "What is it that people want out of life?"

I will share my conclusions to both questions below based on the best empirical research I could get my hands on.

Why Do Problems Go Unsolved?

Where proven and pragmatic answers do exist, here are the suppositions I tested:

Problems are not solved when an individual

- is ignorant of the answers;
- does not seek the answers;
- does not know how and where to seek answers;
- does not have access to the answers;
- implements the wrong answers;
- as a free-will agent, despite knowing the answers, does not know how to act on them;
- lacks a meaningful purpose to help her or him ask the right questions.

Let's look at these in greater detail.

Does Not Know the Answers (The Oblivious)

The fact that you and I do not know the answer to a problem does not mean a solution does not exist. The answer is either available somewhere or it has not been discovered or invented yet. That being the case, *life calls us to the task of discovering, finding, or inventing the solution.* For Christopher Columbus, it was discovering a shorter route to India. For American scientists challenged with the goal "of landing a man on the moon and returning him safely to the earth,"[7] it required finding solutions and doing what had never been done before in space exploration. For Alexander Graham Bell, it was revolutionizing interactive voice-communication technology through the invention of the telephone.

> "We say that human beings are prone to make the same mistake because of their common lack of understanding."
>
> Alfred Adler

Simply stated, your and my problems are unanswered questions. Some problems can be difficult and challenging while others require simple solutions. Regardless of their level of difficulty, life is calling each of us to seek and act on the question posed. Finding and acting on the eventual answer is a meaningful and worthwhile effort. The unpleasant option is to victimize ourselves, to feel miserable and negative, and to give up when things become difficult. This unpleasant option is a segue to the second reason problems are not solved.

Does Not Seek Answers (The Procrastinator)

Something else I concluded from my research was that *consciously or subconsciously, who we are and what we experience in life is the result of*

7 John F. Kennedy on May 25, 1961, before a Joint Session of Congress.

what we have intended to be and to do. A lot of our behavior is purposeful, even when it is self-damaging.

There are various possible reasons an individual would intend not to seek answers to her problems. One of those reasons, according to the Transactional Analysis (TA) psychological method, is that people's autonomous lives are prevented from evolving naturally due to distorted subconscious **psychological scripts** or life plans. A "Script is the repetition in the here-and-now of archaic decisions, that the child made in order to protect and fulfill his/her need for recognition."[8]

Claude Steiner, author and TA psychologist, explains the origin of a script:

> In a life course which develops normally, a decision of such importance as what one's identity is to be and what goals one will pursue should be made late enough in life so that a certain measure of knowledge informs the choice. In a situation where a youngster is under no unreasonable pressure, important decisions about life will occur no earlier than adolescence.
>
> A script results from a decision which is both premature and forced, because it is made under pressure and therefore long before a decision can be properly made.[9]

In other words, people can lose their autonomy or the ability to choose their own actions because of a subconscious decision made in early childhood, a decision made too early to be well thought out and self-

> The style of life decides.
>
> Alfred Adler

8 Novellino, Michele, "On Closer Analysis: Unconscious communication in the Adult ego state and a revision of the rules of communication within the framework of Transactional Psychoanalysis." In *Ego States (Key Concepts in Transactional Analysis),* ed. Helena Hargaden and Charlotte Sills (London, UK: Worth Publishing, 2003), 154.

9 Claude Steiner, *Scripts People Live* (New York: Grove Press 1974), 69.

determined. That decision, whatever it is, could override what we may as adults define as "doing what makes sense."

Let's see the example of imaginary Paul, who was raised in a home where his mother and sisters took care of many of his responsibilities. The life script for him is that he doesn't have what it takes. So when he is faced with challenging life circumstances, he obsesses and worries about them instead of taking action (the procrastinator) because he is living the life script that he doesn't have any influence over his life and what happens to him.

One of the problems of hidden scripts is that, like a bad spirit, they do not easily relinquish their grip on the individual. Adler agrees. "By the time a child is five years old his attitude to his environment is usually so fixed and mechanized that it proceeds in more or less the same direction the rest of his life."[10] This helps explain why a person, like in the example of Paul above, would not seek answers to troubling questions and situations—he or she does not have the script's permission to do so. In spite of this reality there is hope because people can rewire themselves. In logoteleology this is known as *reforming*, a method to be discussed later.

> **Teleology:** the fact or character attributed to nature or natural processes of being directed toward an end or shaped by a purpose.
>
> www.merriam-webster.com/medical/teleology

I like Steiner's *Scripts People Live* because of its simplistic explanation of the choices people make and why they make them. It clearly explains how people's biases and assumptions can prevent them from avoiding and solving problems. Yet, as we will discover, Transactional Analysis is not the only psychological theory that points to the role and influence of

10 Heinz L. Ansbercher and Rowena R. Ansbacher, eds.*The Individual Psycology of Alfred Adler*, 189.

the subconscious in purpose-driven or **teleological** behavior. Additional theories will be discussed later, including logoteleology.

Does Not Know How and Where to Find Answers (The Disheartened)

The term "information explosion" was coined in 1970 by Alvin Toffler in his book *Future Shock*. Toffler predicted the rapid surge of knowledge and information and its impact on what we today call information overload. It is both a problem for those who want accurate information quickly and an opportunity to those dedicated to manage, package, and sell information readers can trust. In a free society, information is accessible through the Internet, professional journals, television, radio, books, academia, and experts, among others. It is not the intent of this book to tell people how to research information; rather, the task here is to point to the difficulty that some might encounter finding answers to their problems. However, if this problem applies to the reader, he is encouraged to ask himself the right question: "How do I learn to research information?" Life presents us with the opportunity to pause, think, and formulate the right question.

Does Not Have Access to the Answers (The Frustrated)

It is possible that in a totalitarian system, such as North Korea, people are banned from gaining access to answers. It is also possible that one's socioeconomic situation and other physical and mental barriers can pose a challenge in the search for solutions. And since access to information and answers is a problem in need of a solution, some of us have made it our life's purpose to make them available to others. And so can you. Fortunately, if you are reading this book you are probably not in North Korea or a country with similar restrictions on human rights and freedom of the press. It can, however, apply to situations in a free society where physical, technological, and socioeconomic barriers might be present, such as limited access to the Internet due to affordability or availability.

Mental barriers are another way people are prevented from having access to answers. This is through blind spots caused by psychological conditioning and prejudices. It is possible for a tangible stimulus to be present and still not be perceived. In psychology this phenomenon is known as a *scotoma,* or a mental blind spot where the individual is unable to understand or perceive certain matters.

For instance, stereotyping women has been associated with the glass ceiling and lower compensation for equal work as men. How is it possible that women are relegated to such handling after the many years that the unfair impact of this stereotyping has been glaringly clear?

Also, the psychoanalyst is no stranger to *resistance* and *repression* or the patient's opposition and inability to make what is unconscious conscious. Thus, an individual can be deprived of information and insight by both external and internal forces.

Implements the Wrong Answers (The Challenged)

Experience might not always be the best teacher, but it does teach lessons to the willing learner. Experience can point to what works and does not work, allowing us to continue a path to personal growth and en route for the discovery of the ultimate working solution. After all, according to James Joyce, "Mistakes are the portals of discovery."

On the other hand, Josh Jenkins also stated, "To err is human, but when the eraser wears out ahead of the pencil, you're overdoing it." Consequently, when a problem has not been solved despite one's best effort, the action to take is to stop the problem-solving process in order to discover why the current approach is not working. Process takes priority over content. In other words, a new and more important question takes precedence and requires a solution, and it might be—among other options—to discover and implement a better problem-solving approach. In case of personal difficulties, that might include getting professional help from a licensed health professional.

> "The greatest mistake you can make in life is to be continually fearing you will make one."
>
> Elbert Hubbard

I can't emphasize enough the importance of paying attention to what one is paying attention to. People err in solving their most pressing life problems because they get distracted by and pay attention to objects and situations irrelevant to their original purpose. For instance, in my practice I many times encounter people who divert their attention away from what is important in order to focus on the fear of failure. Rather than solving the problem, the individuals pay attention to and get distracted by the fear of solving it. As a result, since dealing with fear and anxiety take precedence, the problem is not solved.

Let's take the case of Anthony, who believes he is math-incompetent and has so far avoided taking his math college courses. He knows he will have to deal with it sooner or later if he plans to graduate. During counseling, Anthony is encouraged to think of ways in which he can build his confidence solving math problems, such as being tutored or using self-paced methods for learning. Anthony, however, diverts the conversation to disheartening "what if" scenarios or to dreadful past situations to why he is not good with math. As long as Anthony's attention is on his fear, he will not be able to successfully meet his academic goals.

Another reason people implement the wrong answers is due to faulty assumptions. I have found exploring one's set of suppositions and changing one's perspective go a long way to overcoming this problem. For instance, for many years I believed intelligence was fixed. You were either born with the capacity to be bright and smart or you were condemned to be slow and dumb; or you could be somewhere in between. And in case you were fed that fib, join me in getting rid of it because it is not true. IQ, regardless of age, can be improved by most people.

Finally, people fail to reach the right answer because they start from an ill-defined problem statement. It is important to learn how to state a well-defined problem statement. Learning problem-solving methods can quickly correct faulty approaches.

Despite Knowing the Answers, Resolves Not to Act on Them (The Disoriented)

Being aware of what the right thing is and then choosing not to act on it is an example of the dark side of Life Scripts. There are various reasons this happens, and there are degrees of severity. These come from three script categories of mental disturbances, which Steiner labeled as No Love, No Mind, and No Joy. An interesting side note is that these three are compared to three characters from *The Wizard of Oz*: the Tin Man lacking a heart (No Love); the Scarecrow having no brain (No Mind); and the Cowardly Lion being fearful and lacking courage (No Joy).[11]

"No Love" is the inability to maintain a loving relationship with another. The failure to be fully present with another person is due to self-absorption or a disturbance in the sense of self. The "No Love" scripted person is tasked to push others away and to be lonely. Thus the individual has difficulty committing to a trusting and lasting relationship, cannot give his or her authentic emotional self to another in passionate love, and is challenged in getting along with people. People with no love in their lives have no one to live for.

For instance, I am reminded of the poem "Richard Corey" by Edwin Arlington Robinson[12] (a musical version of it was popularized by Simon and Garfunkel):

> Whenever Richard Cory went down town,
>
> We people on the pavement looked at him:

---

11 I heard this comparison from Dr. Lou Tice, president of the Pacific Institute, Seattle, Washington.

12 PoemHunter.com. Accessed March 22, 2013. http://www.poemhunter.com/poem/richard-cory/

He was a gentleman from sole to crown,
Clean favored and imperially slim.

And he was always quietly arrayed,
And he was always human when he talked,
But still he fluttered pulses when he said,
"Good-morning," and he glittered when he walked.

And he was rich—yes, richer than a king—
And admirably schooled in every grace:
In fine, we thought that he was everything
To make us wish that we were in his place.

So on we worked, and waited for the light,
And went without the meat and cursed the bread;
And Richard Cory, one calm summer night,
Went home and put a bullet through his head.

"No Mind" is the incapacity to deal with real-world, everyday situations, and results in a lack of control over one's life. At the root of this is the individual's inability to think and reason, to figure things out, and to cope intelligently with daily tasks and problems. Extreme cases are the mentally incompetent and the socially deviant who generally find themselves in mental and correctional institutions. But milder symptoms are observed in those with low degrees of self-efficacy and self-esteem. A "No Mind" scripted person could be tasked to confirm one's incompetence and low self-worth. Other symptoms display an internal battle driven to prove the opposite view—that the individual is competent and his or her life is worthwhile (despite another part of his or her personality believing the contrary).

Take Sally, for example: she was raised in a home where her father was overly critical and a perfectionist and told her over and over again that she would amount to nothing. This concept unfortunately became her life script. So when faced with problems, Sally has to overcome her life script that she is incapable in order to muster the courage to solve the right problems in her life.

"No Joy" is the inability to have full control of one's emotions and bodily feelings. Rather than being in touch with and exploring feelings in a genuine way, individuals select stupefying options from a proliferation of "emotional insteads" designed to control our moods and spirits. *Emotional insteads* is a term used to explain the replacement of a healthy authentic emotion with an inappropriate one. For example, in a situation that requires a person to feel the authentic emotion of happiness and pride, he or she instead experiences the unauthentic and inappropriate feeling of embarrassment.

An example of selecting a stupefying option is when we experience the symptoms of a headache, where we ask, "Where is the aspirin bottle?" rather than asking "*Why* do I have a headache?" Because the wrong question is being asked—"Where is the aspirin bottle?"—the root cause is ignored (the source for the pain) and the problem remains unsolved (since the potential of repeating itself remains). In this case the aspiring plays the role of an emotional instead tasked with dulling the senses from an important symptom.

"No Joy" is also seen in self-destructive behaviors and habits such as through the use of illicit drugs, cigarettes, and the abuse of alcohol, among others. The "No Joy" scripted person is driven to desensitize feelings and/or pursue unauthentic or false happiness, a hopeless attempt to have happiness.

Lacks a Meaningful Purpose (The Lost)

> So, again, why don't people do the right thing? According to Logoteleology, what the three types of scripts share in common is the absence of a meaningful purpose that gives one's existence a worthwhile reason to live for and to express it.

So, again, why don't people do the right thing? According to logoteleology, what the three categories of scripts share in common is the absence of a meaningful purpose that gives one's existence a worthwhile reason to live for and to express it. This worthwhile life purpose is matched by a style of life that counters the three Life Scripts—No Love, No Mind, and No Joy—by way of loving relationships, a sound mind, and a state of happiness. And these right reasons to live help us build and wisely use our determination to act.

Logoteleology advocates that people are innately called to discover and commit their lives to what is meaningful. Without such an aim and compass individuals run the risk of living a life that is scripted, directionless, and unfulfilling. Having a clear and meaningful purpose can help a person ask the right questions in order to stay on course and thus fulfill his or her life's goals. Without a clear and meaningful purpose to guide behavior, humans are generally lost, as evidenced by the poor choices they needlessly select.

So what is one to do about these seven obstacles to problem solving?

1. If you are ignorant of the answers, strive to learn.
2. If you are not inclined or motivated to seek the answers, determine why. The chapter "The Will to Meaning" provides some answers.
3. If you do not know how and where to seek answers, search and learn from those who do.

4. If you do not have access to the answers, dedicate your life to discovering, finding, and inventing solutions.

5. If you implement answers that do not work, learn from your mistakes and keep exploring alternatives until you succeed.

6. If you know the right answer and have difficulty acting on it, or choose not to act on the way out, you are missing all the good things life has to offer. Get help from a professional coach or counselor. This book will provide helpful ideas.

7. If you lack a meaningful life purpose to guide you, I invite you to consider and apply what you will learn from this volume.

Once intrinsically motivated to act for the right meaningful purpose, the obstacles discussed above under "Why Do Problems Go Unsolved" (see Page 5) are usually conquered. Further, with the removal of obstacles to solving our pressing problems, better and more desirable options can be implemented. But what are those better and desirable options we all yearn for?

What People Want from Life

Fundamentally, based on the best empirical research available, I have concluded that people want Five Meaningful things from life. I call these the Five Meaningful Life Strivings:

1. To love and be loved by others

2. To have peace of mind

3. To experience a state of happiness

4. To be challenged with interesting experiences

5. To prosper

According to logoteleology, these are worthwhile goals and existential states that life calls us to pursue and achieve individually and collectively.

What I have recognized and will demonstrate later in the book is that, to achieve those five states, we must first develop an individual life purpose dedicated to bringing love, happiness, and peace of mind, stimulating challenge, and bringing prosperity *to others.* One can only experience a real, meaningful, and worthwhile life by being other-directed. This does not mean it is at one's expense, however. If it would be at our expense, then we ourselves could not experience love, peace, happiness, excitement, and prosperity. Meaningfulness is a win-win proposition.

One can only experience a real meaningful and worthwhile life by being other-directed.

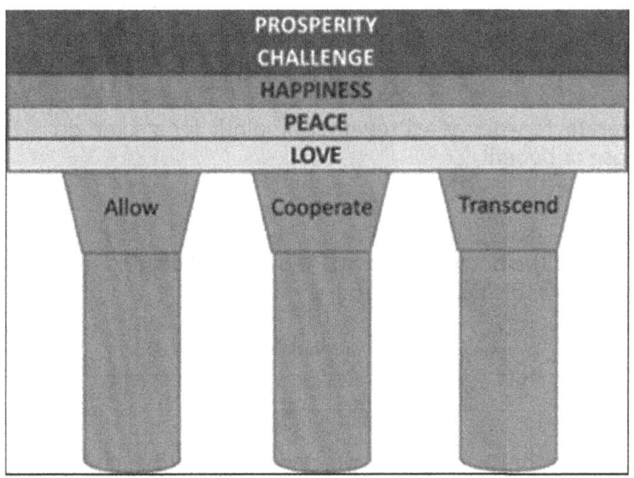

Figure 1: Logoteleology's Three Pillars of Success and the Five Meaningful Life Strivings

These meaning states are achieved when we *allow* others to be their best, when we *cooperate* with others, and when we—in truly altruistic fashion—*transcend* ourselves. I will later expand on these three terms, which I call the **Three Pillars of Meaningful Purpose**. For now, what I mean by *allowing* is the act of actively supporting others' inherent right to achieve their individuality and potential. *Cooperation* is the practice of shared interdependence or mutual aid toward a common purpose. An appropriate synonym for cooperation is *mutualism. Transcendentalism,* on the other hand, is a selfless act where a person rises above or goes beyond what is expected in the service of others. An appropriate synonym for transcendentalism is *altruism,* or the selfless concern for others.

From here forward I will use the acronym ACT for "allow, cooperate, and transcend."

According to the logoteleology theory, ACT and the five strivings are the best and most effective options for successful living. Let's review what the biological sciences and psychology tells us about the way in which species can coexist and why the alternatives to ACT and the five strivings are ineffective.

To **allow** is to actively support others' inherent right to achieve their individuality and potential.

Cooperate: to work or act together or jointly for a common purpose or benefit.

dictionary.reference.com

Mutualism: the doctrine or practice of mutual dependence as the condition of individual and social welfare.

www.merriam-webster.com/dictionary/mutualism

Altruism is the principle or practice of unselfish concern for or devotion to the welfare of others.

www.Dictionary.com

Transcend: (1) to rise above or go beyond the limits of; (2) to outstrip or outdo in some attribute, quality, or power.

merriam-webster.com/dictionary/transcend -

The Symbiotic Alternatives

There is much we can learn by observing and learning how organisms relate to one another. The description of that interaction is known as *symbiosis*. There are seven types of applicable dealings in nature between living beings, including human beings.[13]

Mutualism is an interaction where both parties benefit. In the transaction there is a win-win outcome. Mutualism can also be described as cooperation and collaboration, as when two neighbors help build each others' homes.

Commensalism happens when one person benefits and the other is unaffected. This can be observed when a person allows another to be, to grow, and to succeed on his or her own terms. An example of commensalism is when a classroom teacher accommodates her or his students' learning styles by placing more importance on learning than on an unyielding method.

Similar to commensalism in some ways is one added by logoteleology: *transcendentalism,* or the practice of altruism. Here one person is serving another without expecting anything in return. Different from commensalism, when transcending, the contributor is unselfishly taking an active part helping another. This is also observed when a person loves another.

Amensalism is a symbiotic relationship where one person is harmed or inhibited and the other individual is unaffected. A simple example is when a country with more buying power unknowingly or with no ill intent hordes food, and others with fewer resources starve. At a more personal level this can be observed, for instance, when an adult, due to

13 In the biological sciences, "symbiosis is always 'inter-specific'; that is, it occurs only between different species; intra-specific relationships (relationships within a single species) cannot be described as symbiosis" (http://www.ms-starship.com/sciencenew/symbiosis.htm). However, in logoteleology psychology, there is such license.

ignorance, withholds giving attention to a child who needs recognition and nurturing.

Parasitism happens when one person or group of people benefit and others are harmed. This explains an individual with a sense of entitlement who expects to be supported without contributing in a worthwhile form. Examples of extreme cases of parasitism are the practice of stealing, slavery, human trafficking, and the abuse of social welfare benefits. Milder versions can be observed at work when an individual intentionally does not carry his or her fair share of work.

Competition is the rivalry between two or more persons or groups for a common desired prize that usually results in a victor and a loser but not necessarily involving the destruction of the latter. Competition can be positive when the parties follow fair rules and strive toward the common good of the ultimate customer or beneficiary. We also know of healthy competition between sports teams. The same can be said in commerce and industry where competing organizations can share a consumer market and thrive through innovation. In this case, positive competition generates great ideas for the general betterment of society.

The dark side of competition is observed in the case of war among nations and cut-throat competition among individuals, companies, and countries. This follows a win-lose symbiotic type of interaction that can potentially result in lose-lose outcomes. This type of competition is similar to parasitism—for instance, when practicing industrial espionage, stealing intellectual capital, and practicing unfair currency manipulation.

Neutralism is a symbiotic relationship where neither party is affected. This is most apparent in the observance of tolerance, as when individuals with different religious orientations commune properly and peacefully in a community.

The table that follows illustrates the types of symbiotic interactions between Person "A" and Person "B," where

"Win" denotes benefit to one party.

"Neutral" denotes no positive or negative effect.

"Lose" denotes an undesirable effect of the interaction.

Type of Symbiosis	Results (Win, Lose , Neutral) for Person "A"	Results (Win, Lose, Neutral) for Person "B"
Mutualism	Win	Win
Commensalism	Win	Neutral
Transcendentalism	Win	Neutral / Win
Amensalism	Lose	Neutral
Parasitism	Win	Lose
(Unfair) Competition	Lose / Win	Lose
(Fair) Competition	Win	Win / Neutral
Neutralism	Neutral	Neutral

Table 1 Symbiotic Relationships

It should be apparent that mutualism, commensalism, fair competition, neutralism, and transcendentalism are positive types of symbiotic relationships for humans. On these five types lay the Three Pillars of Meaningful Purpose, or ACT. These are the foundations to realizing the states promised by the five strivings. On the other hand, those oriented toward (cutthroat and unfair) competition, amensalism, and parasitism, for obvious reasons, should be avoided at all cost.

Yet while the positive types of symbiotic relationships are common sense options, why does the human species so frequently select the ones that are counterintuitively harmful? I provided above some preliminary thoughts (i.e., "Why Problems Go Unsolved") as to why. I also offered initial positive alternatives to remedy human suffering and strife. Let's now turn to the four fundamental questions that, I believe, most people would like answers to.

The Four Questions

Logoteleology proposes that to achieve the states of love, happiness, and peace, as well as stimulating challenge and prosperity (i.e., the five strivings), four fundamental questions must be answered:

- Who am I?
- What matters in life?
- Why am I here?
- How do I go about fulfilling my life purpose?

These questions are or should be central and fundamental concerns. It is my strongly held belief that in their answers lay the solution to the fundamental problems facing humanity. As will be explained, their answers are relevant and practical to all matters related to the human experience.

What about you? Do you know who you are? *Really* know?

Do you know what matters in life? And if so, is your style of life fitting to the positive, symbiotic types? If you do know what matters in life, do you give it the right priority and attention?

Do you know what life is calling and asking you to do? Do you know how and where you fit? Are your actions meaningful, as defined by the types of symbiosis?

If you are one of the few who know why you are on this planet, are your actions aligned with what is meaningful to you and others?

If you need help answering the above questions, this book provides answers using the best empirical research I could get my hands on, as well as my own experience developing the theory. Again, this book is concerned with answering why people too frequently make poor choices and what they can do to make better ones.

Review

This book is designed to help people answer questions related to their identity, what gives life meaning, what is the purpose of life, and how to succeed in one's meaningful purpose.

Logoteleology, or the science of meaningful purpose, accepts the principle that there are answers to people-related problems. The thesis is twofold:

First, that mankind suffers unnecessarily.

Second, that solution to mankind's challenges and opportunities are readily available, thus they can be found; and when not, solutions may be discovered and can be invented.

Logoteleology proposes that the reason problems are not solved is because people

- are ignorant of the answers;
- do not seek the answers;
- do not know how and where to seek answers;
- do not have access to the answers;
- implement the wrong answers;
- as free-will agents, despite knowing the answers, do not to act on them; and
- lack a meaningful purpose to help her or him ask the right questions.

Logoteleology is an optimistic solution to human suffering. Fundamentally, it proposes that people are called by life to develop and follow an individual existential purpose that provides Five Meaningful psychological states or experiences through the three pillars for successful living. The three pillars (i.e., ACT) allow others to be and to flourish, to cooperate, and to transcend. The Five Meaningful strivings for worthwhile existential states are the following:

1. Loving, and receiving love from others
2. Having peace of mind

3. Experiencing genuine happiness

4. Participating in, as well as growing and succeeding through, challenging, stimulating, and meaningful tasks and experiences

5. Living prosperous lives

There are seven types of symbiotic relationships (as previously described) humans can choose from. The types of symbiotic relationships that best serve people are mutualism, commensalism, positive competition, and transcendentalism or altruism. Those that harm are amensalism, parasitism, and unfair competition. Logoteleology proposes that the latter are causes of human misery.

Finally, there are four questions all human beings should answer satisfactorily in order to meet the requirements of the three pillars and five strivings:

1. Who am I?

2. What matters in life?

3. Why am I here?

4. How do I go about fulfilling my life's purpose?

Why Is Logoteleology Relevant?

Why is meaningful purpose important, and what application does it have on peoples' real-life problems?

Let us revisit the fundamental hypothesis that started this journey of mine: *Mankind, I concluded, does not suffer for lack of answers. Rather, it suffers despite the answers being available.*

As the proverbial saying goes, "Let's get real." I will provide a global example and then one closer to home.

In 2010, a staggering 925 million people went hungry throughout the world, according to www.worldhunger.org. Children carry the brunt of these statistics, with five million deaths a year due to malnutrition. And this happens despite the fact that the world produces sufficient food for all.

In the United Kingdom (according to guardian.co.uk on Friday, February 5, 2010), insolvency at both the individual and corporate levels is dismal. "Today's figures show a total of 74,670 individuals were declared bankrupt last year, a rise of 10.7% on 2008's figure." And how do corporations fare? "Meanwhile, the number of companies going into liquidation also increased in 2009, rising to 19,077 – the highest figure since 1993."

And how does the world, and the United States, fare? According to Standard and Poor's, "In 2011, 53 global corporate issuers defaulted …" This is considered good news since defaults were "down from 81 defaults in 2010 and the record high of 265 in 2009."[14] According to the US courts, as of June 2011 there were 1,529,560 total business and non-business bankruptcy filings.[15] In addition, as of 2007, 1 percent of Americans have 33.8 percent of the wealth, and half of America has 2.5 percent of the wealth.[16] This gap between the top 1 percent and everyone else hasn't been this bad since the 1920s.

How do these financial statistics relate to relationships? Approximately 40 to 50 percent of first-time marriages will result in divorce within

---

14 standardandpoors.com. 2011 Annual Global Corporate Default Study and Rating Transitions. Accessed March 31, 2013. http://www.standardandpoors.com/ratings/articles/en/us/?articleType=HTML&assetID=1245330814766

15 Uscourts.gov. Bankrupcy Filings Down From 2010 Levels. Accessed March 31, 2013. http://www.uscourts.gov/News/NewsView/11-08-05/Bankruptcy_Filings_Down_From_2010_Levels.aspx

16 Gus Lubin, "15 Mind Blowing Facts About Wealth and Inequality in America" (April 9, 2010): http://www.businessinsider.com/15-charts-about-wealth-and-inequality-in-america-2010-4#half-of-america-has-25-of-the-wealth-2.

fifteen years. One of the most significant root causes is financial difficulties.[17]

These statistics might or might not affect you directly, but in some way they do impact all of us indirectly, even if it is just a simple annoyance. Though I am an optimist believing we can solve these and other problems, I could continue adding statistics and sharing evidence of serious difficulties facing humanity. The question still begs for an answer. If there are solutions to these and many other problems, why do they persist?

What if you could discover, invent, and implement the right solutions to *your* problems and they were never to return? Would the effort be worthwhile? If your answer is the affirmative, this and future books will then help you. This book offers a range of answers, from the fundamental reason for your existence to ways in which you can improve your life's circumstances for the better. And I hope that you can take an active part in improving others' life conditions for the better. In my opinion, there is nothing more important and relevant than knowing who you are, what is important in your life, what the purpose of your life is, and how to achieve it successfully. The path to meaningful purpose is through the commitment to learn how to live a successful, fulfilling and prosperous life. And a good first step is talking about identity and defining who you are.

What's Next?

Here are the highlights for chapter 2, "Identity: Who Am I?" It provides the process to accurately self-identify or know who you are. Using the latest research, I also explain what makes you the unique person you are today and how to best leverage your potential.

17 Divorceline.org. Causes of Divorce. Accessed March 31, 2013. http://divorceline.org/blog/causes-of-divorce/.

Chapter 2: Identity—Who Am I?

He allowed himself to be swayed by his conviction that human beings are not born once and for all on the day their mothers give birth to them, but that life obliges them over and over again to give birth to themselves.—Gabriel García Márquez, *Love in the Time of Cholera*

How would you describe yourself? What does it mean to be you? How are you getting along in life? How satisfactory and fulfilling has your life been?

In the spirit of these questions, this chapter defines identity, describes three types of identities, and explains why identities matter. I also answer where identities come from and what they are made of. In addition, I share ways in which you can apply the content of this chapter. I will then share some of the progress I have made in my own personal journey as a result of what I learned about identity.

Identity Defined

> Meanings are a person's attributes, beliefs, attitudes, values, feelings and aims.
>
> Meaning sets is what makes one's identity recognizable.

Identity is what makes us recognizable to self and others. In other words, identity is how we self-describe and how others describe us. When we complete the sentence "I am _____," we are defining our self-concept. Psychologically, an identity is the set of expressed personal attributes, beliefs, attitudes, values, feelings, and aims that identifies an *individual's* uniqueness, her or his *social* membership in a given group, and the *roles* she or he occupies in society.[18] The personal attributes, beliefs, attitudes, values, feelings, and aims are *meanings.*[19, 20, 21] As we will see later, meanings are expressed with the assistance of motivation and purpose.

But let's first understand what is meant by attributes, beliefs, attitudes, values, feelings, and aims.

First, a singular and individual attribute, belief, attitude, value, feeling, and aim is a *meaning type.*

An *attribute* is a defining and inherent characteristic or quality of a person. For instance, a person could have the attribute of being intelligent or moral.

Belief is a firmly held opinion or conviction, a view of what is true or real. The persuasion that one should not steal is an example of holding a belief. As such, beliefs serve as inner guide and conscience.

A singular and individual attribute, belief, attitude, value, feeling, and aim is a *meaning type.*

Attitude is the learned, relatively stable tendency to respond to people, concepts, objects, and events in an evaluative way, such as the tendency of a person to have a positive disposition of working with children or the negative disposition of eating frog's legs.

18 Burke, Peter J. and Jan E. Stets, *Identity Theory* (New York: Oxford University Press, 2009), 3; 112–29.

19 Markus, H., and E. Wurf, "The Dynamic Self-Concept: A Social Psychological Perspective." *Annual Review of Psychology* 38 (1987): 299–337. These meanings are also known as *schemas.*

20 In logoteleology, meanings are generally grammatically articulated in adjective form.

21 Nevis, Edwin C., Ed., *Gestalt Therapy* (New York: Gardner Press, 1992), 69.

Value is the relative importance that is given to an object, situation, or person. Value describes what is useful, desired, or esteemed. An example of a person expressing a value is when she or he places great importance on reading a book over playing computer games.

Feelings describe how we feel about something or someone. They are a meaning in the sense that they help answer the question, "What does this feeling mean?" Feelings mean something.

Finally, in logoteleology meaning *aims* are aspirational strivings. It explains what an identity intends to become and do. Aims are different from purpose since in teleotherapy[22] aims are aspirations while purpose is an active state of movement toward a goal. Again, I will say more about purpose later.

Meanings help explain why people act the way they do. Meanings are accomplished through purposes in action. In other words, we first give meaning to something or someone, and the meaning fuels an action. For instance, let's pretend a chef is in a bookstore and happens to find a book on Caribbean cuisine containing interesting and unique recipes. Such is her interest that she is encouraged to purchase the book.

Knowing that purpose is triggered by meaning can be significant for people who want to understand and improve their behavior. By answering, "When I took this action (acting on a purpose or goal), it was in order to fulfill which meaning?" you and others can evaluate the quality of your meaning intentions. In logoteleology, meanings precede purpose. Purpose answers "what" and meaning answers "why." Purpose (what) cannot happen without a meaning (why).

To improve our identity and impact, we need to enhance our ability to do the following:

1. Build a meaningful "why"
2. Plan and implement effective "what" strategies

22 teleotherapy means therapy *for meaningful purpose*

Meaning Set

The combined meanings in an identity are known as a *meaning set.* To expand, a meaning set is a collection of organized meanings that highlight the uniqueness of a person's identity. For instance, an *individual* can self-describe with a meaning set that includes attributes such as being caring, helpful, and moral.

As a *social* member of a group, such as a member of a political party, the meaning set can have meanings that describe the individual as patriotic, conservative or progressive, and dedicated.

The combined meanings in an identity are known as a meaning set.

In a *role*, such as manager, the descriptions in the meaning set could be fair, structured, and driven. Thus, in this sense, a meaning set is the equivalent to a person's unique psychological signature. Meaning sets make one's identity recognizable.

For our purpose, and based on the distinctions made above, it is important to understand and differentiate the individual's uniqueness from her or his *social* membership, as well as the *roles* she or he plays in society. When talking about an individual's uniqueness separated from his or her memberships and role, I will use the term "person identity." The other two I will here refer to as "Social or Group Identity" and "Role Identity."[23] Let's review in greater detail the distinctions among person, social, and role identities. I will also explain why the distinctions are relevant.

Person Identity

Person identity is formed in early life by the biogenetic DNA,[24] the psychosocial upbringing at home and the immediate community, and the sociocultural heritage of the nation state. However, identity

---

23 Burke, Peter J. and Jan E. Stets, *Identity Theory*, 112–13.

24 Identities can also be shaped by health conditions or illnesses, such as "I am myopic" and "I am a cancer survivor," but these will not be addressed in this book.

formation is not static; rather, it has the capacity to evolve based on past and present life experiences as well as by our future aspirations. Said differently, the person identity can and should grow in order to help the individual thrive, succeed, and fulfill her or his potential. In short, identities are shaped by our DNA, our family, our culture, life experiences, expectations, and continuous improvement.

Each person's identity is different and unique and cannot be replicated. Think of how your life experience is different from other's. Your view of the world is unique. Your presence on this planet is historically, psychologically, and physically distinct, exceptional, and irreplaceable. In other words, you are positively extraordinary. Your distinct and unique identity with all its potentiality cannot be duplicated. Fortunately, because you are unique, you are not expected by life to be an impersonator, or worse, an impostor. This is what makes human life priceless, the fact that no person can take another's place or fulfill the duty that life asks of him or her to fulfill. Think about it: there is and will only be *one model* of each human being—past, present, and future. There is only one you. What you are called to do by life no one can do in your stead.

This is what makes human life priceless, the fact that no person can take another's place nor fulfill the duty that life asks of him or her to fulfill.

Though each of us is unique, as human beings we all share common qualities. For instance, we are generally identified by meaning attributes such as gender, color of our skin, nationality, place of birth, and language. As psychological beings we humans share common mental processes, yet each of us is unique because of our "meanings imprint"—the meanings we give to our unique identity that cannot be duplicated.

In summary, a *person's identity* has physical and psychological dimensions, as a coin has two sides.[25] In this whole lies the individual's self-concept—how the person explains herself or himself. The meaning set in an identity is the person's psychological signature or what makes him or her recognizable. Finally, the meaning set is what makes the person

- unique;
- autonomous and self-sufficient;
- claim his or her distinct calling in life.

Social Identity

As *social* members, people associate and want to be part of a group in order to express their meanings. We all share the need to relate. But the truth is not all our social memberships are voluntary. People end up as members of a group identity category either by default, by obligation, or by voluntary choice.

Default Group Identities

We are all born into default groups. *Default group identities* include race, gender, place of origin, nationality, family, and clan. In vernacular language you are "stuck" with your default identities. For instance, I am a white male Latino, born a US citizen in Puerto Rico and of the Marrero family. I cannot change that historical and biological reality. These default memberships can be a source of pride as well as being divisive, and even, unfortunately, a source of discrimination. Default groups can build a person's self-worth when their common meanings have a positive impact on its members and others. They are divisive

25 Costello, Stephen J., "An Existential Analysis of Anxiety: Frankl, Kierkegaard, Voegelin." *Journal of Search for Meaning*" 34, no. 2: 65–71. Frankl, however, like Kierkegaard construed the human being as *soma* (body), *psyche* (soul), and *noös* (spirit), the first two dealing with the temporal realm and the third with the eternal realm. We will only deal here with the first two.

when used as an excuse to do harm to others—for instance, by not giving all peoples unconditional regard.

Obligatory Group Identities

Obligatory group identities, as the title suggest, are generally imposed by an external pressure. For instance, an employee can be "volunteered" to be in a committee regardless of interest and desire, with a negative consequence imposed if participation is refused. I have friends who, due to cultural expectations, were guided and influenced by their parents to follow a "prestigious and good-paying career path," which they did not enjoy or find meaningful. So memberships that are meant to meet others' expectations are a form of extrinsic motivation. In some form or other these external and extrinsic expectations are ultimately resented and resisted. And that is what makes the obligatory membership potentially unpleasant.

Voluntary Group Identities

A third category is known as *voluntary group identities,* which involves memberships of our own choosing and free will. For instance, one can choose to join a company as an employee, to belong to a particular religious faith, to be member of a club, to decide on one's career path, and to choose to associate with valued friends.

Logoteleology claims that voluntary identities—where members willingly join and are able to freely express themselves in a meaningful way to achieve common goals—are more sustainable, engaging, and productive than those in obligatory group identities.

Since default group identities are capable of inspiring pride and loyalty, such as being a member of a family or as citizen of a country, they too can build strong bonds as in voluntary group identities.

All three identities—default, obligatory, or volunteer—provide group members a degree of shared meanings or common bonds. Of course when in an obligatory situation, the shared meanings will possibly be few and far between.

In a nutshell, social identity explains what membership an individual holds, it describes the meanings tied to such a membership, and it explains what the person has in common with other members. Maintaining a meaningful social identity builds a person's sense of self-worth or the sense that what one does is valuable and found to be worthy.[26] Voluntary identities are more intrinsically motivating than those with compulsory tendencies such as in obligatory identities. For the reason that default identities can generate feelings of pride, self-satisfaction, and loyalty, they—as in voluntary identities—can also be highly meaningful to members.

We will be identified by -- and our reputations will be tied to -- the groups we belong to.

Whatever our memberships, we will be identified by—and our reputations tied to—the groups we belong to. That is why it is important to be selective of groups and people we associate with. It is my belief that much can be accomplished when two or more people collaborate to fulfill a purpose that is meaningful for all concerned, and meaningful outcomes are frontrunners to a reputable standing.

The Dark Side of Groups

Groups, however, also have their dark side. For instance, Irving Janis introduced the term **groupthink** as the tendency of groups to suppress dissent for the sake of maintaining group harmony.[27] There are multiple historical accounts of groupthink disasters such as Pearl Harbor in World War II, the Bay of Pigs Invasion, the Vietnam War, and the recent war in Iraq. But group self-censorship is one of other types of possible problems with groups. Burke and Stets highlight that "memberships

26 Stets, Jan E. and Peter J. Burke, "*Identity Theory and Social Identity Theory.*" *Social Psychology Quarterly* 63 (2000): 224–37.

27 Janis, Irving L. "*Victims of Groupthink*" (New York: Houghton Mifflin, 1972).

imply an ingroup and an outgroup, and, correspondingly, a sense of 'us' versus 'them.'"[28] This can lead members in the ingroup to see themselves in a positive light and identify and evaluate members of outgroups in a negative way, with all its potential adverse consequences.[29]

To avoid such tendencies, it is important to keep in mind what constitutes meaningful and meaningless behavior. When meanings in a person's identity become negative, gloomy, and draining for either self or others, I describe them as *meaningless*. On the other hand, meanings that are received as positive, mutually beneficial, transcendental, and replenishing are *meaningful*. As I stated in chapter 1, logoteleology is in the business of reducing meaningless actions and promoting meaningful deeds.

As explained above, people can be members of many groups. The groups a person belongs to are part of his or her *social or group identity* or *group set*. A *group set* is the combined social identities an individual holds. Comparing and evaluating a person identity with her or his group set can help determine meaning satisfaction, alignment and fit. Logoteleology believes that the greater the alignment between a *person's identity* meaning set, and her or his *group set*, the stronger the experience of relatedness, harmony, and sense of belonging. Many of us know this intuitively. For instance, it is common practice for company representatives to interview candidates to determine cultural fit in the belief that employees who share the company's values will perform best. Also, friendships, business deals, and political alliances are built based on shared meanings.

A group set is the combined social identities an individual holds. Comparing and evaluating a person identity with her or his group set can help determine meaning satisfaction, alignment and fit.

28 Burke, Peter J. and Jan E. Stets, *Identity Theory and Social Identity Theory,* 118.

29 Hogg, Michael A. "Social Identity Theory." Burke, P. J., Ed. *Contemporary Social Psychological Theories* (Stanford: Stanford University Press, 2006), 111–36.

Let me explain why I believe this is so relevant and important to our daily lives. List the groups you belong to, voluntary, default, and obligatory. Now see if you can give positive answers to the following. Does membership in this group

Analyzing one's group set can help determine which memberships can best meet meaning needs and meaning expression.

- encourage me to be myself?
- make me feel welcome and accepted for who I am?
- bring out the best in me?
- allow me to do meaningful things for myself and others?
- feel like we are all working toward the same purpose?
- allow me to grow and thrive?
- feel like we all share a common meaning and bond in what we do?
- encourage collaboration and interdependence?
- offer me a source of pride?

Analyzing one's group set can help determine which memberships can best meet meaning needs and meaning expression. We can evaluate and select those groups that will best help us answer the above questions in the affirmative. It is important to understand that many memberships are not necessarily helpful. Selecting a few meaning-complementary groups and members can do much to enhance one's quality of life, particularly when the goals of the group do well to its members and others.

Logoteleology encourages forming group identities that

- allow members to be who they are as individuals;

- welcome and accept members for who they are;
- bring out the best in all members;
- encourage members to do meaningful things for all and toward the greatest good;
- partner to work toward the same purpose;
- allow and encourage all members to grow and thrive;
- share and work toward a common meaning and end;
- build a positive reputation and legacy; and
- make people feel proud of their impact and legacy.

Evaluating your group memberships will allow you, like a good gardener, to prune those associations and so-called friendships that are not allowing you to meet the criteria previously listed. Moreover, you can form new groups—professional, civic, spiritual, and social—chartered to do meaningful things that benefit the many. Logoteleology believes The Three Pillars of Meaningful Purpose and the Five Meaningful strivings are important norms that help build such memberships.

To review:

- Humans are social beings with a social identity.
- Forming a group allows its members to exchange and find expression in their common meanings.
- Membership impacts its members' reputations through association.
- When membership is chosen freely, it is said to be desired and voluntary. On the other hand, obligatory memberships are extrinsically motivated and compulsory.

- Default memberships can be a source of pride and inspiration and bring out feelings of loyalty.
- Overall, social identities can build feelings of self-worth.
- Healthy groups have members who are interdependent and work together to achieve meaningful ends.
- All group types also have a potential dark side such as groupthink and negative competition and strife.
- A person's collective group membership is called a *social or group identity* or *group set.*
- Compatible person identity and group identities increase the odds that individuals will experience higher degrees of satisfaction, productivity, and fit.
- Logoteleology encourages people to determine how meaningful their memberships are, and to carefully select their associations. Further, they are encouraged to replace ineffective associations to form new groups that achieve meaningful ends through meaningful means.

Role Identity

People join groups to have meaningful experiences, including satisfying their social needs. There is also an expectation that the new members will contribute to the common purpose. Members fulfill that expectation through *role identities.* Expectations in roles determines what it means to be, for example, a spouse, a son or daughter, the committee chair, a friend, a third baseman, a team lead, or a bus driver. In logoteleology, role identities are designed to fit with and complement other roles, like interlocking pieces in a jigsaw puzzle. For instance, in my role as employee in relation to the role of my supervisor, some of the activities are about expectations such as "produce a report" and "keep me informed." The meanings of being in a role as an employee reporting to a supervisor

> In logoteleology, role identities are designed to fit with and complement other roles, as interlocking pieces in a jigsaw puzzle.

include expectations such as being supportive, timely, confidential, and courteous. Thus, roles have their own set of assumptions, norms, and boundaries. Simply stated, being in a role means there are expectations conveyed through meanings and tasks. Moreover, operating in a role explains what it means to be part of someone's life. Thus, "the price of admission" to the social relationship entails supporting the common meaning, tasks, and members' expectations.

Benefits and Opportunities of Role Identities

There are benefits to having a clear and meaningful role identity. When we are in a role that is complementary to another, it can have a positive effect on our self-esteem.[30] In other words, the role incumbents—to some positive degree—are able to allow, cooperate, and transcend (ACT) as well as practice the "five strivings."[31] We can find comfort and assurance that research provides ample evidence of the benefit of ACT and the five strivings on self-esteem.

In addition, successful performance in a role requires having competencies and meaningful aims. Said differently, you need to be good at something that makes a positive difference to you and others. Again, I believe that to achieve such success and to make a positive difference, ACT and the five strivings will have to play a central part. For instance, referring to one of the five strivings, "interesting challenges," what better way to make life remarkable and stimulating than to self-monitor your performance and competence and to strive to learn and grow? Self-monitoring benefits the role occupier by way of a higher sense of power and control over her or his destiny.

---

30 Dweck, Carol, *Self-Theories* (Philadelphia: Psychology Press, 2000), 131.

31 The five strivings define what is meaningful. They are acts and relationships that bring about love, peace and peace of mind, happiness, interesting challenges, and prosperity.

Another benefit of having a clear and meaningful role identity is that we can select to be in roles where we can be our authentic selves, where we can express our aspirations and gifts to make life better for all. Role identities are empty and unfulfilling shells when they lack a clear, meaningful person identity as context. A goal of logoteleology is to help people stay aware of and be guided by their authentic person identity or true self with all its potentiality. That is why logoteleology believes groups and roles can be ideal platforms to strengthen self-determination and mastery at all three identity levels—person, group, and role. Let's review a few examples.

> Roles are empty and unfulfilling shells when they lack a clear meaningful person identity as context.

Role Identity in Organizations

Logoteleological organizations[32] aim to build work cultures and to design roles that follow ACT and the five strivings for practical reasons. For instance, logoteleology's organization development (OD) method aims to create cultures and complementary roles that build great products, deliver excellence service, and achieve robust financial results. To achieve these results, complementary roles are designed to perform as interlocking pieces where allowing, cooperating, and transcending, as well as the five strivings, are a central part of the role design. Said differently, organizational roles at all levels are intentionally designed to generate meaningful value.

So, for instance, a leader would have quick answers to the following:

- Why do I lead?
- What is the meaning or brand of my leadership?

32 Excellent examples of leaders of meaningful purpose organizations are Japan's Kazuo Inamori, chairman of Kyocera and DDI Telecommunications; and Gurnek Bains, CEO of the British Consulting firm YSC Business Psychologists.

- How does my leadership benefit those I work with at all levels inside and outside my organization?
- How do I measure the meaningfulness of my leadership style?[33]

Role Identity in Families

Families can also benefit from a meaningful role identity. By embracing ACT and the five strivings, individual members can answer questions such as

- What is the meaning of my being a spouse?
- What is the meaning of being a member of a family?
- What is the meaning of being a father or mother? What's in it for the children?
- What meaningful things will I contribute as a husband, wife, or child in this family?

Digressing for a moment, I have found in my practice and life experiences that relatively few people have thought about the meaning of their person, associations, and roles. Few people, in my experience, can satisfactorily answer the above questions with in-depth understanding and consequence. As previously mentioned, a lot of people's behavior is scripted and on "autopilot." Not many people can answer with confidence and certainty the four fundamental questions of life:

- Who am I?
- What matters in life?
- What is the purpose of my life?
- How do I successfully achieve my life's purpose?

---

33 I will go into greater depth on the subject of logoteleology's contribution to organizations in a future volume.

And hence, again, this explains the meaningful purpose and contribution of logoteleology on people's lives.

We have so far covered the definition of an identity and the three types of identities. But are there identities that are more important than others? If so, why?

The Preeminence of Person Identity

While all identities are important and play a significant part in personality, person identity has preeminence over social and role identities, as seen in figure 2. Why? Because a person identity has the original, foundational, or higher order meaning set. That means that first and foremost we are unique individuals with a unique meaning set or meaning DNA. And as unique individuals with a base person identity, what we do—the actions we take—is expressed through the roles we play within our associations. In other words, I always bring "me" to the group through the role I chose to play, but I am not first and foremost the group or the role.

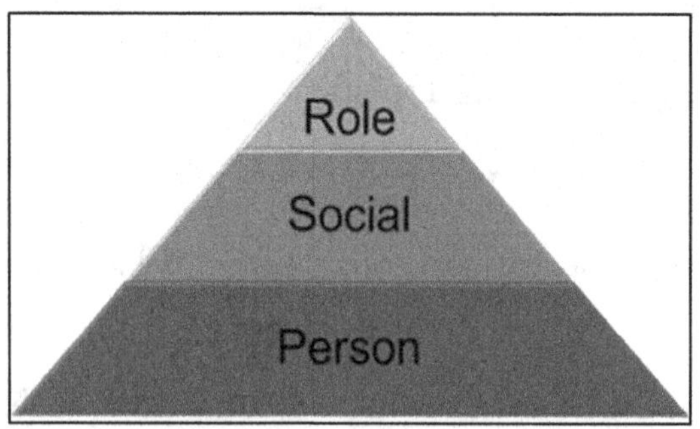

Figure 2 Preeminence of Identities

Ideally, people would select membership and roles based on their self-determined person identity meanings. And why "ideally"? Because many times the memberships and roles we engage in are not consciously freely chosen (e.g., default and obligatory). And as previously covered, people can also be misguided by scripts.

Thus, logoteleology studies how people express their person identity meaning set through their associations and roles. To what end? To help people

- form and develop healthy person identities; and
- find channels to do meaningful things in groups through roles.

Let's see how.

Role Sets

In this section I will explain what a role set is and describe the value of studying roles in personality.

The various roles a person occupies in life are called the role set. For instance, among other things I am a consultant, son, brother, husband, father, colleague, friend, and author. All those roles in my life are part of my role set. One of the things a logoteleologist does is review, compare, and evaluate a person's identity with his or her group and role sets to determine the type and degree of meaning expression, harmony, and growth. The conviction is that *a high degree of role meaning expression, harmony, and growth are signs of a healthy identity. Contrary, low degrees could reveal an identity with psychological disturbances.*

In regard to meaning expression:

The various roles a person occupies in life are called the role set.

- Is the individual committed and able to express his or her person identity meaningful goals through group memberships (group set) and in the roles he or she plays?

  For instance, does the individual *consistently* express the value of being an empathic listener as a judge, mother, wife, and president of the PTA? Or does she make exceptions where being empathic finds expression on some roles but not on others?

- Are some groups and roles better than others in allowing members to use their unique talents and gifts?

For instance, do organizational leaders encourage team members to contribute based on strengths and talents?

Pertaining to meaning harmony:

- Are there common meaningful themes among the groups and roles?

  For example, do all or most of the groups a person belongs to meet his or her need to build lasting and uplifting friendships? Can he or she do the same for others in all or most of the groups?

Related to meaning growth:

- Are some groups and roles better than others in nurturing person identity formation and development?

  For example, do I come out feeling like a better person each time I engage with my groups and through the roles I play?

Logoteleology also believes that worthwhile meanings that are consistently applied on all roles are generally self-determined and authentically grounded on the person identity. On the other hand, when individuals make exceptions, it is possibly due to introjects[34] and their subsequent scripts at the person identity level. Such exceptions can lead to cognitive dissonance or conflict between two held beliefs. Again, that is why in the logoteleology method, analyzing the degree of consistent role meaning-expression can help to diagnose the health of the personality.

Moreover, when meanings are self-determined, aligned, harmonious, and robust as well as filled with vitality, they express the identity's reason, or *raison d'être,* to live for. The person's style of life, as a theme,

---

34 Introjection: generally the process by which aspects of the external world are absorbed into or incorporated within the self, the internal representation then taking over the psychological functions of the external objects. Source: *The Penguin Dictionary of Psychology.*

embodies what she or he lives for. It expresses the person's life ideology. It answers the question, what is my life worth living for?

> When meanings are self-determined, aligned, harmonious, and robust as well as filled with vitality they express the identity's reason, or raison d'etre, to live for.

What about you? When you think about the different roles you play in life, are there roles that stand out as indifferent and inconsequential to who you truly are or wish to be?

Summarizing, people assume roles in groups. These roles are known as role identities. They can be voluntary, default, or obligatory. A role identity brings with it the following:

- The expectations that tasks will be fulfilled. Membership entails working and contributing in some significant way.
- Demands of competence. In order to fulfill tasks members need knowledge, skills, and experiences.
- Adherence to assumptions, norms, and boundaries. Incumbents will have to find common agreement on what the rules of engagement are in order to work harmoniously.

Clear and meaningful roles complement one another toward a common purpose. Logoteleology believes that when the social and role identities are aligned and supportive of the person identity's meanings, the individual experiences a high sense of self-determination in life. For that reason people are encouraged to set goals that complement as well as maintain consistency and coherence between their person, social, and role meanings, in that order.

People belong to many groups and hold various roles in life. The groups a person belongs to are called *social or group identity,* or *group set.* The social and role identities are ways in which the person identity expresses its core meanings. For that reason the person identity has preeminence over the other two identities as shown in figure 2. Psychologically healthy individuals seek memberships and engage in roles that are consistent with the long-range meaningful purpose and supportive goals of their person identity.

A *role set* contains all the roles a person takes part in life. Role identities are empty and unfulfilling shells when they are disconnected from the person identity meanings. The logoteleologist evaluates how consistent meaning-expression is across roles in order to help solve identity personality issues or to improve current performance and quality of life. The goal is to build meanings that give people a worthwhile reason to live for.

Why Do Identities Matter?

We all have identities, but many might not know what they are and why they are important.

Identities matter for the following eight reasons:

1. *Identities provide meaning to life.* Burke and Stets[35] best described why identities matter.

   A life without meaning is a life that is full of anomie; it has no purpose, no structure, and no framework. Without meaning, people have low self-esteem. Thoits[36] and a number of other researchers suggest that identities provide a sense of purpose and meaning in life, integrating us with the actions and expectations of others. Identities do this because they define who we are as well as how and why we are to behave in normatively specified ways. Identities thus increase self-esteem and reduce depression and anxiety.[37]

35 Burke, Peter J. and Jan E. Stets, *Identity Theory and Social Identity Theory*, 146.
36 Thoits, Peggy A., "Multiple Identities and Psychological Well-Being: A Reformulation and Test of the Social Isolation Hypothesis." *American Sociological Review* 49 (1983): 174–87. Also: "Multiple Identities: Examining Gender and Marital Status Differences in Distress." *American Sociological Review* 51 (1986): 259–72.
37 Thoits, Peggy A. "Multiple Identities and Psychological Well-Being: A Reformulation and Test of the Social Isolation Hypothesis."

In addition to giving meaning to life, identity describes a person's potential and direction. Identity reflects our life theme. It is the center of our awareness, life purpose, and vigor. We are self-transformational beings charged to become and enjoy our best. Identity yearns to achieve meaningful ends; and such a pursuit can build confidence and self-regard. Identity formation, through ACT and the five strivings, is the path to a meaningful purpose; and by being cognizant of our outcomes, experiences, and moods, we can determine if the direction we are following is making the most of our potential. Identity also claims the contribution we are going to make in life. Ultimately we cannot answer "Who am I?" without first answering "Why am I here?"

2. *You either shape or control your identity or someone or something else will.* If you do not claim and take conscious charge of your identity, as a puppet—others, circumstances, or your introjected scripts—will pull your strings to control you. I say "consciously" because taking claim of one's identity starts with and entail deliberate attention, focus, and decision making. Otherwise our unconscious and hidden life scripts will run their introjected course.

Let's be reminded of logoteleology's basic proposition ten, *The individual's meanings—conscious or not—influences every psychological process.* The fact that a person is not aware of his or her life script does not mean he or she does not have one.[38], [39], [40] Aware or unaware of what we are doing, we *do* act out our scripts. Clinical psychologist and transactional analyst Claude Steiner wrote "Berne thought scripts were the result of the repetition compulsion, a psychoanalytic concept which postulates that people have

Ultimately we cannot answer "Who am I?" without first answering "Why am I here?"

38 Frankl, Viktor, *Man's Search for Ultimate Meaning* (Boston: Beacon Press, 2006), 32.

39 Ansbacher, Heinz L. and Rowena Ansbacher. 1956. 93.

40 Steiner, Claude, *Scripts People Live* (New York: Grover Press, 1974), 51.

a tendency to repeat unhappy childhood events".[41] University of Iowa's Johnmarshall Reeve reminds us that "People engage in external and introjected regulation largely out of compliance and because they have to (i.e., they are being controlled), while people who engage in identified and integrated regulation do so largely because they want to and chose to (i.e., they act autonomously)."[42] [43]I will say more about identified and integrated regulation later in this volume.

The point is that people should strive to have a clear identity in order to build their self-efficacy[44] and strengthen their self-determination[45]; otherwise, other forces will take them in a different direction. Stated differently, people's meanings should ideally be autonomously decided in order to build competence and confidence, and in order to achieve important ends. Logoteleology is committed to helping people be more intentional and deliberate, building meaning-rich, ideal, aspirational, and achievable identities.

3. *Identities are self-regulating and self-fulfilling.* Identities steer behavior. Burke and Stets claim, "People act in ways such that the meanings of the behavior reflect the meanings they hold for themselves in their identities."[46] This supports logoteleology's sixth basic proposition: *humans are teleological or purpose-driven.*[47] We have a mental teleological or self-directing mechanism employed to maintain environmental consistency with identity meanings. We cannot help but act as we self-describe through

41 Ibid., 13.

42 Reeve, Johnmarshall, *Understanding Motivation and Emotion* (New Jersey: John Wiley and Sons, Inc., 2005), 154.

43 Introjected regulation is an extrinsic type of motivation. An individual responding to introjected regulation does so out of obligation, and because it is what is expected.

44 Self-efficacy is the belief that one is capable of achieving predetermined goals.

45 Self-determination is making choices based on personal beliefs and values rather than on the basis of external pressures.

46 Burke and Stets, *Identity Theory*, 84.

47 Teleology is the science of ends and purposes. Logoteleology describes goal-directed behavior.

our identities—consciously or involuntarily. We are wired to find ways to act according to our self-concept[48] and to fulfill our self-image.[49] Hence, person and role identities are inherently teleological.

Role identities interact with other roles in order to achieve ends. I agree with Alfred Adler that, "A person would not know what to do with himself were he not oriented toward some goal. We cannot think, feel, will, or act without the perception of some goal."[50] More recently, Reeve affirmed that, "Defining or creating the self shows how *self-concept* energizes and directs behavior."[51] In short, we are goal-directed.

4. *Identities can help us detect and follow what matters and avoid distractions.* Given that identities are made of purposes, motivations, and meanings, we can proactively decide what meanings to pursue and avoid. As I stated in logoteleology's first basic proposition, *Logoteleology proposes that as an adult, the individual is tasked with finding, creating, or inventing meaning in order to regain autonomy and control over his or her life.* This lifelong task requires evaluating external demands and internal wishes to determine if they support one's self-determined core meanings. It also requires making choices that are attuned with one's person, social, and role identities.

Meaningful and conscientious identities remind us what matters and what deserves our attention, and what does not. I am reminded of Harvard's Clayton M. Christensen's July 2010 article titled "How Will You Measure Your Life?" where he lamented the state of his fellow classmates:

> Over the years I've watched the fates of my HBS classmates from 1979 unfold; I've seen more and more

---

48 Self-concept is one's own description of the self.

49 Self-image describes the self in evaluative ways, positive or negative.

50 Ansbacher, Heinz L., and Rowena R. Ansbacher, Eds., *The Individual Psychology of Alfred Adler* (New York: Harper and Row, 1964), 96.

51 Reeve, Johnmarshall, *Understanding Motivation and Emotion,* 261.

> of them come to reunions unhappy, divorced, and alienated from their children. I can guarantee that not a single one of them graduated with the deliberate strategy of getting divorced and raising children who would become estranged from them. And yet a shocking number of them implemented that strategy. The reason? They didn't keep the purpose of their lives front and center as they decided how to spend their time, talents, and energy.[52]

It is refreshing to see Christensen and others calling attention to the role of purpose and meaning in daily life and that they support paying attention to what really matters in life, as I will explain in greater detail here and in the chapter related to meaning.

5. *Your identities set you apart from others.* As mentioned previously, you are unique. There are things that only you can do for others and that no one else can do on your behalf. Logoteleology is an optimistic science that believes you can shape your identity with confidence and fulfill the meaning that life expects only of you. Again, you are not called by life to be a replica or image of another person. Nor are you called by life to meet the selfish needs of others. As social beings our role is to serve and complement one another, not to be misused by others or by our own introjected life scripts.

6. *Identities remind us of our common humanity.* Different people communing in confidence and harmony are best expressed in the Latin *E pluribus unum* (out of many, one.). Psychological and social health depends on our ability to simultaneously acknowledge our individual uniqueness, our group identity, and our common humanity.[53] Alfred Adler stated, "The only individuals who can really meet and master the problems of life,

---

52 Cityofseekers.com. How Will You Measure Your Life? Accessed March 31, 2013. cityofseekers.com/wp-content/uploads/2011/11/how-will-you-measure-your-life.pdf

53 Ibid. 2005. 354.

however, are those that show in their strivings a tendency to enrich all others, who go ahead in such a way that others benefit also. All human judgments of value and success are founded, in the end, upon cooperation; this is the great commonplace of the human race."[54]

This supports logoteleology's second basic proposition, *All meaning-fulfillment is social, transcendental, or other-directed and required for social and psychological adjustment.* Cooperation is not just good common sense for interpersonal interactions, it is crucial, for instance, for mental health. This should remind us of chapter 1's explanation of the types of symbiotic relationships that will help us and others succeed. It is also a reminder of the relevance of ACT and the five strivings.

> Different people communing together in confidence and harmony are best expressed in the Latin *E pluribus unum* (Out of many, one.).

Our common humanity should also remind us that we are called to care for our shared ecological environment.

7. *Identities can fulfill our affiliation needs.* Being a member of a respected and recognized group has a positive effect on self-esteem.[55] There are two types of affiliation needs: *intimacy* and *approval.* Intimacy is based on interdependence where attention is given to building warm and close friendships for their own sake.[56] In interdependence we have a greater sense of belonging. In opposition, people with strong affiliation needs that are driven by the need for approval, acceptance, and security hold

---

54 Ansbacher, Heinz L. and Rowena R. Ansbacher, *The Individual Psychology of Alfred Adler* (New York: Harper and Row, 1956), 255.

55 Stets, Jan E., and Peter J. Burke, "Identity Theory and Social Identity Theory." *Social Psychology Quarterly* 63 (2000): 224–37.

56 McAdams, D. P., "A Thematic Coding System for the Intimacy Motive." *Journal of Research in Personality* 14 (1980): 413–32.

meanings that are rooted in a fear of interpersonal rejection.[57] That is why it is important to carefully assess the quality of our affiliation meanings and goals, and how they are expressed.

To have a robust identity that fulfills our affiliation needs we should want to follow logoteleology's fourteenth basic proposition, *We have three authentic tasks to fulfill in life: to allow, to cooperate, and to transcend.* A psychologically healthy person legitimizes others' identities and becomes a catalyst for others' self-improvement and self-fulfillment goals.

8. *Healthy identities achieve productive ends.* Individuals and groups with a healthy social identity, agenda and competence can achieve synergy and prolific results. For instance, there is evidence that organizations with healthy meanings tend to outperform the S&P 500 by more than an 8-to-1 ratio, a significant proportion.[58] Individuals with a healthy and secure identity also achieve great things and built positive reputations. I am particularly impressed with Kazuo Inamori,[59] the founder and CEO of Japan's Kyocera, and with Gurnek Bains[60], CEO of YSC Business Psychologists, for their commitment to build meaningful and profitable organizations and who are dedicated to having a positive social impact. Many are also familiar with CNN's Heroes, where individuals are acknowledged for doing something meaningful that improves conditions in the world.

Not only can meaningful identities achieve productive ends that benefit others, they build the giver's self-concept.[61] Myers explains: "Recognized

57 Heckhausen, H., *Motivation and Handeln* (New York: Springer-Verlag, 1980).

58 Sisodia, Rajendr S., David B. Wolfe, and Jagdish N. Sheth, *Firms of Endearment* (New Jersey: Wharton School Publishing, 2007), 16.

59 Inamori, Kazuo, *For People and For Profit* (Tokyo: Kodansha International Ltd., 1997).

60 Gurnek Bains et al, *Meaning, Inc.* (London, UK: Profile Books, 2007).

61 Steger, Michael F. and Joo Yeon Shin, "The Relevance of Meaning in Life Questionnaire to Therapeutic Practice: A Look at the Initial Evidence." *The International Forum of Logotherapy: Journal of Search for Meaning* 33, no. 2 (2010): 95–104.

> A psychologically healthy person legitimizes others' identities and becomes a catalyst for others' self-improvement and self-fulfillment goals.

achievement boosts self-concept because we see ourselves in others' positive appraisals. When people think well of us, it helps us think well of ourselves."[62]

Summary

To review, identities matter because they answer what the meaning and purpose of life are. As in the precaution to avoid identity theft, it is important that you claim and manage your identity, or someone or something else will. Once you self-determine, your teleological or self-regulating system will guide your identity to achieve its purpose. This teleological system can help you identify and do what matters as well as avoid distractions. In other words, it makes choice selection easier.

Your identity is what sets you apart. It reminds you that you are unique, and that you are not expected or called by life to imitate others. Yet while you are unique, identity also reminds us that we share a common humanity with our fellow men and women. Our meanings should be purposed to allow, to cooperate with others, and to transcend ourselves in the service of fellow human beings and nature. Doing so can help fulfill our affiliation needs. These affiliations are our sources to loving relationships, happiness, peace of mind, interest, and prosperity. Finally, your affiliation needs will help you achieve productive ends that can build your self-esteem.

What Is Identity Made Of?

Logoteleology's basic proposition three affirms that *Telos (Purpose or Ends), Thelos (Will), and Logo (Meaning or Reason) are three distinct mental functions in a psychological system called identity.* These three mental functions are core to identity formation and health. I will explain in greater detail these mental functions and how we can leverage them

---

62 Myers, David G, *Social Psychology* (New York, NY: McGraw-Hill ,2005), 45.

to our advantage in the chapters related to Meaning, Purpose, and Will. For now I will introduce the simple form of the identity formula:

$$I = P + Me$$

I = Identity, P = Purpose, and Me = Meaning. I subsequently will expand the formula to address the role of the Will.

In logoteleology, identity or our self-concept is expressed in the grammatical form of a noun or pronoun. Remember that a self-concept answers the question "I am __." As a noun, we use role identities or labels such as student, parent, doctor, weather forecaster, etc. Subsequently, the self-concept begs the question, "What do you do as a student, parent, doctor, or weather forecaster?" This "what" question is about the *purpose* of the role. Logoteleologically, the request demands an action verb for an answer. I will use the weather forecaster's role to explain the formula. Combining the noun role (weather forecaster) with the action verb, a reasonable answer could be "I am a weather forecaster who *reports* weather conditions." So the *purpose* of this person's role—the "what" of being a weather forecaster is to *report* (an action verb) on weather-related matters.

The next question could be any of the following: "Why should I care? What's so important and meaningful about reporting weather conditions? Why did you pick that role for a career?" Those questions are about the reasons "why" one would do something. They define the meaning of—or what is *meaningful* about—"reporting weather conditions." So our imaginary forecaster could provide the short answer, "To help people plan their daily lives." Meanings are generally expressed through adjectives; but they can also be conveyed through adverbs and prepositional phrases. Explicitly, here is how the formula I = P + Me works with our imaginary weather forecaster.

In logoteleology, identity or our self-concept is expressed in the grammatical form of a noun or pronoun.

The **identity** is the role in noun form "weather forecaster."

The **purpose** of the identity is grammatically expressed as an action verb, "reports." It answers "what" the weather forecaster does.

The **meaning** of reporting weather conditions is stated through the prepositional phrase "to help people plan their daily lives." It answers "why."

If you notice, we know what the role identity title is (weather forecaster), *what* the person in the weather forecaster role does (report), and *why* the weather forecaster role is meaningful (help people plan their daily lives).

But does the weather forecaster enjoy his craft? How meaningful is this career role for him? Does he want to do this? Is it fun for him to do this reporting day in and day out? These questions are about the weather forecaster's motivation or willingness to do the reporting. In other words, these questions can help explain how intrinsically motivating the job of reporting weather conditions is. Thus I introduce the expanded form of the formula:

$$I = P + Mo + Me$$

I = Identity, P = Purpose, Mo = Motivation, and Me = Meaning.

So let's assume for the sake of our example that the imaginary weather forecaster is very motivated by the meanings of his career. Let's complete this particular career role identity statement. "I am a weather forecaster who *deeply enjoys* reporting weather conditions in order to help people plan their daily lives."

The **identity** is the role in noun form: "weather forecaster."

The **purpose** of the identity is grammatically expressed as an action verb: "reporting."

The **meaning** of reporting weather conditions is stated through the prepositional phrase "to help people plan their daily lives."

The **motivation** (as in willingness) to report weather conditions are affectively communicated through the expression "deeply enjoys."

Let's review logoteleology's Proposition Number Five, "*Will responds to and is energized by the degree of meaningfulness of an outcome.*" In other words, the *will* is animated as a response to the strength of the meaning. Thus, using the previous example, the power of a meaning (to help people plan their lives) determines the energy level invested by the will (deeply enjoys) in order to fulfill a purpose (report). Another way of saying it is that meanings energize motivation; and motivation brings about purpose. As a formula, reading from right to left, it is expressed as

$$P \leftarrow Mo \leftarrow Me$$

The effectiveness of an identity is determined by the motivational effect of meanings on the will (as in "willingness to") in order to carry out a purpose. This means that people who have powerful reasons to succeed are generally motivated to act on and achieve their goals.

The Study of Identities

In the identity formula, for diagnostic, treatment, and scholarship purposes, "meaning" can be studied as a singular attribute, belief, attitude, feeling, value, or aim—or a *meaning type.* Meanings can also be studied as a collection of organized meaning types, which we have defined as a *meaning set.* Logoteleologists study individual meaning types, such as an attitude, or the interaction of different meaning types in a meaning set (for instance, telling the story about how a belief triggers a feeling that shapes an attitude).

The flexibility of being able to study and treat clients' individual meaning types as well as their meaning sets facilitates the diagnosis of behavioral phenomena, as in scripted behavior.

But how does this identity formula help the teleotherapist diagnose and treat identity-related concerns? Also, how does it aid individuals who want to understand and improve their identities?

First, the formula provides a way of understanding behavior as a causal flow in the identity system. Basically, meanings influence motivation to purpose (P ← Mo ← Me).

Second, it helps to analyze input meanings, their effects on motivation, actions, and the impact of outputs. For instance, if an employee is not producing reports on time, we could discover that she or he gives a low-meaning priority to generating reports and thus is amotivated[63] from writing them. Simply stated, the low meaning given to writing reports does not motivate the individual to put pen to paper.

> Meanings energize motivation; and the motivation brings about purpose.
> P ← Mo ← Me

Third, the identity formula is a pragmatic visual tool that can strengthen self-determination through meaning:

- analysis: to determine meaning set content
- validation: to determine meaning set quality
- replacement: to improve meaning set quality

The hypothesis is that identities are formed by and improved first and foremost through meanings. With a clear and determined meaningful "why" in play, the most energizing and effective "what" or purpose can be planned, skilled and implemented. In addition, helping people surface, explore, and understand the implications of their subconscious meanings (i.e., deepening their self-awareness) can help them replace unhealthy meanings with more effective ones.

63 http://encyclopedia.thefreedictionary.com/Amotivational+syndrome. Amotivational syndrome is a psychological condition associated with diminished inspiration to participate in social situations and activities, with lapses in apathy caused by an external event, situation, substance (or lack of), relationship, or other cause.

In summary, an identity is formed of a purpose, motivation, and meaning(s). An identity is articulated through the formula

$$I = P + Mo + Me$$

Purpose, motivation, and meaning are three separate mental functions in a system known as identity. Meanings energize the motivation, and the motivation brings about purpose. It is expressed through the formula

> The hypothesis is that identities are formed by and improved first and foremost through meanings.

$$P \leftarrow Mo \leftarrow Me$$

Healthy identities can be built, reconstructed, realigned, and improved.

Application: Who Am I? Claiming Your Identity

Throughout this chapter I have defined what an identity is, why identity matters, and described its construct. To describe who you are, you will need to fill in the elements of the identity formula (I = P + Mo + Me). After my example below, follow the steps so you can determine and claim your identity. This might take a few attempts. Start with a working draft. As you read other chapters, you can come back to this exercise to continue refining your description until you find a meaning and purpose fitting of your potential and calling in life.

In the example, you will read that my life purpose is *to be genuinely devoted to allow, to cooperate, and to transcend in order to improve the quality of life of the willing through meaningful purpose.*

Identity	Luis A. Marrero
Purpose	to allow, cooperate, and transcend through meaningful purpose
Will	genuinely devoted
Meaning	to improve the quality of life of the willing

Table 2 Example of a Life Purpose

1. List and prioritize no fewer than fifteen meanings (attributes, beliefs, attitudes, values, feelings, and aims) that best describe your person identity. Use word adjectives for your descriptions. For instance, intelligent, worrisome, handsome, moral, etc.

2. Evaluate which of those meanings you and others consider positive and negative or that work in or against your favor, and then separate and place the positive and the negative meanings in two columns.

3. Replace the negative meanings with positive meanings. For instance, if you listed "arrogant," you can replace it with "humble." The goal is to commit to operate out of positive meaning sets and purge those meanings that do not help you and others.

4. Review the new list of positive meanings. Add new ones if you find it helpful. Take time to ponder what the combined list tells you about

    a. what is important to you
    b. who you wish to be
    c. what you want people to say about you (your reputation)
    d. what is going to be your life's achievements and legacy

5. Once you have built a preliminary meaning set, choose a purpose to carry it out. For instance, in my case, I selected a life purpose that could be applied to each and every role I occupy in my life: to *allow, cooperate, and transcend through meaningful purpose* (which assumes the five strivings).

6. *Feel* how motivating the purpose is. Is it something you feel passionate about? If not, either change the purpose or go back to improve your meaning set.

7. Now, fill the table with the understanding that you will be refining and improving over time.

Identity	
Purpose	
Will	
Meaning	

Table 3 Description of Your Identity

Learning from My Journey

In chapter 1 I introduced the circumstances that led me to invest with renewed interest to study psychology—particularly to understand the relationship and functions of identity, purpose, motivation, and meaning in behavior. I believe answers do exist for humanity's fundamental problems and that logoteleology can make a difference providing solutions. These problems apply to all facets of our lives. I have found this human predicament both bewildering and fascinating to explore and understand. Imagine: it is like being a prisoner in a jail, having the key to freedom in our pocket yet choosing to remain incarcerated as if we had no option. I strongly believe that for various reasons, as a species, we have not yet found the collective will to solve these vital difficulties.

> At the heart of humanity's inability to solve its fundamental problems lies a lack of understanding of who we are and what we are here for. As a species we suffer of an identity crisis.

You will recall from chapter 1 that I found seven fundamental reasons problems go unsolved. These are because people

- are ignorant of the answers;
- do not seek the answers;
- do not know how and where to seek answers;
- do not have access to the answers;
- implement the wrong answers;

- as free-will agents, despite knowing the answers, do not to act on them;
- lack a meaningful purpose to guide them; thus, its absence makes it difficult for them to ask the right questions.

I also believe that at the heart of humanity's inability to solve its fundamental problems lies a lack of understanding of who we are and what we are here for. As a species, we suffer from an identity crisis. I firmly believe the field of psychology is called to make a special contribution to meet this challenge. As an outcome, my research and learning drove me to find the answers about our identity through four basic questions:

- Who am I?
- What matters in life?
- Why am I here?
- How do I go about fulfilling my life purpose?

This chapter started answering the first question, "Who am I?"

As I organized findings and reached conclusions, I followed through with my commitment to act on my new awareness in order to test hypothesis and to improve as a person. I am my own guinea pig and observer. And to use myself as instrument of observation and research, you will recall, I committed to the following process:

- identify and prioritize areas to improve upon
- seek answers
- take action on the answers
- observe and learn from the results
- repeat successful practices

- if not successful, go back to step two
- if successful practices can be improved; go back to step one

So how has my learning about identities helped me?

- I can explain myself clearly and unequivocally.
- I am wiser and more intentional about choosing my friends and memberships. I am also more selective, purposeful, and adept at nurturing authentic relationships with others. I work and share my life only with the willing.
- Through the identity formula I can better understand where my actions come from. I know how the meanings I give to situations influence what I do. This understanding gives me the tools and confidence to improve.
- Knowing about identity helps and allows me to assist the willing build their unique self.

What's Next?

This chapter provided a psychological answer to who we are through the understanding of identities. We know there are three identities: person, social, and role. We also learned why identities matter. We know how identities are formed. We also learned that each person is extraordinary and irreplaceable. In addition, you had an opportunity to apply some of the concepts to evaluate and—where called for—enhance your identity. Finally, I shared some of the ways that I have been helped by understanding identities.

Chapter 3, "Meaning—What Is It?" will build on chapter 2, particularly explaining what a meaning is and what its origins are.

Chapter 3: Meaning—What Is It?

Without continual growth and progress, such words as improvement, achievement, and success have no meaning.—Benjamin Franklin

I stated in the previous chapter that at the heart of humanity's inability to solve its fundamental problems lies a lack of understanding of who we are and why we are here. I believe that as a species we suffer from an identity crisis.

To solve this identity problem, my research drove me to find the answers to four fundamental, meaningful questions:

- Who am I?
- What matters in life?
- Why am I here?
- How do I go about fulfilling my life's purpose?

The previous chapter addressed the first question, "Who am I?" The next two chapters will define meaning and address "What matters in life?" More specifically, I will cover the following six topics, as specified:

In chapter 3:

- What is a meaning?

- Where do meanings come from?

In chapter 4:

- What is meaningful and meaningless?
- What role do emotions play in meaning sets?
- Why does meaning matter?
- What is the meaning of life?

In addition, as with the previous chapter, I will propose ways in which you can benefit from the content of these chapters. I will also describe how learning about meaning has been useful to me and valuable to those with whom I interact.

What Is Meaning

In the previous chapter, *meaning* was defined as the expressed *attributes, beliefs, attitudes, aims, feelings, and values in an identity.* It is important to explain that these six elements, while unique and distinct, are not isolated and independent of one another. They are an organized and interactive synergetic *set.* For instance, values influence attitudes and aims. I reached that conclusion after reviewing multiple definitions that, taken as a whole, were insightful and comprehensive. Meaning sets can be simple, as seen in figure 3, or complex, which would include many more meanings, as seen in figure 4.[64]

64 The logoteleologist studies meaning sets in order to understand behavior.

The context for the proposed definition is the person, social, and role identities I previously discussed. However, there are other definitions for meaning beyond that framework. Some authors have suggested descriptions linked to the interaction between individuals. Other researchers study meanings as a system. Here are a few of these definitions.

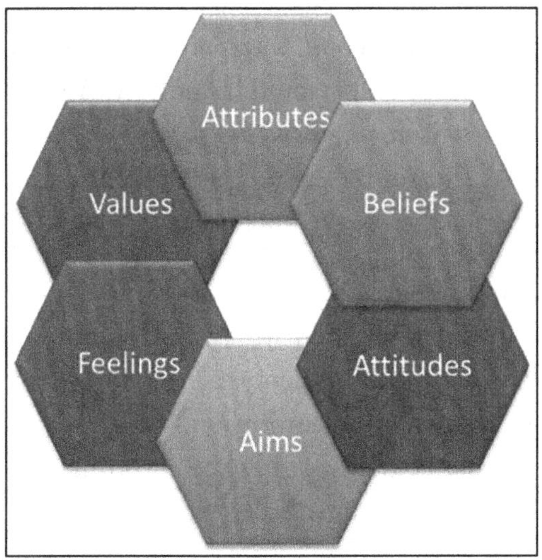

Figure 3: The Meaning Set

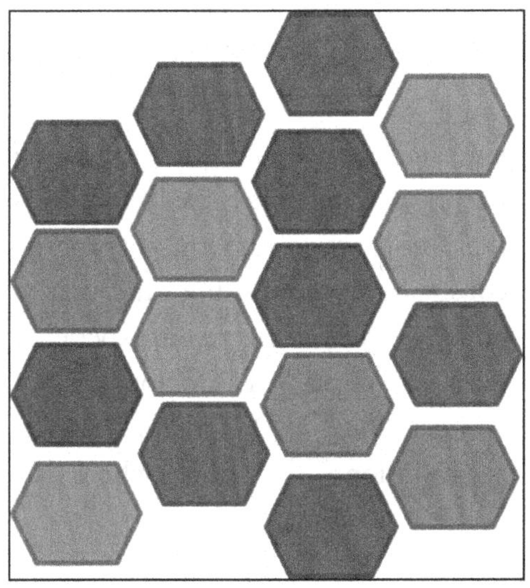

Figure 4: A Complex Meaning Set

According to Frankl, as a stimulus, "*Meaning is what is meant,* be it by a person who asks me a question, or by a situation which, too, implies a question and calls for an answer."[65] And, "There is only one meaning to each situation, and this is its true meaning."[66] Taken this way, meaning answers the question, *What is the meaning of the sender's message or of the situation?*

The listener's task is to interpret correctly what he or she hears so that its meaning is clearly understood. Burke

65 Frankl, Viktor E., *The Will to Meaning: Foundations and Applications of Logotherapy.* (New York: Meridian, 1998), 62.
66 Ibid., 60.

and Stets defined meaning as "a set of responses that people make to a stimulus or a sign."[67] For instance, if I am introduced to a visitor and she smiles and extends her hand toward me, I could interpret those actions as friendly intentions, or it could mean the person is friendly. Meaning, in this sense, answers, *What is the meaning I give to this situation/person?* Hence there is the meaning of the source (as per Frankl) and the meaning decoded by the receiver (as per Burke and Stets).

Making reference to semantics and systems theory, the British analytical psychologist Dale Mathers summarizes well what the combined intended meaning and the decoded meaning denote: "Meaning is an act of communication, rather than a communication."[68] The act of communication is a two-way exchange that requires the encoding and the deconstruction (or decoding) of meanings. Adler expands:

> A private meaning is, in fact, no meaning at all. Meaning is not only possible in communication, for a word which meant something to one person only would really be meaningless. It is the same with our aims and actions, since their only meaning is their meaning for others.[69]

Dale Mathers adds, "Internally generated meanings require validation by the collective, to avoid solipsism (private language)." He later affirms that "we share co-responsibility for the construction of meaning" and that to do so "we must engage in our experience with a kind of democracy of appreciation."[70] This democracy of appreciation—the space where the

> "A private meaning is, in fact, no meaning at all"
>
> Alfred Adler

67 Burke, Peter J., and Jan E. Stets, *Identity Theory* (New York: Oxford University Press, 2009), 93.

68 Mathers, Dale, *Meaning and Purpose in Analytical Psychology* (Philadelphia: Taylor and Francis, Inc., 2001), 3.

69 Ansbacher, Heinz, and Rowena Ansbacher. 1956. 156.

70 Mathers, Dale, *Meaning and Purpose in Analytical Psychology,* 11.

parties are co-responsible for the construction of meaning—requires mutual trust.[71]

But why does this matter? How is sharing co-responsibility for the construction of meaning relevant? And isn't this obvious?

It matters because it reminds us that in order to survive and thrive as a civilization, we need shared meanings to get things done. It is relevant because unless we take personal responsibility to act, cooperate, and transcend, we are not going to be able to appreciate one another. What *is* obvious is that, too frequently, we are still failing in great measure to solve our most pressing problems.

Meanings and Emotions

Decoding meanings includes understanding the emergence of feelings[72] in a transaction. Previously quoted Gestalt practitioners Joseph Melnick and Sonia March Nevis affirm, "Labeling of a sensation is one way to define 'meaning.'"[73] This means that when people face a situation, their emotional reaction means something worth understanding. Thus, in this sense, meaning is the labeling of a sensation. It answers, "What does this feeling mean?"

For instance, let's imagine a worker we will call Julie. Her boss never calls her unless it is to give her "constructive feedback" pertaining to her performance. Upon returning to her office from a business trip, Julie finds a message from her boss in her voice mail's inbox asking her to call him as soon as possible. Julie's stomach turns and feelings of anxiety surface. Her feelings are telling Julie based on past experiences that no good will come from this call. Thus, her feelings are conveying meanings.

Taking all of the above definitions in consideration, it can be said that

71 Ibid., 115.

72 In logoteleology feelings are evaluative affective experiences, and emotion is energy that sets motion or motivation.

73 Nevis, Edwin C., Ed., *Gestalt Therapy* (New York: Gardner Press, 1992), 69.

meaning is also an inner guidance *system* that pays attention to, collects, and stores relevant information in order to appraise and make decisions. It scans, draws, and filters important incoming data. Thus, the *meaning system* manages our attention. As a system it analyzes the implications of incoming information and considers options.

In an identity meanings set the agenda.

Once incoming data is understood, the meanings become instructions, expectations, and aims. Consequently, in an identity, *meanings set the agenda*. But why do meanings set the agenda? To what end are they met and for whom? Rychlack explains that "meaning is an organization or pattern that extends its significance to some relevant target."[74] Meaning provides the "why" a situation or person deserves our attention. As will be explained in greater detail in the chapter related to the Will, *if the reason* (i.e., *Why* do it?) *is strong and meaningful enough it will instruct our motivation to energize and direct action toward a target*[75] (i.e., *What* action will I take?). Said differently, meaning is a prerequisite condition to motivation, and motivation is a required condition for purpose. As was explained in chapter 2, meanings find their expression through purposes. That is why and how meanings become instructions, expectations, and aims.

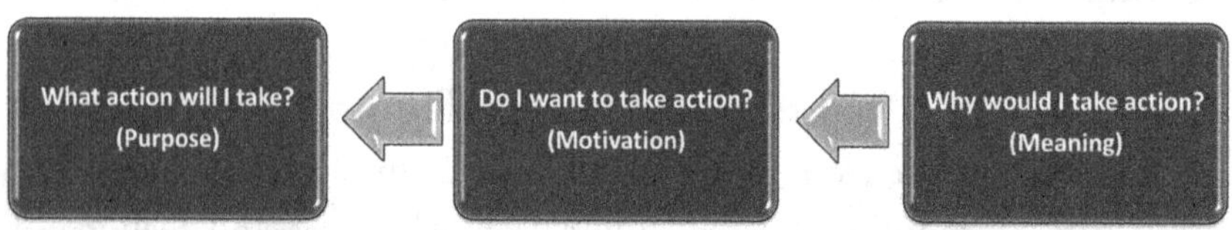

Figure 5 The Influence of Meanings on Motivation and Purpose

Hence, a *meaning system* in an identity receives, decodes, stores, builds upon, encodes, and sends information by way of attributes, beliefs, attitudes, values, feelings, and aims (i.e., meanings) in order to fulfill

74 Rychlack, Joseph F., *Logical Learning Theory: A Human Teleology and Its Empirical Support (*Lincoln: University of Nebraska Press, 1994), 316.

75 *Target* is meaning fulfillment, the object of our meanings.

a purpose or goal. According to Dr. Dweck, meaning systems help "people develop beliefs that organize their world and give meaning to their experiences."[76]

But meaning systems—being part of a larger and open system—do more than to help us transact with the outer world. The exchange of information continuously builds and shapes identity, as in building knowledge and character.

We now have working definitions for meaning within the contexts of identity and transactions (see table 4, below), as well as the description of a meaning system. With those explanations as background, let's review and learn more about where meaning comes from. I will also broaden understanding about the role of meaning systems in an identity.

Scope	Definition	Sample Questions
Identity	Attribute	What qualities and characteristics best describe me?
	Beliefs	What do I accept as true? What moral and ethical compass do I follow?
	Attitude	What is my emotional investment and disposition? What am I disposed to pursue and avoid? What is my outlook toward life and situations?
	Value	What is important and esteemed? What do I want? What am I living for? What significance does my life have?
	Feelings	What emotional state or mood best describes me? What feelings affect my world outlook and approach? What do feelings say about my self-esteem?
	Aims	What do I aspire to? What do I deserve to be and do? What do I want out of life?

76 Dweck, Carl S., *Self-Theories: Their Role in Motivation, Personality, and Development.* (Philadelphia: Psychology Press, 2000) , xi

<table>
<tr><td rowspan="5">Transactional</td><td>What is meant by other</td><td>What is the meaning of the sender's message or situation?</td></tr>
<tr><td>What is interpreted</td><td>What is the meaning I give to this situation/ person?</td></tr>
<tr><td>What is felt</td><td>What does this feeling mean?</td></tr>
<tr><td>What I mean</td><td>What understanding do I choose to communicate?</td></tr>
<tr><td>What is aimed</td><td>What influence do I want my communication to have on me and/or the receiver?</td></tr>
</table>

Table 4 Meaning Definitions

Where Do Meanings Come From?

Where do your meanings in the form of attributes, beliefs, attitudes, values, feelings, and aims come from? How did they find their way into your mind? And how do they influence you? You will recall from the chapter on identity that we give meaning to significant events and what we judge those events say about us, others, and situations. Therefore, *meanings derive from the conclusions and affirmations people make about themselves, others, and situations.* These conclusions and affirmations are answers to questions intended to help us make sense of the world around us (i.e., "What is the meaning of this?").

> Meanings derive from the conclusions and affirmations people have made about themselves, others and situations

Next, let's deepen our understanding of how meanings originate from the conclusions and affirmations people make about themselves, others, and situations.

The Meaning System

Each time people go through a significant event, the mind, through the meaning system, attempts to make sense of the situation through a version of the question, "What is the meaning of this?" The incoming input must be interpreted and tested for veracity by the receiver. That is why Frankl asserted, "Meanings are discovered but not invented."[77] In other words, it makes no sense to give meaning to someone else's input and expect it to be accurate without first asking or checking for verification. We learned that a meaning that is not verified would be a private interpretation and not a shared meaning.

Mathers adds, "my meaning and purpose are no one else's."[78] In other words, *a* meaning is not "my" meaning because someone else, in the form of a projection, says so. Also, *my* meaning is not "your" meaning until you can understand and validate mine. This means that when engaging with another individual, each person has the duty to be "responsible for giving the *right* answer to a question, for finding the *true* meaning of a situation."[79] Said differently, it is impossible to "be on the same page" with another person unless honest answers are given.

By the way, without such shared understanding it is difficult to allow, cooperate, and transcend. And for obvious reasons, it is difficult to have a shared mindset with another unless ultimately the meanings are mutual, confirmed, and settled. For instance, we can make sure a meaning is mutual by (a) paraphrasing what was heard and (b) by genuinely reflecting what was felt by the sender. That way the receiver can validate with the sender if the meaning has been correctly interpreted. The ideal end goal of civil and goodwilled people is to reach a state of "our meaning." ACT and the five strivings are excellent enablers for goodwilled people.

---

77 Frankl, Viktor, *The Will to Meaning,* 60.

78 Mathers, Dale, *Meaning and Purpose in Analytical Psychology,* 27.

79 Frankl, Viktor, *The Will to Meaning,* 62.

Meaning is an individual attribute, attitude, belief, value, feeling, and aim in a person's identity. Meanings come from the conclusions and affirmations people have made about themselves, others, and situations through the meaning system based on biogenetic temperaments plus past and current life experiences. As a result, meanings create the agenda in an identity. They express our needs and wants. In logoteleology, meanings are generally expressed in adjective form.

A collection of attributes, attitudes, beliefs, values, feelings, and aims (i.e., meanings) in a person's identity makes a **meaning set**. **The construct of a meaning set** contains the psychological instructions used in the development and functioning of a personality or identity, much like the DNA has the genetic instructions of a person. Meaning sets can be studied in their simple or complex forms.

A **meaning system in an identity** *receives, decodes, stores, builds upon, encodes, and sends information by way of meanings. These meanings become expectations and instructions that influence decision making and choice.* It is through meaning systems that we make sense of experiences. In other words, meaning systems help people analyze situations, exercise choice, and take appropriate action.

Adler, Frankl's predecessor, had much to say about meaning and where meaning comes from.

> No human being can escape meanings. We experience reality only through the meaning we ascribe to it; not as a thing in itself, but as something interpreted.
>
> Moreover, he stated,
>
> If we closed our ears to words and concentrated on observing actions, we would find that each person has formulated his own individual "meaning of life," and that all his opinions, attitudes, movements, expressions,

> mannerisms, ambitions, habits, and character traits are in accordance to this meaning. [80]

This means each person has either an operating self-determined conscious meaning or a scripted unconscious meaning for her or his life. We have already discussed the adverse consequences of negative scripts in personality. That explains why logoteleology is in the business of building self-determined identities.

> "The ancestor of every action is a thought."
>
> Ralph Waldo Emerson, Essays, First Series, 1841

But is there research to further substantiate that *meanings derive from the conclusions and affirmations people have made about themselves, others, and situations?* The answer is affirmative. Finding meaning has been determined to be an active process in which people interpret the events in their lives,[81] find value in these events,[82] and discover the significance of what happens to them."[83], [84]

Stanford University's Carol Dweck's landmark studies on meaning systems also give weight to the proposed definition for meaning. She and others have researched and reported convincing findings about "how people's beliefs, values, and goals set up a meaning system within which they define themselves and operate."[85]

To sum up, meanings come from conclusions and affirmations people have made about themselves, others, and situations through the

---

80 Adler, Alfred, *What Life Could Mean to You* (Center City, Minnesota: Hazeldn, 1998), 1.

81 Taylor, S. E., "Adjustment to Threatening Events: A Theory of Cognitive Adaptation." *American Psychologist* 38 (1983): 1161–73.

82 Davis, C. G., S. Nolen-Hoeksema, and J. Larsen, "Making Sense of Loss and Benefiting from the Experience: Two Construals of Meaning." *Journal of Personality and Social Psychology* 75 (1998): 561–74.

83 Park, C. L., and S. Folkman, "Meaning in the Context of Stress and Coping." *Review of General Psychology* 1 (1997): 115—44.

84 Reeve, Johnmarshall, *Understanding Motivation and Emotion*, 431.

85 Dweck, Carol S., *Self-Theories,* 138–39.

meaning system based on biogenetic temperaments plus past and current experiences. Self-determined individuals can be purposeful and aware of their individual meaning of life. Otherwise, for the less fortunate, what life means will remain scripted and unaware. Logoteleologists are committed to helping people be self-determined.

Leveraging the findings of the previous authors and researchers, let us now take a look at logoteleology's building blocks of meaning systems.

What Are Meaning Systems Made Of?

In logoteleology, a meaning system in an identity has five core components:

- Meaning Antecedents
- Meaning
- Meaning Sets
- Emotional Attitudes
- Meaning Motives

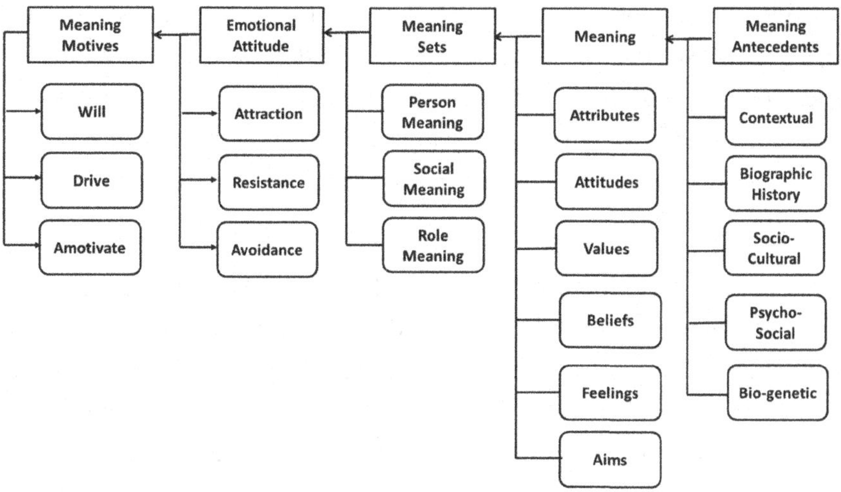

Figure 6: Logoteleology's Meaning System

Meaning Antecedents: The Sources of Meanings

The meaning system can be seen in graphic form above, in figure 6. On the extreme right are the factors that influence identity formation that were covered in chapter 2. I mentioned that identities come from our DNA, our family (psychosocial), culture (sociocultural), accumulated life experiences, and current situations or context. That makes us biopsychosocial organisms.[86] These shapers of identities are **meaning antecedents**. These meaning antecedents, which are unique for each human being, help organize people's worldview and give significance to their daily lives. These meaning antecedents form **meanings** in the identity.

The Meaning Set

Meanings are grouped to self-identify us. You will recall from the previous chapter that the combined meanings in an identity are known as a **meaning set**. We select, organize, and form meaning sets to define and express our unique person, social, and role identities. These also

86 Myers, David G., *Social Psychology*, 9.

provide the platform and lens whence we interpret and face people and situations. The meaning set ultimately defines a person's quality and vitality of life. Moreover, as in the case of DNA, meaning sets are meaning strands with the psychological instructions used to develop and function. Therefore, *meaning sets are made of meanings and operators* (e.g., if … then).

Thus, meaning set constructs are *not* random, accidental, or unsystematic. The construct has a specific organized pattern and subsequent agenda and aim. Meaning sets are appropriately configured to influence motivation and ultimately define a purpose and an orientation. The meaning segments carrying this psychological inherent information in the brain are called *neural networks*. At the risk of being overly simplistic, below (figure 7) is an example of a mind map of a meaning set related to being wealthy (operators excluded).

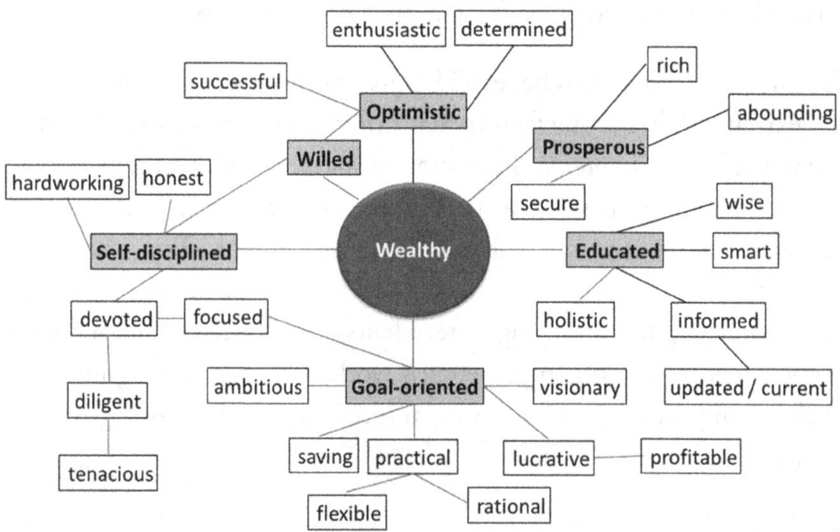

Figure 7: Meaning Set of a wealth oriented identity

Emotional Attitude

Our next component in the meaning system is an **emotional attitude,** or the emotional disposition toward a situation, person, or task. As we interact with people and deal with situations, we feel emotions. Dweck agrees with previously quoted Gestalt practitioners Melnick and Nevis when she reminds us that "people tend to feel positive or negative emotions because of the meaning they give to something that has happened." Further she states, "They are things that we can *become* aware of, but at any given moment we may not realize that they're present and how they are affecting us."[87]

These emotions plus the meanings that triggered them prompt an attitude toward the situation or person. The type of attitude that is urged will predispose a response. Zajonc proposed that there are stimuli features, which he called *preferenda,* that when combined with emotions allow people to make evaluations of the sort known as attraction, repulsion, pleasure, and so forth in eight hundred milliseconds or fewer.[88] In other words, *emotional attitude* is the innate affective evaluation of a meaning related to a situation, person, or task. The emotional disposition incites emotional attraction, avoidance, or resistance. The speed of processing the evaluation explains in part why the feeling can remain at the unaware level.

Meaning Motives

The meaning set influenced by the emotional attitude toward a target arouses an operator (e.g., if/then)—which I call **Meaning Motives**—to select from three motivational alternatives: *Will, Drive,* and *Amotivate.*[89]

87 Dweck, Carol S., *Self-Theories,* 139.

88 Zajonc, R. B., "Feeling and Thinking: Preferences Need no Inferences." *American Psychologist* 35 (1980): 159.

89 Hereafter, Meaning Motives Will, Drive, and Amotivation will be capitalized.

The Will

Simply stated, *Will* is an energetic and enthused "I want to!" In this situation motivation is intrinsic and self-determined.

The Drive

Drive, on the other hand, is a reluctant "I have to, so I will do it. But if I had the choice, I would not do it." In this case, motivation is extrinsic and a response to an introjection or a coercive demand by an external power. In logoteleology, Drives are not responses to satisfy intrinsic needs and wants; rather, they are motivated to avoid (i.e., avoidance) a negative consequence or to earn a reward (i.e., scripted attraction) by outside forces. They could also be compulsions and impulses at the unaware level. In this case the unconscious drive would claim "I have to or something terrible will happen to me."

The Amotivation

Amotivation is the inability or an unwillingness to engage in the situation or with the person. The amotivated individual procrastinates and resists while protesting "I won't do it!" as a rebellious stance. It can also be the case of helplessness where the answer is "I can't do it!" A third option is based on boredom and apathy, where the situation does not generate interest. It answers "I am not interested." In summary, amotivation is the result of a rebellion against an internal drive or external imposition (a counterinjunction), the outcome of learned and real helplessness, or apathy.

Will is self-determined intrinsic motivation and *identified motivation.* Identified motivation is expressed when an individual is committed to action because, while not intrinsically motivating, the outcome of the effort is perceived as meaningful. Identified motivation encourages people to cooperate and transcend. It is expressed as "I want to do it."

In logoteleology *Drive* is introjected extrinsic motivation or a compulsion where an individual is compelled to act against his or her own wishes. A drive can be an impulse or sudden incitement to act with little or no conscious control. It is expressed as "I have to do it."

Amotivation is the inability or unwillingness to engage in normal social situations. It is a counterinjunction to an internal drive or an external imposition. Amotivation can also be experienced as learned and a real sense of helplessness, and apathy. It is expressed as "I won't do it," "I can't do it," or "I am not interested."

Summary

Meaning Motives are decision-making operators that select a motivational approach (Will, Drive, and Amotivate) based on the emotional attitude given to a target (e.g., I will follow this approach because of how I interpret the situation [i.e., meaning given] and because of the emotional attitude I feel [attraction, avoidance, or resistance generated by the meaning] about the target).

> What is necessary to change a person is to change his awareness of himself.
>
> Abraham Maslow

It is important to emphasize that *meaning motive types determine the motivational option-response that best supports the meaning given to the situation and the emotion it arouses.* Operationally, in a meaning system, meaning motives do not stimulate an individual to act; rather the meaning motive assigns the fitting *motivational* approach—either to will, to drive, or to amotivate.[90], [91], [92], [93], [94], [95], [96]

I will expand on the relationship between the meaning system and the role of motivation in the chapter related to the will.

Utility of Meaning Systems

Finally, how is the meaning system useful? And what is the practical use of this model?

In my practice I have found that when clients are made aware of the process of meaning formation and meaning expression, they gain the renewed power of being more self-determined. Put differently, clients are more receptive to believe in their capacity to control and improve their meanings and outcomes.

For instance, using the meaning system model, they can

- become aware of the type of motivation that is influencing their behavior (Will, Drive, or Amotivate);
- label the emotional attitude (attraction, resistance, avoidance);

---

90 This is consistent with differential emotions theory where emotions act as motivation systems that prepare the individual to perform in adaptive ways. See Izard, C. E. 1989. "The Structure and Functions of Emotions: Implications for Cognition, Motivation, and Personality." Cohen, I. S., Ed. The G. Stanley Hall lecture series, *American Psychological Association* 9: 39–73. Washington, DC.
91 Izard, C. E., and C. Z. Malatesta. 1987. "Perspectives in emotional development: I. Differential emotions theory or early emotional development." In J. D. Osotsky (Ed.), *Handbook of Infant Development,* 2nd ed. 494–554. New York: Wiley-Interscience.
92 Izard, C. E., *The Psychology of Emotions* (New York: Plenum, 1991).
93 Izard, C. E., "Basic Emotions, Relations among Emotions, and Emotion-Cognition Relations." *Psychological Review* 99 (1992): 561–65.
94 Izard, C. E., "Four Systems for Emotion Activation: Cognitive and Noncognitive Development." *Psychological Review* 100 (1993): 68–90
95 Arnold, M. B., *Emotion and Personality* (Vols. 1 and 2). (New York: Columbia University Press, 1960)
96 Arnold, M. B., "Perennial Problems in the Field of Emotion." Arnold, M. B., Ed. *Feelings and Emotions* (New York: Academic Press, 1970), 169–85.

- describe the emotion felt that elicited the type of motivation;
- recall the role, situation, or context where the emotion was experienced;
- discover and describe what attributes, attitudes, beliefs, feelings, and aims (i.e., meanings) triggered the whole sequence;
- select a more appropriate meaning set for the situation.

For readers who might be interested, I have added an example of a discovery process below under the heading "Example of Discovery Process."

Example of Discovery Process

This section illustrates the discovery process using the example of the weather forecaster from chapter 2. Let us assume the weather forecaster is being coached by a teleotherapist and that the conversation revolves around why he likes his job.

Teleotherapist: Now that you understand the meaning system, what type of motivation best describes you in your role? (Meaning Motive Type)

Weather Forecaster: Oh! Definitely *Will*! I love my job! (Meaning Motive Type)

Teleotherapist: Go on. You are doing fine. Follow the model. You started describing the emotions that drive your will ... (Emotional Attitude)

Weather Forecaster: Well, I feel a sense of pride, that I am making a difference in people's lives. Helping and being useful is part of my core self; it makes me feel good. Being a member of a community dedicated to serving others, particularly through the role of weather forecaster gives me great satisfaction. (Emotional Attitude)

Teleotherapist: So you love doing what you do and feel pride doing something meaningful to your core self. I also heard you say you can express what is meaningful to your core self (personal identity) as a member of the meteorological community (social identity), and in your role as a weather forecaster (role identity). You experience alignment and fulfillment in your career. (Meaning Set: Personal, Social, and Role Identitities)

Weather Forecaster: That's right. When I am in the studio, in front of the camera, I experience deep gratification. (Emotional Attitude)

Teleotherapist: How does being a weather forecaster play to your strengths? (Meaning Antecedent and Attribute Meaning Type)

Weather Forecaster: As far back as I can remember I have always loved the sciences, particularly related to weather. It is a system, and I enjoy figuring things out in complex situations such as one experience in meteorology. (Meaning Antecedent and Attribute Meaning Type)

Teleotherapist: No wonder you have such a positive attitude toward meteorology! (Emotional Attitude)

Weather Forecaster: Oh, yes. I gravitate toward anything related to my craft! (Emotional Attitude)

Teleotherapist: So the payoff of your aim is clear to you. (Emotional Attitude)

Weather Forecaster: Actually, in two ways. The deep satisfaction I derive from it as well my aim and desire to make a difference in people's lives. (Emotional Attitude and Meaning Types: Values and Beliefs)

Teleotherapist: And how else does your job fit with your attributes, particularly your (biogenetic) temperament? (Meaning Antecedent and Attribute Meaning Type)

Weather Forecaster: Well, while I like to be in front of the camera and enjoy the attention a forecaster gets, I am really an introvert. So working at the station is just perfect because I have my private space, and people respect my research time. It allows me to prepare for my segment. So

I have the best of both worlds. (Smiles) (Meaning Antecedent and Attribute Meaning Type)

Teleotherapist: Let's go to the Meaning box labeled "values." Say more about what is important to you. (Meaning)

Weather Forecaster: I believe in doing something valuable for others. It is not just about me. Service is one of my values. Second, I work with and enjoy being part of a team. I value partnering with others to make our news program unique, relevant, fun, and interesting. Part of doing something valuable for others is cooperating with my team to plan and offer a program worthwhile to our public and sponsors. (Meaning Set)

Teleotherapist: You seem to be grounded on your values. You are also able to live them through your work, allowing you to do what matters. (Meaning Set)

Weather Forecaster: Yes. (Meaning Set)

Teleotherapist: Where do these values come from? Do you remember when you claimed them to guide your life? (Meaning Antecedents)

Weather Forecaster: Oh, I am sure from Mom and Dad; church also. But when I claimed them? I never thought of it that way, as a claim…. Yet, I must have since values do influence my choices. I would attribute any claim as part of growing up, and maturing as a person. (Meaning Antecedents)

Teleotherapist: You are not alone. I have found that many people have not thought much about their values in an intentional way. Generally they seem to surface and express themselves without much thought and validation. Yet I do encourage people to think about what matters in life, what their beliefs are, and what principles would best guide their behavior toward a meaningful end. I believe that it makes life easier and more fulfilling.

Weather Forecaster: I would find that to be an interesting exercise …

As you can determine from the previous interaction, the meaning system guides self-awareness. Meaning motives can be studied, the emotions and meanings that precede them can be evaluated, and future options can be considered. The awareness and use of the model by the client encourages self-determination with minimal intervention by and dependence on the counselor or coach. The goal of the coach and process is to empower the clients to select those meanings that bring about the right and optimistic feelings. In turn, the positive emotions encourage the selection of the Will over the other two motivation options (i.e., Drive and Amotivation). This act of self-determination helps individuals relate well with others and soundly deal with life's challenges.[97] There is strong evidence from researchers Peter J. Burke and Jan E. Stets that "People act in ways such that the meanings of their behavior reflect the meanings they hold for themselves in their identities."[98] Hence, helping people select healthy options through the meaning system strengthens their ability to act autonomously and enhances their self-esteem with an overall improvement of their identity.

Application

Now that you have a deeper understanding of meanings and where they come from, what new awareness do you have about who you are and what your life means?

---

97 Feldman, D. B., and C.R. Snyder, "Hope and the Meaningful Life: Theoretical and Empirical Associations between Goal-Directed Thinking and Life Meaning." *Journal of Social and Clinical Psychology* 24, no. 3 (2005): 401–21.
98 Burke, Peter J., and Jan E. Stets, *Identity Theory,* 84.

My Journey

Some of the most significant lessons I learned were through the meaning set. In particular I learned to

- appreciate and respect my unique attributes;
- understand at a deeper level that others have their own uniqueness and that our differences are meant to complement, not divide us;
- pay attention to what I value;
- be clear about my beliefs since these influence my attitude and outlook on life;
- consider and remain aware of what my aims and motives are and of their consequences;
- pay attention to what my feelings are telling me.

Chapter 4: Meaning—What Matters in Life?

From all this we may learn that there are two races of men in the world, but only these two -the "race" of the decent man, and the "race" of the indecent man. Both are found everywhere; they penetrate into all groups of society. No group consists entirely of decent or indecent people.—Viktor Frankl

In this chapter we will address

- What is meaningful and what is meaningless?
- What role do emotions play in meaning sets?
- Why does meaning matter?
- What is the meaning of life?

What Is Meaningful and What Is Meaningless?

In chapter 2 I shared that when meanings in a person's identity become negative, gloomy, and draining, I describe them as *meaningless*. On the other hand, meanings that are positive, mutually beneficial, transcendental, altruistic, and replenishing are *meaningful*.

More specifically, according to logoteleology, there are Five Meaningful strivings that make life fulfilling and meaningful. A vibrant, meaningful life is measured by the degree in which we accomplish those five strivings. These are the meaning bliss or standards of meaningfulness.

In sequential order, these are

1. being in loving relationships;
2. fostering harmony and having peace of mind;
3. making others happy;
4. living, learning, working, and sharing a stimulating, productive, and interesting life with others;
5. building and securing prosperity for oneself and for others.

On the other hand, a meaningless life is the contrary, its symptoms being

1. lacking loving relationships;
2. tormented by one's conscience and introjects, as well as living in strife;
3. sad and emotionally depressed;
4. unable to enjoy life or experience success;
5. economically depressed and destitute.

But before we go further, what is a *striving*? And how does it differ from a goal? University of Iowa's Johnmarshall Reeve explains:

> Personal strivings are not goals per se but, instead exist as subordinate aspects of the self that organize and integrate the many different goals a person seeks. Thus, general strivings reflect general personality dispositions, whereas goals reflect situationally specific objectives.[99]

99 Reeve, Johnmarshall, *Understanding Motivation and Emotion,* 212.

Strivings are the springs that spawn and spur individual daily goals. For instance, I can express my striving of making others happy by setting the goal of making my home environment rich in laughter and harmony. The value of the five strivings is that they provide the framework for goal setting, a topic I will discuss further in the chapter related to purpose.

To review, we know meaning antecedents shape the meaning sets that ultimately select a type of motivation to either

- will toward the meaningful; or
- drive and amotivate toward the meaningless.

Allowing, cooperating, and transcending—the Three Pillars of Meaningful Purpose covered in chapter 1—are methods that will the Five Meaningful strivings.

Let's take a look at ACT and the Five Meaningful strivings through table 5 to illustrate what separates what is meaningful from what is not.

Meaningful is when the individual is …	*Meaningless* is when the individual is …
The Pillars	
Allowing, cooperating, and transcending (or being altruistic).	Preventing others from being themselves and from reaching their potential as well as hindering, disengaging, and underperforming.
Meaningful:	*Meaningless:*
The Strivings	
Love: Being outwardly focused and other-oriented. Practicing empathy, respect, consideration, and compassion. Caring for others.	Alone and inwardly focused and self-oriented. Indifferent, aloof, and uncaring toward others.

Peace: Fostering harmony and doing things that bring peace of mind. Communicating to build meaningful bridges and shared understanding.	Being tormented by one's conscience and introjects, as well as living in strife. Communicating and acting in order to resist, attack, demean, and deceive.
Happiness: Making others happy. Being reasonable and acting in ways that are level-headed and "make sense" to others. Life is oriented foremost toward people as a source of happiness versus a preferred orientation toward objects and impersonal objectives.	Being sad and emotionally depressed. Acting toward others in confusing and unreasonable ways. Being difficult, arbitrary, and irrational toward others. Living an existence that is oriented to value objects and impersonal objectives (i.e., things) over people as a source of happiness.
Interest: Living, working, and sharing a stimulating, productive, and interesting life with others. Experiencing more intrinsic than extrinsic motivation.	Unable to enjoy life, to work, and to relate well with others. Lacking a sense of direction and progressive success. Experiencing more extrinsic than intrinsic motivation.
Prosperity: Building and securing wealth for oneself and others.	Remaining economically depressed and destitute.

Table 5 Describing the Meaningful and the Meaningless

Let's deepen understanding on each.

Allowing, Cooperating, and Transcending

Allowing. Allowing is the path of self-determination and self-definition.[100] When we respect others' meanings, we allow. Allowing is also valuing others' right to choose, to grow, and to evolve organically at their own readiness and pace. Allowing entails having the wisdom to know when to back down, yield and walk away without giving it a competitive meaning of surrender or defeat. To allow is to work with the willing without the expectations that others have to support our agendas. In allowing there is no coercion. Neither is this autonomy-supportive description meant to be "permissive" or laissez-faire. The goal of allowing is not to leave the person alone; rather, it is to have the individual interact more effectively with others through cooperation and transcendence.[101]

> *"The only individuals who can really meet and master the problems of life, however, are those that show in their striving a tendency to enrich all others, who go ahead in such a way that others benefit also. All human judgments of value and success are founded, in the end, upon cooperation; this is the great shared commonplace of the human race."*
>
> Alfred Adler

Cooperating. A tenet of self-determination theory asserts that one of the basic psychological needs that must be met for human growth and well-being is relatedness.[102] Relatedness refers to experiencing a

100 Self-definition: definition of one's identity, character, abilities, and attitudes, especially in relation to persons or things outside oneself or itself. http://www.thefreedictionary.com/self-definition.

101 Skinner, Ellen, and Kathleen Edge. "Self-Determination, Coping, and Development," Deci, Edward, and Richard M. Ryan, Eds., *Handbook of Self-Determination Research* (New York: The University of Rochester Press, 2002), 297–337.

102 Deci, Edward L., and Richard M. Ryan, Eds., *Handbook of Self-Determination Research* (New York: The University of Rochester Press, 2002), 6.

sense of community and belonging with others.[103], [104] This sense of community involves the pursuit of a common and shared meaning by two or more people. This sense of community requires collaboration and teamwork.

Cooperation encourages each individual to offer their talents and competences in service to a common cause and for the general good. Besides helping to achieve a goal, cooperation is fulfilling because it meets people's basic need to socialize and interact with others. Research shows that the social support that is experienced through cooperation acts as a buffer against psychological distress. It helps reduce the possibility of depressive episodes and loneliness while contributing to a positive self-image.[105], [106], [107], [108], [109], [110] Cooperation is meaningful because it follows the doctrine of mutualism, interdependence, and mutual aid. Cooperation also entails shared leadership, where members are encouraged to take the lead when required and appropriate, as well as to exercise authority in order to forward the group's agenda.

---

103 Baumeister, R., and M. R. Leary, "The Need to Belong: Desire for Interpersonal Attachments as a Fundamental Human Motivation." *Psychological Bulletin* 117 (1995): 479–529.
104 Ryan, R. M., "Psychological Needs and the Facilitation of Integrative Processes." *Journal or Personality* 63 (1995): 397–427.
105 Cohen, S., D. R. Sherrod, and M. S. Clark, "Social Skills and the Stress-Protective Role of Social Support." *Journal of Personality and Social Psychology* 50 (1986): 963–73.
106 Lepore, S. J., "Social Conflict, Social Support, and Psychological Distress: Evidence of Cross-Domain Buffering Effects." *Journal of Personality and Social Psychology* 63 (1992): 857–67.
107 Pierce, G. R., B. R. Sarason, and I. G. Sarason., "General and Relationship-Based Perceptions of Social Support: Are Two Constructs Better than One?" *Journal of Personality and Social Psychology* 61 (1991): 1028–39.
108 Pierce, G. R., B. R. Sarason, and I. G. Sarason, Eds., *Handbook of Social Support and the Family* (New York: Plenum Press, 1996).
109 Reis, H. T., and P. Franks, "The Role of Intimacy and Social Support in Health Outcomes: Two Processes or One?" *Personal Relationships* 1 (1994): 185–97.
110 Sarason, B. R., et al., "Perceived Social Support and Working Models of Self and Actual Others." *Journal of Personality and Social Psychology* 60 (1994): 273–87.

Transcending. While allowing and cooperating are laudable and effective meaningful actions, transcending is the ultimate expression of being humane. Frankl, making reference to Abraham H. Maslow's work on motivation, stated, "What is called 'self-actualization' is ultimately an effect, the unintentional by-product, of self-transcendence."[111] Said differently, the life task of building a self-determined and healthy identity that transcends in the service of others ultimately leads to self-actualization. Self-actualization is the self-determined attainment of one's full potential by way of

- unbiased self-awareness;
- the commitment to doing meaningful things;
- the intrinsic motivation to succeed;
- the understanding of how to effectively maneuver through the complexities of life in the real world.

> Psychologically, the ultimate meaning and purpose in life for all humans is to master the abilities and attitudes to allow, to cooperate, and to be altruistic; to transcend.

Thus, psychologically, the ultimate meaning and purpose of life for all humans is to master their abilities and attitudes in order to allow, to cooperate, and to be altruistic; to transcend. As stated previously, we can master these abilities and attitudes through the practice and perfection of the Five Meaningful strivings.

Striving One: Loving Relationships and Being Outwardly Focused and Other-Oriented

True and authentic love is other-oriented. It gives life meaning.[112] In addition, love is more than an emotional experience; it is a biological imperative. For instance, psychiatrist John Bowlby's research on the

111 Frankl, Viktor E., *Man's Search for Ultimate Meaning,* 84.

112 Frankl, Viktor E., *The Will to Meaning,* 69–70.

mental health of homeless children revealed, "Intimate attachments to other human beings are the hub around which a person's life revolves. ... From these intimate attachments [people draw] strength and the enjoyment of life."[113]

Common to all true loving relationships is mutual understanding, a supportive orientation, and enjoying the loved one's company.[114] In other words, in loving relationships people seek, claim, and nurture strong shared meanings.

In addition, being outwardly focused has its benefits. For instance, when individuals have a social orientation and are assertive and have a positive and stimulating disposition, they experience greater satisfaction in life.[115], [116]

Also, extroverts are happier and enjoy more positive moods than do introverts.[117], [118], [119] Compared to introverts, extroverts are prone to experience a higher degree of enjoyment when socializing with others.[120],

---

113 Bowlby, John, *Loss, Sadness, and Depression. Vol. III of Attachment and Loss* (London: Basic Books, 1980), 442.

114 Myers, David G., *Social Psychology,* 453.

115 Depue, R. A., and P. F. Collins, "Neurobiology of the Structure of Personality: Dopamine Facilitation of Incentive Motivation and Extraversion." *Behavioral and Brain Sciences* 22 (1999): 491–569.

116 Watson D., and L. A. Clark, "Extraversion and Its Positive Emotional Core." Hogan, R., J. Johnson, and S. Briggs, Eds. *Handbook of Personality Psychology* (San Diego, CA: Academic Press, 1997), 767–93.

117 Costa, P. T., and R. R. McCrae, "Influence of Extraversion and Neuroticism on Subjective Well-Being: Happy and Unhappy People." *Journal of Personality and Social Psychology* 38 (1980): 668–78.

118 Diener, E., and E. Sandvik, et al., "Extraversion and Subjective Well-Being in a US National Probability Sample." *Journal of Research in Personality* 26 (1998): 205–15.

119 Lucas, R. E., and F. Fujita, "Factors Influencing the Relation between Extraversion and Pleasant Affect." *Journal of Personality and Social Psychology* 79 (2000): 1039–56.

120 Ibid.

[121] This does not mean, however, that introverts are self-centered and incapable of being other-oriented. Their temperament after all is based on genetic factors.[122] The good news is that introverts who are outwardly focused do experience some of the same emotional benefits as extroverts.[123] The point is, regardless of whether we have an extroverted or introverted temperament, we cannot have meaningful experiences in isolation from others, at least not for too long.

Meanings can be found in the fulfillment of others' needs, and if we are going to experience a meaningful existence, we will have to focus our attention on others and their needs as much as and even more so than on our own. Frankl believed the more an individual "forgets himself"—giving himself to a cause or another person—the more *human* he is. And the more he is immersed and absorbed in something or someone other than himself, the more he really becomes *himself*.[124] This describes what it means to be altruistic or transcendental.

> Meanings can be found in the fulfillment of others' needs; and that requires that if we are going to experience a meaningful existence we will have to focus our attention on others and their needs as much as and even more than our own.

On the other hand, choosing to be isolated has negative consequences, including suffering from depression.[125] And with depression come various

121 Elliot, A. J., and T. M. Trash, "Approach-Avoidance Motivation in Personality: Approach and Avoidance Temperament and Goals." *Journal of Personality and Social Psychology* 82 (2002): 804–18.

122 Pederson, N. C., et al., "Neuroticism, Extraversion, and Related Traits in Adult Twins Reared Apart and Reared Together." *Journal of Personality and Social Psychology* 55 (1988): 950–957.

123 Lucas, et al., "Factors Influencing the Relation between Extraversion and Pleasant Affect".

124 Frankl, Viktor E., *Man's Search for Ultimate Meaning,* 84–85.

125 Rychlack, Joseph J., *Logical Learning Theory,* 278.

illnesses.[126], [127] For example, those who live a life of distress are most likely to die at an earlier age than those that do not.[128] Also, chronically lonely people are inclined to engage in self-defeating behaviors.[129]

This helps clarify my previous explanation of psychological scripts as an introjected life plan with three potential negative themes, one being No Love. The other two—No Mind and No Joy—are generally outcomes of the first. People who make their life task to love others can make great strides toward becoming script free. Loving others can also help stop the scourge of intergenerational transfer of scripted personalities.

In conclusion, people who enjoy a meaningful existence do so because they are loving and other-oriented. They strive toward mutual understanding and have an encouraging orientation. On the other hand, people who are self-centered and isolated suffer physiological and psychological ills.

Striving Two: Fostering Harmony and Having Peace of Mind

Unfortunately, since the beginning of recorded history, peace has eluded most Homo sapiens. Peace and peace of mind are by-products of love, which is followed by happiness, the third striving. Achieving the state of peace and peace of mind requires identities with a collective harmony-enhancing meaning set. It requires the intentional strive to build societies and group identities that teach and practice productive and harmonious interactions that are free of toxic introjections and life scripts. It must be said, however, that conditions of peace cannot be

126 Anda, R., et al., "Depressed Affect, Hopelessness, and the Risk of Ischemic Heart Disease in a Cohort of US Adults." *Epidemiology* 4 (1993): 285–94.

127 Freasure-Smith, N., et al., "Gender, Depression, and One-Year Prognosis after Myocardial Infarction." *Psychosomatic Medicine* 61 (1999): 26–37.

128 Valliant, G. E. 1997. "Report on Distress and Longevity." Paper presented during the American Psychiatric Association convention.

129 Anderson, C. A., et al., "Behavioral and Characterological Attributional Styles as Predictors of Depression and Loneliness: Review, Refinement, and Test." *Journal of Personality and Social Psychology* 66 (1994): 549–58.

achieved unilaterally. Research has shown countless times that those who practice the strategy of appeasement and remain 100 percent cooperative often get exploited.[130] Peacemakers must also practice self-respect.

While it is best to know how to foster peace and prevent conflict, there are tools that thwart the escalation of tension, such as the GRIT (graduated and reciprocated initiatives in tension reduction) methodology that has shown promising results in laboratory conditions[131] as well as in international conflicts.[132]

> If we have no peace, it is because we have forgotten that we belong to each other.
>
> Mother Teresa

My goal, however, is not to use this volume to delineate methods for peace building. Those tools do exist. Again, going back to the central thesis of this book, mankind does not suffer for lack of answers, but it does suffer despite those answers being available. What I am encouraging is that we build collective identities with meaning sets that help us to

- learn peacemaking;
- ask the right questions using ACT and the five strivings as standards;
- practice and enjoy the benefits of peaceful living;
- have peace of mind.

I strongly believe we need to make peacemaking a central learning agenda of a free democracy and a free world.

---

130 Myers, David G., *Social Psychology*, 558.

131 Osgood, C. E., *An Alternative to War or Surrender* (Urbana, IL: University of Illinois Press, 1962). Osgood, C. E. 1980. "GRIT: A Strategy for Survival in Mankind's Nuclear Age?" Paper presented during the Pugwash Conference on New Directions in Disarmament, Racine, WI.

132 Etzioni, A., "The Kennedy Experiment." *The Western Political Quarterly* 20 (1967): 361–80.

In conclusion, to achieve a state of harmony and peace of mind requires choosing supportive peace-oriented meanings and building a collective will. It involves building communities that teach and practice productive and harmonious interactions, de-escalate tensions, and foster tolerance. ACT and the five strivings are useful enablers to building harmony.

Striving Three: Making Others Happy

I cannot think of a better disposition after love and peace of mind than being in a state of happiness. Happiness can be experienced as a mood that stems from mental events that last for hours or perhaps days. Happiness can also be understood as an emotion that is tied to a significant life situation and how we judge the circumstance to benefit our overall well being.

While moods are steady states, emotions are usually short-lived, lasting no more than a few seconds or minutes.[133] Either as a long-term mood or short-lived emotion, happiness is an outcome of what people do. Frankl emphasized that "pleasure and happiness are by-products. Happiness must ensure. It cannot be pursued. It is the very pursuit of happiness that thwarts happiness."[134] Trying to be happy does not have a lasting effect. Happiness is considered to be a by-product of life's satisfaction, triumphs, and positive relationships.[135] Logoteleology proposes that some of the actions we can take to make people happy is to care for them, to give others peace of mind, and to help them succeed. This entails giving them our unconditional regard, encouragement, and support.

Logoteleology proposes that one of the actions we can take to make people happy is to help them succeed. It also helps to give them our unconditional regard, encouragement and support.

133 Eckman, P., "All Emotions Are Basic." Eckman, P., and R. J. Davidson, Eds. *The Nature of Emotion: Fundamental Questions* (New York: Oxford University Press, 1994), 15–19.

134 Frankl, Viktor, *Man's Search for Ultimate Meaning*, 90.

135 Izard, C. E., *The Psychology of Emotions.*

While it might be obvious to some, there are multiple benefits to being other-oriented. For instance, research has demonstrated that supporting others has a positive impact on their well- being.[136] Colorado State University at Fort Collins's Michael Steger and Joo Yeon Shin presented a strong case in favor of doing meaningful things that profit others.

> Presence of meaning has been positively associated with many other indicators of well-being, including positive effect, self-esteem, life satisfaction, optimism, hope, happiness, curiosity, self-actualization, and daily positive social interactions, in addition to more positive perceived health. [137]

Moreover, the Framingham studies by University of Pennsylvania's Positive Psychology guru Martin Seligman have clearly demonstrated that moods—positive or negative—are contagious.[138] Thus, acting meaningfully toward others can be spread across groups and communities; it benefits the welfare of the many.

To summarize, happiness can be short-lived or long-lasting. Emotions are short-lived and episodic, while moods are longer-lasting and reflect our general state of mind. Happiness is the outcome of the things we do. To make others happy we can give them our unconditional regard and support, do things that bring them peace of mind, and help them succeed. Happiness can be spread and can benefit the many. Anything less than the above is meaningless.

Striving Four: Living a Stimulating Life

Is your life interesting and stimulating? The answer to the question depends on

- the quality of your meaning set;

---

136 Seligman, Martin E. P., *Flourish* (New York: Free Press, 2011), 16–26.

137 Steger, Michael F., and Joo Yeon Shin, "The Relevance of the Meaning Questionnaire to Therapeutic Practice: A Look at the Initial Evidence." *The International Forum for Logotherapy* 33 (2010): 95–104.

138 Seligman, Martin E. P., *Flourish*, 146.

- the amount of meaningful actions you contribute.

As previously discussed, life is worth living when you do meaningful things. Particularly when you

- love and care for another;
- pursue peaceful ends;
- help others;
- make others laugh and bring joy to their lives;
- foster creativity, innovation, and productivity;
- enjoy all the positive and interesting things life has to offer;
- do smart work and invest wisely in order to be prosperous.

Anything we consider worth accomplishing can and will be found to be meaningful and, as a result, intrinsically motivating. I believe life calls us to create intrinsically motivating and friendly environments where we and others can flourish. This will require we do the following:

- Commit to a clear and worthwhile life purpose
- Commit to achieving goals that are aligned with that life purpose
- Build the right competence to achieve the goals
- Give others and ourselves autonomy and reasonable control over actions
- Enjoy what life has to offer

Let us understand these aims in greater detail.

A Clear and Worthwhile Life Purpose

We are born with an innate, vivid, and exciting disposition to shape and fulfill our self-chosen mode of existence. And as previously noted, it is also worthwhile and meaningful to support others in shaping and fulfilling their inborn potential through their self-chosen way of life. That belief explains why logoteleology encourages each person to define who they are through the answer to the question, "Why am I here?" Ultimately, who we become will be defined and determined by our actions and legacy. Having a meaningful "why" or reason to live for makes daily existence stimulating.

Valuable Goals to Achieve

Humans are wired to solve problems and fulfill goals. Logoteleology proposes that once we define our life purpose, we have the responsibility of choosing those goals that best meet the criteria of the

- life purpose;
- Three Pillars of Meaningful Purpose (i.e., ACT [allow, cooperate, transcend]);
- the five strivings (i.e., love, peace, happiness, interest, and prosperity).

Fulfilling a self-determined life purpose through supportive goals and actionable tasks can and should be a fulfilling experience. Interesting tasks inherently satisfy our innate needs and wants. Having something worthwhile to accomplish brings about feelings of enthusiasm, interest, and commitment.

Building Competence

It serves people well to aim high and to build self-efficacy or the optimistic belief and assurance in one's competence and effectiveness.[139] Life is more enjoyable when we approach it with the goal of learning and growing

139 Maddux, J. E., and J. T. Gosselin, "Self-Efficacy." Leary, M. R., and J. P. Tangney, Eds., *Handbook of Self and Identity* (New York: Guilford, 2003), 57.

with hard-won achievements. When all the meaningful conditions are present, people can experience a greater sense of competence. This is particularly true when contexts, individuals, and activities are experienced as organized, predictable, reliable, and consistent.[140, 141, 142, 143, 144, 145]

Autonomy and Reasonable Control over Actions

In addition to being competent, being self-determined and self-accountable allows people to have a greater sense of control over their destiny. Actually, people who feel in control of their lives enjoy life and exhibit better mental health.[146]

> "...people who feel in control of their lives enjoy life and exhibit better mental health."
>
> Tangney, J. P., Bauemeister, R. F., & Boone, A. L.

There are benefits to promoting and creating conditions where others can

---

140 Bandura, A., "Self-Referent Thought: A Developmental Analysis of Self-Efficacy." Flavell, J. H., and L. Ross, Eds. *Social Cognitive Development: Frontiers and Possible Futures* (Cambridge, UK: Cambridge University Press, 1981), 200–239.

141 Carton, J. S., and S. Nowicki, "Antecedents of Individual Differences in Locus of Control of Reinforcement. A Critical Review." *Genetic, Social, and General Psychology Monographs* 120 (1994): 31–81.

142 Gunnar, M. R., "Contingent Stimulation: A Review of its Role in Early Development." Levine, S., and H. Ursin, Eds. *Coping and Health* (New York: Plenum, 1980), 101–19.

143 Schneewind, K. A., "Impact of Family Processes on Control Beliefs." Bandura, E., Ed. *Self-Efficacy in Changing Societies* (New York: Cambridge University Press, 1995), 114–48.

144 Skinner, E. A., J. Zimmer-Gembeck, and J. P. Connell, "Individual Differences and Development of Perceived Control." *Monographs of the Society for Research in Child Development*, no. 204 (1998).

145 Suomi, S. J., "Contingency, Perception, and Social Development." Sherrod, L. R., and M. E. Lamb, Eds. *Infant Social Cognition: Empirical and Theoretical Considerations.* (Hillsdale, NJ: Erlbaum, 1980)

146 Tangney, J. P., R. F. Bauemeister, and A. L. Boone, "High Self-Control Predicts Good Adjustment, Less Pathology, Better Grades, and Interpersonal Success." *Journal of Personality* 72 (2004): 271–324.

experience greater autonomy. For instance, within organizations, there is credible research that management practices and leadership styles that promote personal control foster health and happiness[147] and improve morale.[148] This in turn can reduce voluntary turnover and absenteeism with a positive impact on productivity.

Autonomy and control, of course, should be strengthened with the individual's level of competence and maturity. The wise path for those lacking knowledge, skill, and experience is to practice cooperation by following and learning from others. This is because there are situations where, in order to gain autonomy and greater control of our actions, we will need to follow in order to learn until we reach a level where we can operate independently of others. In other words, we would be working *with* rather than *for* others.

The Ability to Enjoy What Life Has to Offer

We can also add spice to life through our own wish list or "bucket list." Such a list could include interesting activities and goals pertaining to

- our professions;
- hobbies;
- places to visit;
- meeting and learning from thought-provoking people;
- being curious and doing extraordinary things.

We can also invest in helping others enjoy life by being inclusive and engaging. In a way, we too could be great examples of meaningful purpose by having others experience us as uplifting and helpful. There is credible research, such as that of Tim Kasser, associate professor of

147 Deci, E. L., and R. M. Ryan, "The Support of Autonomy and the Control of Behavior." *Journal of Personality and Social Psychology* 53 (1987): 1024–37.
148 Miller, K. I., and P. R. Monge, "Participation, Satisfaction, and Productivity: A Meta-Analytic Review." *Academy of Management Journal* 29 (1986): 727–53.

> ...those who strive for "intimacy, personal growth, and contribution to the community" are happier and experience an overall higher quality of life.
>
> Tim Kasser, Knox College

psychology at Knox College, Illinois, where he offers that those who strive for "intimacy, personal growth, and contribution to the community" are happier and experience an overall higher quality of life.[149], [150] Thus, seeking ways to serve and learn from others has its benefits.

Professor Kasser also reminds us that materialism—placing high value on money and possessions—is a symptom of a people who feel insecure, unsafe, and disadvantaged. The satisfaction created by having wealth is brief. Still, paradoxically, many college students prefer to pursue education with the goal of making more money over values such as "develop a meaningful philosophy for life," "becoming an authority in my own field," "helping others in difficulty," and "raising a family."[151] Those in pursuit of happiness through material gain over meaningful values are in for a rude awakening.

To summarize, in order to experience a stimulating life, people need to select and live a worthwhile life purpose and supportive goals. They also need to build competence and take responsibility and control for their actions and outcomes. It also helps to add pizzazz to their lives through stimulating and challenging personal and professional tasks and interests. In addition, there is value in allowing and encouraging others to enjoy a purpose-fulfilling life. This also entails supporting their competence building and cheering them along so they can enjoy all life has to offer.

---

149 Kasser, T., "Two Versions of the American Dream: Which Goals and Values Make for a High Quality of Life?" Diener, E., and D. Rahtz, Eds. *Advances in Quality of Life: Theory and Research* (Dordrecht, Netherlands: Kluwer, 2000).
150 Kasser, T., *The High Price of Materialism* (Cambridge, MA: MIT Press, 2002).
151 Myers, David G., *Social Psychology,* 650.

Striving Five: Building and Securing Prosperity

I believe striving for financial success and security is meaningful and worthwhile. The alternative is just too unbearable, and here's why: financial problems is fourth on the top ten reasons people divorce in the United States.[152] As I write (the first half of 2013), many countries have problems balancing their budgets and operating within their means. The economic problems facing the globe are creating significant social unrest. Corporations are experiencing low approval by the American public [153] for their contribution to the economic downturn and unethical practices.

To prevent becoming a statistical victim to poor financial management, people need to learn how to create and sustain wealth. I encourage others to make financial prosperity an agenda item of striving toward living a stimulating life. Again, it is not my intent to lecture or explain how to manage your finances. It is worth repeating that the answers and information are available.

In addition to learning, achieving financial success requires building a meaning set that wills you to

- work hard;
- improve yourself;
- save;
- invest;
- build financial capital.

Learning how to prosper will help you achieve those aims and aspirations

152 http://www.top10stop.com/lifestyle/top-10-reasons-for-divorce-and-marriage-breakdowns-stats-from-the-us.

153 Michael Whitney, "Exclusive: New Polls Shows Clear Majorities Distrust Big Corporations, Favor Unions," *FDL:* http://workinprogress.firedoglake.com/2009/10/02/exclusive-new-poll-shows-clear-majorities-distrust-big-corporations-favor-unions/.

that stimulate and enrich life. Knowing you have a long-term plan in place and the resources to give you and your family security in economic downturns will give you security and confidence. Doing so will also give you peace of mind (striving two).

To summarize, become a student of success and prosperity, and build the meaning set that will motivate you to get ahead and flourish.

It is also meaningful to encourage others to learn how to prosper in life. This is an exercise that would have to start at home and be reinforced by schools, businesses, government, and houses of worship.

To Review

This section has defined what is meaningful and meaningless. All meaningful activities are acts of love, foster peace, and bring about peace of mind; contribute to happy emotional states; promote a stimulating life for self and to others; and build and secure prosperity. Any other pursuit or striving is meaningless.

What Other Role Do Emotions Play in Meaning Sets?

Previously I explained that meaning analysis includes making an emotional appraisal of a situation. We ask, "What does this feeling mean?" However, not all emotional states are felt through personal interactions with others. We also feel and make an affective assessment of what we observe in an environment, such as when we are awed by beautiful and inspiring scenery. In this scenic situation the feeling could mean there is more to enjoy in life than just hard work or that there is a Master Designer of all things worth admiring. In addition, emotions can remind us what is significant or meaningful in our lives, and hence direct our attention to pursue what is important and relevant to our and others' well-being. Such emotions influence and govern behavior, as explained by University of Iowa's Johnmarshall Reeve:

> Emotions are short-lived subjective-physiological-functional-expressive phenomena that orchestrate how

we react adaptively to the important events in our lives. That is, emotions organize and orchestrate four interrelated aspects of experience:

- Feelings—subjective, verbal descriptions of emotional experience
- Physiological preparedness—how our body physically mobilizes itself to meet situational demands
- Function—what specifically we want to accomplish at that moment
- Expression—how we communicate our emotional experience publicly to others[154]

According to teleotherapy theory, an individual meaning has an innate emotional tone. To appreciate the concept of meaning and emotional tone, as an exercise, *feel* the individual meaning of words such as romantic, bold, and courageous. Notice how each word prompts an affective image and corresponding feeling(s). As I will describe in greater detail in upcoming chapters, these feelings serve a motivational function.

Moods

Since a meaning set is an organized strand of meanings, and individual meanings have an emotional tone, the collection of feelings in the meaning set constitute a mood. Said differently, we have embedded in our personalities an ever-present signature mood. *A mood is the predominant emotional state of mind of a person.* That explains why moods are longer lasting than emotions. They also influence our view

154 Reeve, Johnmarshall, *Understanding Motivation and Emotion*, 7.

of life, the lens with which we interpret situations, and what we think about.[155]

Meaning sets can be harmonious or dissonant. They influence the Meaning Attitude (attract, resist, or avoid) and consequently the Meaning Motive (Will, Drive, or Amotivate). When meaning sets are dissonant they hold introjected Meaning Antecedents with No Love, No Mind, and No Joy scripts. Harmonious meaning sets, however, express more socially fitting feelings such as love, happiness, peace, interest, inquisitiveness and ambition.

Thus, a meaning set and its corresponding affective mood can be compared to music. Good music has a logical and congruent structure that leads to harmonious sounds. Each meaning's emotion can be compared to a musical note. The combined musical notes in a meaning set can be harmonious (positive mood), dissonant (negative mood), or indifferent (unconcerned mood).[156] Hence, emotions and moods give meaning sets an affective, molar,[157] and unitary quality.

In conclusion, according to teleotherapy theory, an individual meaning has an emotional tone. The collection of feelings in the meaning set creates a mood. A mood is the predominant emotional state of mind of a person. Thus, moods describe the affective tone of meaning sets.

A mood is the predominant emotional state of mind of a person.

155 Davidson, R. J., "On Emotion, Mood, and Related Affective Constructs." Ekman, P., and R. J. Davidson, Eds. *The Nature of Emotion: Fundamental Questions* (New York: Oxford University Press, 1994), 51–55.

156 I credit Barry Hermann's *Team Spirit* workshop for the view of situations being harmonious or dissonant.

157 Molar: pertaining to large units of behavior; related to a whole. Edward Chace Tolman's purposive behaviorism (1932) defined meaningful behavior as molar behavior. To Tolman, it was obvious that all actions of behavior are goal-oriented. See Schultz, D. P., and S. E. Schultz. 2012. *A History of Modern Psychology* (Belmont, CA: Wadsworth, Cengage Learning), 10.

The role of feelings in meaning sets is to

- appraise situations;
- remind us what is important and meaningful;
- direct our attention to pursue what is important and relevant to our and others' well-being;
- adapt to situations;
- manage our behavior.

Why Do Meanings Matter?

First, as previously covered, meanings are important because they shape and set the agenda for our identity. Meanings define how vibrant, positive, and successful our life will be.

Second, meanings explain our personal brand, reputation, and legacy. What people ultimately evaluate and judge about others' actions are their meanings. People pay attention to others' meanings in order to make sense of the individual and what she or he does.

We are generally aware of who we are and what we are all about by how others describe us as individuals. This awareness allows us to make adjustments, to grow, and to successfully coexist with others. Understanding how meanings, meaning sets, and meaning systems respectively operate in an identity gives us the power to shape our character and distinctiveness to our advantage. Logoteleology believes the intentional formation and development of meaning sets can produce healthy personalities.

> "Hindsight bias. The tendency to exaggerate, after learning an outcome, one's ability to have foreseen how something turned out. Also known as the I-knew-it-all-along phenomenon."
>
> David Myers

Third, knowing what meanings are, what they do, and how they function in personality can help us diagnose their quality and better understand our behavior. Moreover, being aware of the meanings that describe us can allow us make changes by replacing negative and unhelpful meanings with positive and constructive ones.

Fourth, meanings and meaning set construct matter because they help explain why—despite answers and solutions being available—individuals', groups', organizations', systems', and humankind's most significant problems are unresolved.

For instance, some readers will find that the content of this book has familiar concepts. Moreover, some might say my conclusions are common sense, psychological notions. Assuming they do not suffer from hindsight bias,[158] these readers might perhaps even conclude that there is not much new or innovative about the theory and methodology. Should that be the case, it would prove the point that, despite the fact so many people are surrounded with available, familiar, and common sense answers and solutions, for some reason these answers go ignored and are not used for personal advantage and benefit—even when paying attention to and acting on the lessons would make a positive difference in peoples' lives! In other words, if these concepts are so obvious, we should honestly ask ourselves why our fundamental problems persist.

Finally, the meaning set, through the *meaning system,* manages our attention and awareness. Meanings signal to the brain what is and is not important and relevant. Thus, the meaning system is given the task of analyzing incoming information, reviewing relevancy, and when important, making us aware.

The key to increasing the odds of solving our core problems rests in evaluating the quality of our meaning sets, building on the strong and healthy ones, and replacing those individual meanings that are weak

---

158 "Hindsight bias: the tendency to exaggerate, after learning an outcome, one's ability to have foreseen how something turned out. Also known as the 'I-knew-it-all-along' phenomenon." Myers, David G. 2005. 18.

and disruptive with better and/or improved options. Among other benefits, building and nurturing our meaning sets can consequently

- improve life's outlook;
- help us value each person's life;
- inspire doing what is important;
- encourage the expression of feelings for good;
- offer a vital reason to live for;
- build shared understanding.

To summarize, meanings matter because they define our life's agenda and its quality. It allows us to define who we are, how we will behave and relate with others, and how much enjoyment we are going to get out of life. We should also care for what meanings do in our personality because they explain how people see and define us and how effective we are relating with others. With an understanding of our impact on others, when appropriate, we can make improvements in order to stay aligned with who we are or wish to be. Meanings also influence our awareness and attention. Finally, understanding meaning systems can help us identify how we prevent ourselves from succeeding, and how to improve.

When Meanings Fail

What are the consequences of the existential vacuum or lack of meaning? To further appreciate why meanings matter, let's review a few examples of what research findings report about people's meaning sets, and their consequences. Here are some sobering statistics.[159]

---

159 Save.com. Suicide Facts. Accessed March 23, 2013. http://www.save.org/index.cfm?fuseaction=home.viewPage&page_id=705D5DF4-055B-F1EC-3F66462866FCB4E6

- Suicide takes the lives of nearly thirty thousand Americans every year.
- The strongest risk factor for suicide is depression.
- In 2010 depression became the number-one disability in the world (World Health Organization).
- Suicide is the eleventh leading cause of death in the United States (homicide is fifteenth) (Center for Decease Control and Prevention [CDC]).
- Suicide is the third leading cause of death for fifteen- to twenty-four-year-old Americans (CDC).
- It is estimated that there are at least 4.5 million [attempted] suicide survivors in this country (American Association of Suicidology [AAS]).
- An average of one person dies by suicide every 16.2 minutes (CDC, AAS).
- Between 1952 and 1995, suicide in young adults nearly tripled.

Other studies claim that patients with mental problems overwhelm hospitals in the United States.[160]

In the United Kingdom, the evidence pertaining to mental health is alarming.[161]

- One in four people will experience some kind of mental-health problem in the course of a year.
- Mixed anxiety and depression is the most common mental disorder in Britain.

---

160 http://www.dispatch.com/content/stories/local/2011/10/09/psychiatric-patients-overcrowd-hospitals.html.

161 http://www.mentalhealth.org.uk/help-information/mental-health-statistics/.

- Women are more likely to have been treated for a mental-health problem than men.
- About 10 percent of children have a mental-health problem at any one time.
- Depression affects one in five older people.
- Suicide rates show that British men are three times more likely to die by suicide than British women.
- Self-harm statistics for the UK show one of the highest rates in Europe: four hundred per one hundred thousand people.
- Only one in ten prisoners has no mental disorder.
- One in four British adults experience at least one diagnosable mental-health problem in any one year, and one in six experiences this at any given time (the Office for National Statistics Psychiatric Morbidity report, 2001).
- Although mental disorders are widespread, serious cases are concentrated among a relatively small proportion of people who experience more than one mental-health problem (The British Journal of Psychiatry, 2005).
- It is estimated that approximately 450 million people worldwide have a mental-health problem (World Health Organization, 2001).[162]

These symptoms are the outcomes of the No Love, No Joy, and No Mind psychological scripts from whence the existential vacuum or the meaningless originate.

And how meaningful is work for the American worker? According to a June 28, 2011, article published by the Gallup Corporation, the Employee Engagement Index for the third quarter of 2011, those

---

162 http://www.mentalhealth.org.uk/help-information/mental-health-statistics/UK-worldwide/?view=Standard.

engaged constituted 29 percent of the workforce, while 53 percent are not engaged, and 19 percent are actively disengaged.[163] Doing the math, 72 percent of the workforce is not producing to its potential because the organizations' work contexts do not provide people with the opportunity to fulfill their needs.

I believe the lack of meaning is one of the worse and most harmful epidemics besetting mankind. As seen by the previous statistics related to mental health and worker dissatisfaction, the lack of meaning is a miserable state. But how is it under a meaningful reality?

When Meanings Generate Success

What are the consequences of having a positive and healthy meaning set? What research is there about affirmative attributes, beliefs, attitudes, values, feelings, and aims and their consequences? What is meaning success?

- People with a self-view of being competent and effective are more persistent, less anxious, less depressed, and live healthier lives.[164]
- Individuals with positive self-meanings experience a stronger locus of control. This is because they believe that what happens to them is a consequence of their own efforts and skills. In addition, they are able to deal more effectively with life

---

163 Blacksmith, N. and J. Harter, "Majority of American Workers Not Engaged in Their Jobs." (October 28, 2011): http://www.gallup.com/poll/150383/majority-american-workers-not-engaged-jobs.aspx.
164 Maddux, J. E., and J. T. Gosselin, "Self-Efficacy." Leary, M. R., and J. P. Tangney, Eds. *Handbook of Self and Identity* (New York: Guildford, 2003), 57.

difficulties and are more inclined to delay gratification in order to attain long-term goals.[165], [166], [167], [168]

- People with a style of life concerned with learning, improving, and reaching one's potential (known as "growth-seeking individuals") are capable of adjusting better to failures than those seeking external validation so as to test their personal worth, competence, or likeability.[169]

- Individuals who imagine having positive self-concept meanings outperform those who imagine being failures.[170]

- Dweck and other researchers found that students who believe intelligence can be mastered are more resilient than those who do not.[171]

These research findings offer strong evidence that meaning sets define the quality and vitality of one's life. Growth-oriented and self-determined individuals, as we have seen from the evidence, enjoy a superior quality of life. In contrast, those described previously as being influenced by a No Love, No Joy, and No Mind life scripts experience a lower quality of life.

---

165 Findley, M. J., and H. M. Cooper, "Locus of Control and Academic Achievement: A Literature Review." *Journal of Personality and Social Psychology* 44 (1983): 419–27.

166 Lefcourt, H. M., *Locus of Control: Current Trends in Theory and Research* (Hillsdale, NJ: Erlbaum, 1982).

167 Milller, P. C., et al., "Marital Locus of Control and Marital Problem-Solving." *Journal of Personality and Social Psychology* 51 (1986): 161–69.

168 Tangney, J. P., R. F. Baumeister, and A. L. Boone, "High Self-Control Predicts Good Adjustment, Less Pathology, Better Grades, and Interpersonal Success." *Journal of Personality* 72 (2004): 271–324.

169 Dykman, B. M., "Integrating Cognitive and Motivational Factors in Depression: Initial Tests of a Goal-Orientation Approach." *Journal of Personality and Social Psychology* 74 (1998): 139–58.

170 Ruvolo, A., and H. Markus, "Possible Selves and Performance: The Power of Self-Relevant Imagery." *Social Cognition* 9 (1992): 95–124.

171 Dweck, Carol S., *Self-Theories,* 5.

The remedy to depression and hollow jobs is the pursuit of meaning. To achieve this end, after assessing their state, all individuals need to replace unhelpful and negative meanings within their meaning sets with constructive and positive ones—for example, by getting rid of the false assumption that intelligence is fixed and cannot be improved. Ultimately, situations will be as bad or good as the meaning given to them. The positive option is definitely more promising.

The option to depression and hollow jobs is the pursuit of meaning.

In light of the above, from a logoteleological perspective, the next section will address what life calls us all to do so that our meanings generate success.

What Is the Meaning of Life?

When I studied the writings of psychology's giants as well as current research, I found *the common denominator to the meaning and purpose of life is to master one's abilities and attitudes in order to allow, to cooperate, and to transcend* (i.e., to ACT). These can be accomplished through the five strivings, which can be considered standards to successful living. Yet this proposed prescription is a framework. Each individual is unique and extraordinary. As a result, she or he is required to find and define *her* or *his* concrete and unique meaning of life and to select a purpose to fulfill it. Nonetheless, I do believe the framework is a useful and important foundation in which to define one's life's meaningful purpose. The framework was influenced by multiple prominent psychologists and authors. Here are a few of their contributions:

> Alfred Adler:
>
> "There has always been people who understood this fact, who knew that the meaning of life was to be

interested in the whole of humankind, and who tried to develop social interest and love."[172]

"Every human being strives for significance, but people always make mistakes if they do not see that their whole significance must consist in the contribution to the lives of others."[173]

"The only individuals who can really meet and master the problems of life, however, are those who show in their striving a tendency to enrich everyone else, those who forge ahead in such a way that others benefit too."

> *The meaning and purpose of life is to master one's abilities and attitudes in order to allow, to cooperate, and to transcend* (i.e., to ACT). These can be accomplished through the five strivings, which can be considered standards to successful living.

"All human judgments of value and success are founded, in the end, upon cooperation; this is the great universal truism of the human race. All that we ask of conduct, of ideals, of goals, of actions, and of traits of character, is that they should serve the cause of human cooperation."

"The neurotic and the criminal … have lost the courage, however, to conduct their lives in a useful way. An inferiority complex tells them, 'Success in cooperation is not for you.'" [174]

Viktor Frankl:

"Men can give meaning to their lives by realizing what I call *creative values*, by achieving tasks. But they can also give meaning to their lives by realizing *experiential values*, by experiencing the Good, the True, and the

172 Adler, Alfred, *What Life Could Mean to You,* 8.
173 Adler, Alfred. 2010. 8.
174 Ibid. 55.

Beautiful, or by knowing one single human being in all his uniqueness. And to experience one human being as unique is to love him."[175]

"Shouldn't the survival of humanity too be contingent on whether or not men arrive at a common denominator of meaning? Shouldn't it be contingent on whether or not people, and peoples, find a *common* meaning, become united in a common *will* to a common meaning?"[176]

Peter Senge:

"But what if humans, as a species, actually have a purpose? What if we have something distinctive to contribute—something to *give* rather than just *take*?"[177]

Martin E. P. Seligman:

"Human beings, ineluctably, want meaning and purpose in life. The Meaningful Life consists in belonging to and serving something that you believe is bigger than the self, and humanity creates all the positive institutions to allow this …"[178]

Carl Jung:

"Trust that which gives you meaning and accept it as your guide."[179]

Johnmarshall Reeve:

"From a motivational point of view, meaning in life grows out of three needs. The first need is purpose. … Connecting the activity of the day with a future goal

---

175 Frankl, Viktor E., *The Doctor and the Soul: From Psychotherapy to Logotherapy* (New York: Vintage Books, 1983), xix.

176 Frankl, Viktor E., *The Unheard Cry for Meaning* (New York: Touchstone, 1978), 36.

177 Senge, Peter, et al., *Presence: Human Purpose and the Field of the Future* (New York: Currency, 2004), 238.

178 Seligman, Martin E. P., *Flourish* (New York: Free Press, 2011), 12.

179 http://www.sonoma.edu/users/d/daniels/Jungsum.html.

> effectively endows day-to-day activity with a sense of purpose it otherwise would not have. The second need is for values. Values define what is good and what is right, and when we internalize or act on a value we affirm a sense of goodness in us. The third is efficacy. Having a sense of competence is important because it enables us to believe that what we do makes a difference. Collectively, a sense of purpose, internalized values, and high efficacy to affect changes in the environment cultivate meaning in life."[180]

Life calls all of us to claim and fulfill a meaningful life purpose.

Life calls all of us to claim and fulfill a meaningful life purpose. It is an innate human need to want meaning and to fulfill it through a purpose. To self-define is to self-mean. Hence, the quality of our life depends on how well we respond to our calling and exercise our unalienable right to fulfill it through meaningful tasks. I go further to propose that it is not only the quality of our life that is at stake, it is also our existence as a species. The logoteleology method is designed to help individuals, groups, and organizations self-mean and hence enjoy all that life has to offer.

Application

Reflect on the content of this chapter. What struck you about it? Recall specific situations that were meaningful to you. Is there a pattern to what has been meaningful to you? Have you thought about the meaning of your life and what you would like it to be? If so, reflecting on the application exercise from chapter 2, what else should be content of your meaning set?

180 Reeve, Johnmarshall, *Understanding Motivation and Emotion* , 431.

My Journey

In light of my research on meaning, here are a few lessons I learned and decisions I made along the way.

- I know what is meaningful in life, and as a result, I am more focused on what matters and less distracted by what does not. My life and my surroundings are more appealing and interesting.
- I have a better perspective and learn from my successes and failures. As a result, I experience less guilt and feel that I am guided by a wiser voice. I have strengthened my resilience. It is easier for me to let go, apologize, forgive, and move on. It is not easy for others to lure me into strife. I accept that I am far from perfect. It allows me to be empathic when interacting with others. I have committed to practice humility and to be teachable.
- Even though for a long time I have been comfortable alone as well as in the enjoyable company of friends and colleagues, both ways of spending time now have greater value and significance. How I spend my time is currently more meaningful and uplifting.
- I know what actions will best meet my life purpose and supporting goals. While I still have room to grow, my intentions are becoming meaningful and focused over time. I have a meaning compass that serves me well.
- Progressively I experience more peace of mind, a stronger self-determination, and fulfillment. However, I must confess that there have been moments when the learning, discovery, and insight have been disturbing. I continue to confront my shadow or dark side.
- Increasingly I experience more love and happiness. On a daily basis I feel more positive than negative moods.
- I ask myself helpful and positive questions that encourage creativity and meaningful resolutions.

Chapter 5: The Will to Meaning

The tragedy of life is not that it ends so soon but that we wait so long to begin it.—W. M. Lewis

Logoteleology's View of Motivation

I approach motivation from the logoteleological perspective that human beings are always displaying energy, direction, and striving for meaning. I have concluded and proposed that *what* motivates people resides within the frame of the Three Pillars of Meaningful Purpose (ACT), and the five strivings. I have also offered that each individual must find his or her specific meaningful purpose within such frame if he or she is to have a meaningful life experience.

But how can we build determination to follow ACT and the five strivings? Also, what additional resources are there to help us find our meaningful purpose? Both questions can be answered with an understanding of the role of motivation in an identity. To do so, this chapter will explain in greater detail logoteleology's view of motivation through the following propositions:

> First, motivation is energized by meaning sets. The quality and staying power of our motivation is intimately related to the strength, vigor and health of our meanings.
>
> Second, motivation is a mental process within an identity. Understanding how this motivational mental

process operates with the meaning set and purpose can help individuals be more self-aware, intentional, and confident.

Third, it is possible to create environmental conditions so natural and inborn striving for meaning can be expressed.

I will address these propositions through the following questions:

1. What is the relationship between meaning sets, motivation, and purpose?
2. What is the construct of motivation as a system, and what are its processes and consequences?
3. What are the best environmental conditions for meaning expression and fulfillment?

Meaning Sets and Motivation

Here I'll address the first question, "What is the relationship between meaning sets and motivation?" Let's first review the concept of a meaning set.

The Meaning Set

I previously covered that the combined meanings in an identity are known as a *meaning set*. Further, I explained that a meaning set is

- the equivalent of a person's unique psychological signature; and
- what makes one's identity recognizable. We select, organize, and form meaning sets to define and express our person, social, and role identities.

What Is Motivation?

Having reviewed meaning sets, let's define motivation. Reeve offers, "The study of motivation concerns those processes that give behavior its energy and direction." Elsewhere he states, "Motives are internal experiences—needs, cognitions, and emotions—that energize the individual's approach and avoidance tendencies. External events are environmental incentives that attract and repel the individual to engage or not engage in a particular course of action."[181]

Based on the previous description, motivation is tasked with providing energy and direction based on a *like/don't like* continuum.[182] Motivation expresses the relative importance of options. Strong importance of an option generates a higher level of motivation while an option with low importance generates lower levels of motivation. Further, Reeve described the study of motivation as "the study of directing purpose in inherently active people."[183] This is another way of saying *humans are teleological or steered by meanings in order to fulfill a purpose.*

> There are two key tasks that motivation is chartered to fulfill: to provide energy and direction based on a like/don't like continuum.

Relying on Reeve's research and conclusions, *logoteleology defines motivation as directed energy.* Energy provides motion and direction based on the *like/don't like* continuum previously referenced. Motivation is ultimately directed by the meaning set.

For research purposes, motivation is represented through the formula

(Motivation = Energy + Direction) or (Mo = E + D)

181 Reeve, Johnmarshall, *Understanding Motivation and Emotion*, 6.

182 See also Ryan, Richard M., Kennon M. Sheldon, Tim Kasser, and Edward L. Deci, "All Goals Are Not Created Equal: An Organistic Perspective of Goals and Regulation." Gollwitzer, Peter M., and John A. Bargh, Eds. *The Psychology of Action: Linking Cognition and Motivation to Behavior*. (New York: The Guilford Press, 1996), 7–26.

183 Reeve, Johnmarshall, *Understanding Motivation and Emotion*, 34.

I will next explain how the meaning set influences the dynamics of energy generation and direction. I will also describe how a meaning-guided motivation steers purpose.

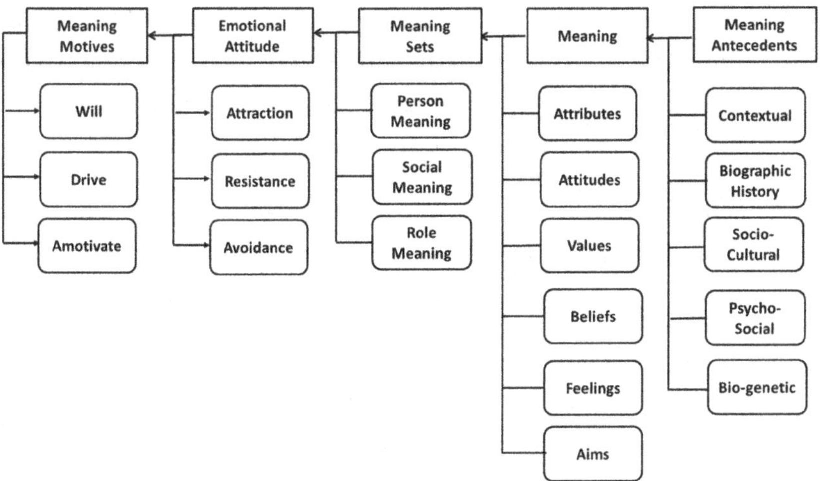

Figure 8 The Meaning System

The Impact of the Meaning Set on Motivation

How do meaning sets interact with and influence motivation?

I explained in previous chapters that meanings set the agenda. I also clarified that identities have a meaning system with five core components, as seen in figure 8, above. They are worth repeating:

- *Meaning Antecedents* originate from our biological DNA, family, culture, or accumulated life experiences, and current situations or context. Meaning Antecedents are unique for each human being. They help organize people's worldviews and give significance to their daily lives through meaning formation.
- *Meaning* is formed by Meaning Antecedents in the form of attributes, beliefs, attitudes, values, feelings, and aims in the identity. They are components of a meaning set.
- *Meaning Set* is a collection of well-organized meaning strands

with the psychological instructions used to develop and function. The construct has a specific organized pattern and subsequent agenda and aim. The construct is made of meanings and operators (e.g., if/then/else). The Meaning Set ultimately defines a person's quality and vitality of life. The Meaning Set finds expression through the three identities: person, group, and role. The content of the meaning set can be modified to improve or to weaken performance and the quality of life.

- *Emotional Attitude* is the affective evaluation or judgment given by a meaning set to a situation, person, or task (i.e., target). The emotional disposition incites emotional attraction, avoidance or resistance.

- *Meaning Motives* are decision-making operators that select a motivational approach or direction based on the emotional attitude assigned to a target. Meaning Motives select from three motivational alternatives or *Types*: Will, Drive, and Amotivate. [184] The type is said to *specify* the direction of the energy. They also *determine* and *regulate* the strength of motivation. However, it is important to emphasize that it is the Motivation System which *generates* motion or motivation, not the Meaning Motive or any other component of the meaning system.

Once the person knows how he or she "feels about" a situation (through the Emotional Attitude) the Meaning Motive is prompted to choose from one of the three alternatives (Will, Drive, and Amotivate).

The Selection of the Meaning Motive Type

This next section will explain how the Emotional Attitude (attraction, avoidance, or resistance) influences the selection of a meaning motive type (Will, Drive, Amotivate).

---

184 Zajonc, Robert B., "Social Facilitation." *Science* 149 (1965): 296–74.

From Attraction to Will

For attraction, the motivational choice will generally be the Will (e.g., I *want* to do it or I *chose* not to do it.). Hence, Will is a decision to either seek out or to avoid a situation, again based on the *like-don't like* continuum. In either case, there is a choice; the decision is self-determined and the motivation intrinsic.

For instance, Mary is a competent bank teller. She also loves arts and is a talented graphic artist. When she learns there is an opening in the graphic arts department in her bank, she feels *attracted* to apply for the job. However, when her branch manager learns of Mary's interest, he offers her a raise in order to retain her as a bank teller. Mary *chooses* not to accept the raise so she can pursue her dream of being a professional graphic artist. She makes her choice because the intrinsic meaningful value of the job in the graphic arts department is greater than the extrinsic value of a higher salary doing a teller's role. As a result, Mary *Wills* to take on the new job in the graphic arts department.

> *Arousal enhances whatever response tendency is dominant.*
>
> Principle in experiential psychology

From Resistance to Drive

Resistance can be the outcome of an extrinsic Drive (e.g., I *have* to do it, so I will do it. But if I had my way, I would not do it.). Such a Drive can be induced by internal introjects or through external (e.g., do it or else) demands.

To illustrate how it applies to a person Driven through introjects, consider a high-level executive named Carlos who is compulsively Driven to work long hours (type-A workaholic). There is a side of Carlos that would like to spend more time with his family; however, he cannot prevent himself from staying long hours at the office and continues to come home late.

On the other hand, Phillip exemplifies the person succumbing to external demands who—under firm but quiet protest—is working hard to meet his manager's compulsory "do it or else" deadline. Phillip is going to meet the minimum expectations and will not do more than required since threats ultimately polarize people.

From Avoidance to Amotivation

For avoidance, Amotivation is an alternative because of feelings of

- helplessness (I don't have the confidence to do this);
- apathy[185] (I am bored by this situation); and
- rebellion (I refuse to do this).

Consider Amanda, a secretary who refuses to compete for a more senior role because she is overcome by feelings of self-doubt. Her helpless self-talk affirms, "I cannot see me doing that role successfully."

> What else is boredom if not the incapacity to take an interest? And what else is apathy if not the incapacity to take initiative?
>
> Viktor Frankl. *The Will to Meaning*

For a situation describing apathy we have Bill, a bright student who is bored by the lack of challenge and the slow pace of his class, which results in his losing interest in the subject.

Finally there is Sean, to illustrate an example of a rebellious stand, who refuses to do his chores at home because his parents will not let him borrow the car for his date.

Other Options

Does the Will resist and avoid? The answer is in the affirmative. However, the Will's resistance and avoidance is a self-determined choice, not the

185 Frankl, Viktor, *The Will to Meaning*, 87.

outcome of introjects and external extrinsic forces. In this sense, a Willed Amotivation is a tactical retreat; while a Willed resistance is expressed as setting valid boundaries based on standards and values (e.g., principles, ethics, etc.).

The next section will explain how the Meaning Set initiates motivation.

The Telosponse

What is the handoff between the meaning system and the motivation system? In figure 9, page 129, related to the Meaning System's Influence on Motivation, the Meaning Motive makes a judgment to

- ascribe the energy level; and
- assign a type of direction (Will, Drive, or Amotivate).

But as previously explained *the Meaning Motive does not generate energy*. That is reserved to the role of the Motivation System. Again, the Meaning Motive *determines* the strength of the meaning (energy level) and assigns direction by selecting the motivation type (Will, Drive, or Amotivate). By *strength of the meaning* (as in meaningfulness for or against the situation) I specifically mean assigning energy intensity to pursue, to resist or to avoid a meaning.

> *In logoteleology, telosponse is the genesis of motivation. Motivation is directed energy.*

In logoteleology, a *telosponse*[186] is a decision to release energy (cathexis[187]) in order to generate directed movement toward a target.

---

186 I owe the concept of *telosponse* to Loyola University at Chicago's Joseph F. Rychlack (1994). He defines it on p. 36 as "the affirmation or taking of a position regarding a meaningful content (image[s], word[s], judgmental comparison[s], etc.) relating to a referent acting as a purpose for the sake of which behavior is then intended. Affirmation encompasses predication."

187 Cathexis: investment of energy: the concentration of a great deal of psychological and emotional energy on a singular goal or on one particular person, thing, or idea.

It can also be said that a telosponse is

- a transition point between the Meaning and Motivation systems;
- the moment a meaning becomes a motive;
- the beginning of motivation;
- a point of mobilization;
- a decision point; and
- a choice.

As a formula, it is represented as follows:

Telosponse = Decision Point + Energy + Direction

or as (T = DP + Mo)[188]

or its more detailed version (T = DP + E + D)

Additional representations of this formula include the replacement of the variable expression "D" (Direction) with the specific Meaning Motive Type, such as (T = DP + E + W), where "W" represents Will. But since this is an introductory book on the fundamental concepts of logoteleology, space will not allow me to provide here a full and comprehensive description of the finer details of the method. These will have to wait for future publications.

For now, the important idea we take from this is that *in logoteleology*

- *telosponse is the genesis of motivation; and*
- *motivation is directed energy.*

188 It has been already established that Mo = E + D.

The Meaning and Motivation Systems

As seen in figure 9 below, the Motivation System takes over once the Meaning System assigns a Meaning Motive Type (to decree the level of energy and direction toward a target). As will be seen in subsequent illustrations, the Will and Drive motivations have a *Point of Mobilization*. Avoidance motivations, on the other hand, have a *Point of Amotivation*. Both point types are *telosponses*.

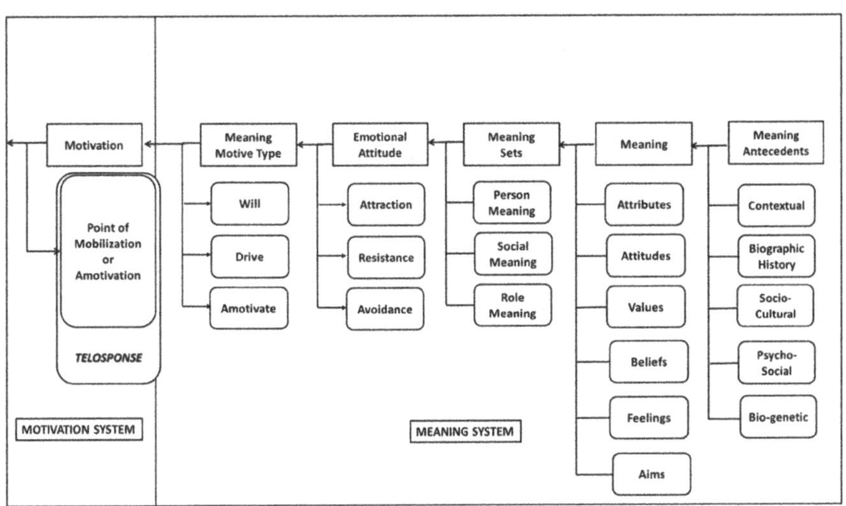

Figure 9 Meaning System's Influence on Motivation

Telosponsivity Scale

Figure 10 below illustrates a generic **Telosponsivity**[189] **Scale**. The Telosponsivity Scale has two extremes: *Intention Awareness* on the left and *Intention in Action* on the right.

Intention Awareness is a mental space, or the field of intentions. It is a readiness state, and no action is observed in this phase. This field of intentions is where the meaning system operates. It is concerned with the "*why* to act."

189 Telosponsivity, or how resolute and persistent performance will be, particularly when facing obstacles.

To its right of the vertical line, *Intentions in Action* is the field where the affirmed meanings are acted and observed (by external people) as overt behavior. This field of action represents the *purpose system's* ground of operation. It is concerned with "*what* we are going to do."

For illustration purposes, the intersect point is the *Point of Mobilization* or telosponse. This is the historical moment when intention becomes energized action. From this point forward the meaning is implemented in some form *through a purpose.* Action is committed.

The vector labeled *meaning significance progression* expresses the intensity of the meaning and explains how it energizes motive. The vector explains how meaning sets influence and energizes motivation.

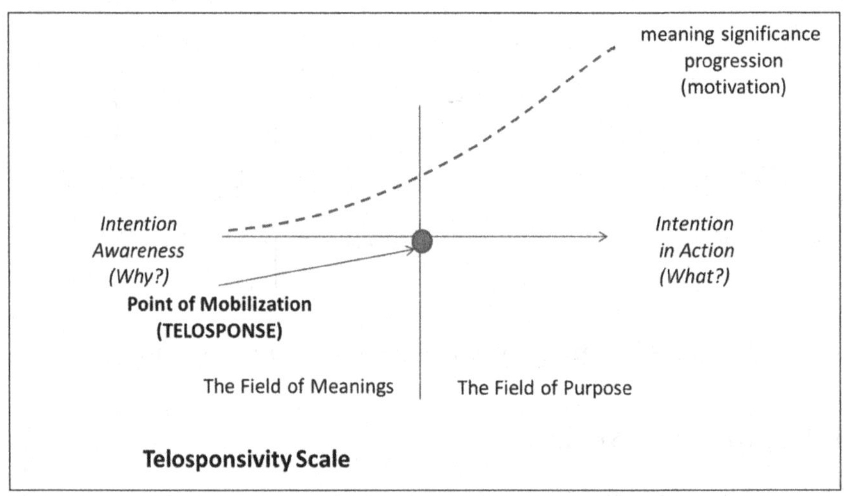

Figure 10 Telosponsivity Scale

Figures 11, 12, 13, and 14 illustrate through a Telosponsivity Scale how Will, Drive, and Amotivation, respectively, energize motivation.

Telosponsivity Scale for Will

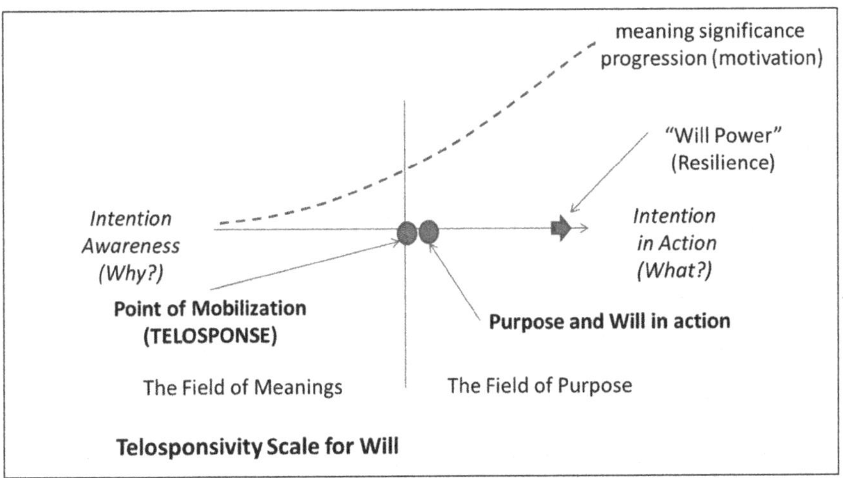

Figure 11 Telosponsivity Scale for Will-Directed Motivation

Starting with figure 11, **Telosponsivity Scale for Will**, once mobilization gains energy (cathexis), the Point of Mobilization (the telosponse) prompts an intention to act or to purpose. *The intention in action entails setting a goal and outlining a plan that is followed by performance movement toward the desired end state.*

The strength of the commitment is expressed by the arrow labeled "Will Power." The arrow represents the performer's willingness to deal with obstacles until the goal is reached. When individuals display this staying power, we call it dedication, resilience, and persistence. In groups and organizations, the Willing employees who eagerly and actively contribute to the organization's agenda are characterized as actively engaged performers.

> Activity Trap: being busy with little or no aim

Telosponsivity Scale of an Extrinsically Motivated Drive

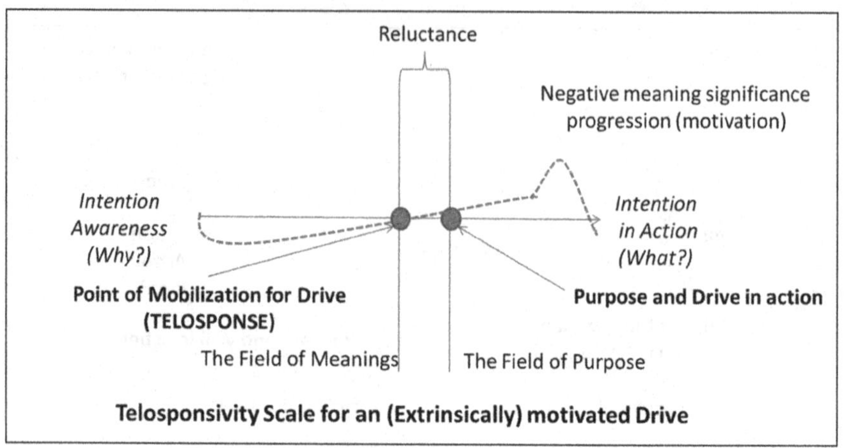

Figure 12 Telosponsivity Scale for Externally Motivated Drive

Figure 12 represents an individual who perceives being required to carry out an unwanted task by external forces. Notice how the vector has an initial negative trend (under the line), with a late energizing significance. Once the point of mobilization has been reached ("do it or else") the example illustrates a reluctance gap ("dragging of the feet") where there is activity but no significant movement (i.e., "activity trap")[190] until finally a plan is put into effect and acted upon. It can be said the individual is fighting amotivation, procrastination, or his or her own reluctance through avoidance. As seen by the vector's drop, as soon as the goal is reached, interest in the task falls (Amotivation).

Many of us have seen this phenomenon in students who wait until the last minute to study for a final exam by cramming and pulling "an all-nighter."

I have also found this to be a common phenomenon in organizations, for example, where workers who feel controlled experience anxiety and pressure. These high-control conditions have been linked with a drop in long-term resolve and determination.[191] Work environments that deny

---

190 Activity trap being busy with little or no aim.

191 Deci, E. L., and R. M. Ryan. 1985. *Intrinsic Motivation and Self-Determination in Human Behavior* (New York: Plenum).

the expression of reasonable levels of autonomy de-motivate workers. Employees under these conditions are described as expressing moderate to low levels of employee engagement or commitment.

Telosponsivity Scale of an Intrinsically Motivated Drive

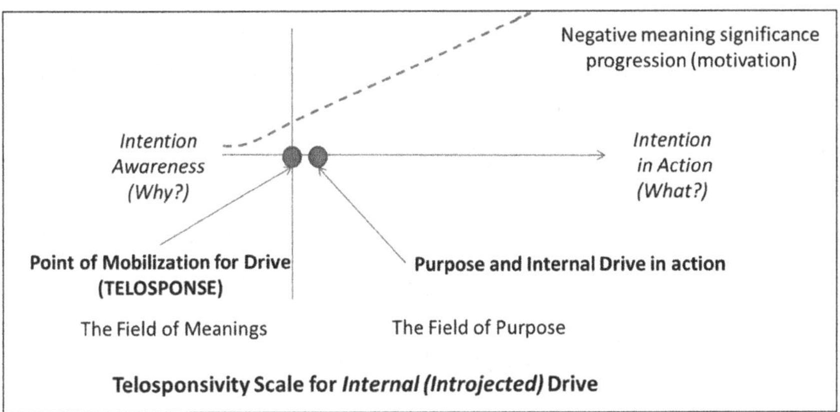

Figure 13 Telosponsivity Scale for Internal (Introjected) Drive

Figure 13 above is another example of a Drive-motivated individual. This graph, however, represents the behavior of an individual that is scripted to react to an internal and introjected Drive. Notice in the scale the close proximity of the *Intention Awareness* to the Point of Mobilization for this Drive. This illustrates the reactive and many times unconscious nature of introjects expressed through Drivers. Individuals that are Driven by introjects are generally not aware of their motives. They do not know *why* they act compulsively and can face difficulty making sense and rationalizing their actions to themselves and to others.[192] Again, this explains why the illustration has such a "short fuse" between Intention Awareness and the Point of Mobilization. The quick action is a Drive compelled to fulfill the required tasks of the introjected script.

Unfortunately, because Drives are determined by an introjected script,

192 I will discuss these disturbances in greater detail in the chapter related to teleotherapy. I will share now, however, that Introjected-driven individuals who act without full awareness of the meaning behind their actions suffer from a purpose-related disturbance.

the relief of finishing the task is temporary. As happens on these types of situations, a new cue will trigger (Drive) another cycle of impulsive responses. Such is the nature of introjected Driven scripts, as in the case of obsessive-compulsive disorder (OCD).[193]

In my professional experience, employees displaying Driven behavior are generally considered engaged employees, but their actions could be more out of necessity and impulse (for instance, they cannot help themselves but work hard). Their engagements respond to introjected Drives and not necessarily because they are fully supportive of the broader organization's agenda in a meaningful way (even when they claim it so). As a result, Driven performers are at risk of carrying out introjects *as if* their motives and goals were compatible with those of the organization.

Telosponsivity Scale of the Amotivated

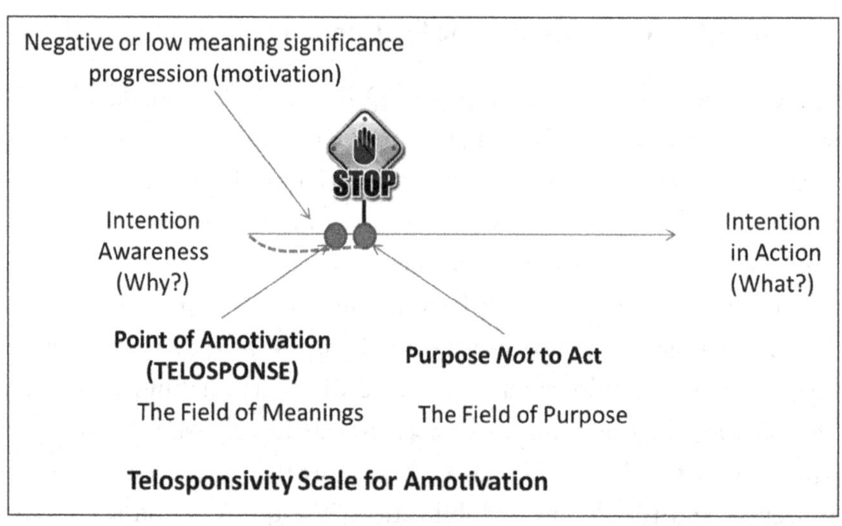

Figure 14 Telosponsivity Scale for Amotivation

Figure 14 illustrates the dynamics of a situation where the choice is not

193 Obsessive-compulsive disorder (OCD) is an anxiety disorder characterized by unreasonable thoughts and fears (obsessions) that lead you to do repetitive behaviors (compulsions). See http://www.mayoclinic.com/health/obsessive-compulsive-disorder/DS00189.

to act. Amotivation—a response to extrinsic forces, either introjected or coerced externally—is an expression of helplessness, apathy, or resistance. The process for all three options, however, is the same. The meaning is either negative and insignificant and thus unable to generate energy for individual action. As a rule, there is no intrinsic value to take action.

Amotivation explains, for instance, what is known as the "active disengagement" of employees in organizations.

Final Observations

We started with the goal of explaining the relationship between meaning sets, motivation, and purpose. It should be apparent by now that

- the meaning set determines the level (strength) and type (direction) of motivation;
- the type and motivational energy (cathexis) is applied to take action or to stand still (inaction); and
- action or inaction is overtly visible to others through a purpose that is determined or absent in fulfilling a meaning, respectively.

This logic was also explained through a version of the identity formula:

$$I = P \leftarrow Mo \leftarrow Me$$

Utility of Telosponsivity Scales

How is understanding the theory of the telosponsive scales relevant and applicable to the daily problems people and organizations encounter?

First, they help explain how meanings—particularly in terms of what is meaningful and meaningless—influence the type of motivation. Understanding these dynamic realities of daily lives can encourage the selection of more effective and wiser options. For instance, as an executive coach I have found that when clients gain a deeper insight of their meaning sets they can "make the connection" between

- their emotional attitude;
- the strength and type of motivation;
- the behavior that follows; and
- the eventual outcomes and consequences.

For these individuals, the result and impact of their behavior on others "makes sense" and opens the door for empathy and personal transformation.

I have also found this process helpful when doing life and career coaching with students. The process encourages students to constructively deal with the emotional pros and cons of the various options before them. Differentiating between Will (attraction), Drive (resistance), and Amotivation (avoidance) and paying attention to the intensity of their motivation toward an action is something they can reason with and feel. I believe awareness of these tools and their usage in effective coaching and therapy can build a stronger sense of self-determination and self-control. This is another area where I encourage more empirical research.

Pertaining to organizations, I have found it valuable when diagnosing the root causes of dysfunctional work cultures—for instance, to help explain the correlation between the culture's meaning set and the degree of employee engagement.

For individuals and organizations, the key to excellence and meaningful performance lies in understanding and improving the content of the meaning sets. For instance, I study the individual and the organization's culture meaning DNA strands, respectively, to assess strengths and opportunities. Assuming the person or organization has determined an ideal state (where I encourage the use of ACT and the five strivings as foundations), the gap between the current and aspirational meanings becomes the space for improvement.

Comparison of Gestalt and Telosponsivity Models

But how does the telosponsivity model compare to other well-known and reputable models?

The Telosponsivity Scale is comparable in some ways to the Gestalt Cycle of Experience (see figure 15 below). I offer this contrast against an established model such as Gestalt in order to exhibit the rigor of the Telosponsivity Scale.

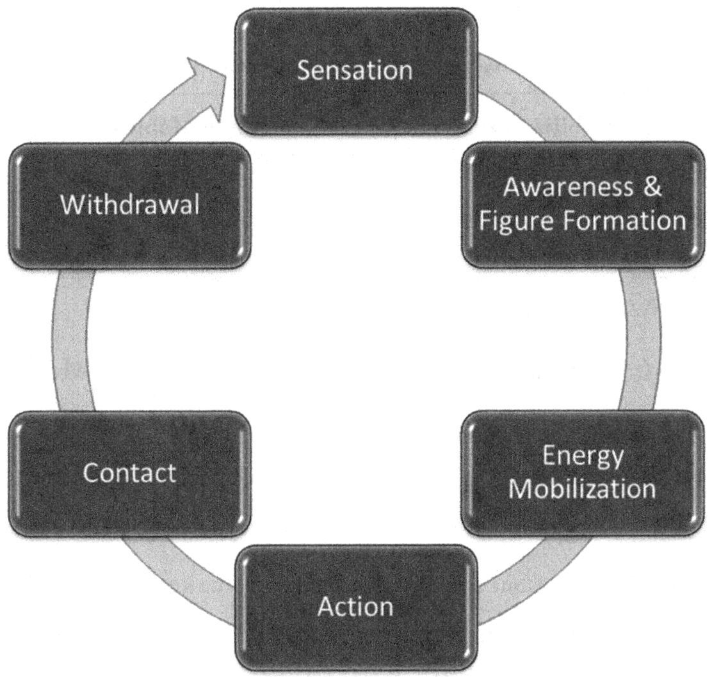

Figure 15 Gestalt Cycle of Experience

The Gestalt cycle starts when a *sensation* disturbs attention through any of the five senses or an internal stimulus. After the new sensation claims attention, the *awareness* is labeled as a *figure* (e.g., "I am thirsty") and thereafter induces an anxiety or excitement that *mobilizes energy* for action. *Action* leads to *contact* or engagement with something or someone in order to satisfy the need. When the need has been satisfied, there is a *withdrawal,* or a state of rest.

Comparing the two models, Gestalt's *Sensation* and *Awareness and Figure Formation* relate to *Intention Awareness* in the Telosponsivity Scale. Gestalt's *Energy Mobilization is* the equivalent to the *Point of Mobilization*. Telosponsivity's *Purpose and Will in Action* are equivalent to Gestalt's *Action* and *Contact,* respectively. By design, there is no equivalent to *withdrawal* on the Telosponsivity Scale. Table 6 below illustrates the comparisons.

GESTALT CYCLE OF EXPERIENCE	TELOSPONSIVITY SCALE
Sensation & Awareness	**Intention Awareness**
Energy Mobilization	**Point of Mobilization**
Action	**Purpose & Will in Action**
Contact	
Withdrawal	**NA**

Table 6 Comparison of Gestalt and Telosponsivity Models

To review, meanings establish the agenda through the meaning system. As seen in figure 9, the Meaning System influences a type of motivation. Specifically,

- the Meaning Set (i.e., the strands that make the Person, Social, and Role Meanings) makes a subjective evaluative judgment and responds with an Emotional Attitude—*Attraction, Resistance,* or *Avoidance;*
- the Emotional Attitude predisposes the individual to adopt one of three Meaning Motives—*Will, Drive,* or *Amotivate*; and
- the Meaning Motive Type designates a direction and the level of energy.

Evident on figure 10 above, related to the Telosponsivity Scale, as meaning significance increases so does the motivation to take action. It answers, "*Why* would I act?" The intensifying motivational energy prompts action at the Point of Mobilization. It answers, "*What* am I going to do about it?" The stronger the level of meaningfulness, the stronger the investment of motivational energy will be. And the stronger the energy, the more resilient the Will Power or determination to follow through will be. The Telosponsivity Scale's validity as a model is strengthened when compared to the Gestalt Cycle of Experience.

Kurt Lewin's work on goal tension systems also gives weight to the argument that a worthwhile goal increases resilience.

> Lewin assumed that behavior is goal driven. The first of Lewin's clues is that adopting a goal sets up a tension state, which remains until the goal is satisfied or the individual gives up the goal (i.e., leaves the field). If the goal is unsatisfied and the goal is not given up, the tension remains, and behavior related to the goal will continue to re-emerge.[194]

We will next address the following two questions, "What is the construct of motivation as a system, and what are its processes and consequences?"

Constructs of Motivation

Through the Meaning System and Telosponsivity Models, I explained how Emotional Attitudes in the form of Attraction, Resistance, and Avoidance influence the selection of a Meaning Motive Type: Will, Drive, or Amotivate. In this section I will explain in greater detail

- What role does motivation play in the identity formula?

---

194 Tesser, A., L. Martin, and D. Cornell, "On the Substitutability of Self-Protective Mechanisms." Gollwitzer, Peter M., and John A. Bargh, Eds. *The Psychology of Action* (New York: Guilford Press, 1996), 51.

- How do people end up selecting one of the three motivation orientations?
- What are the consequences for each choice?

The Role of Motivation in the Identity Formula

We will discuss the first question, "What role does motivation play in the identity formula?"

I previously introduced the formula (I = P + Mo + Me), which states *an identity is the sum of its purpose(s), motivation(s), and meaning sets.*

> *An identity is the sum of its purpose(s), motivation(s), and meaning sets.*

I also explained that motivation provides the identity with energy and direction based on instructions from a meaning set. Direction plus energy is a telosponse. The energy is provided by the level of meaning intensity (i.e., meaningfulness) and the direction by the type of Meaning Motive (Will, Drive, and Amotivation).

Table 7 has the three identity formulas that represent the type of Meaning Motive (direction and energy form) that is cathected, or invested to energize a purpose.[195]

Type of Meaning Motive	Formula Representation
Will	I = P + W + Me
Drive	I = P + D + Me
Amotivation	I = P + A + Me

Table 7 Types of Motivations and Formulas in an Identity

195 Digressing for a moment, the formulas are shared as efficient shorthand representations that describe types of identities for scholarly and diagnostic purposes. Pragmatically, they are designed to affirm and illustrate that while each human is unique, there are sufficient commonalities in human behavior to allow us to develop a set of theories and models to deepen understanding on their logoteleological nature. In this particular case, models allow us to study how the processes and operators in meaning systems make judgments and how they energize motivation.

In addition to studying identity as a sum of its parts, we can study the dynamics of the parts to explain the role of motivation in an identity, as illustrated by the formula

$$I = P \leftarrow Mo \leftarrow Me$$

and narrated as *a meaning set influences motivation (cathexis) to fulfill a purpose in an identity.*

Inversely,

$$I = P \rightarrow Mo \rightarrow Me$$

The formula can also be expressed as *in an identity,* a *purpose is fulfilled through a type of motivation for the sake of a meaning.*

Thus, in the identity affirmation "I am a teleotherapist devoted to coach, train, consult, and publish in order to enhance the quality of people's lives,"[196]

- the identity (who are you?) is "teleotherapist";
- the purpose (what do you do?) is "coach, train, consult, and publish";
- the motivation (how motivated are you to do this?) is "devoted"; and
- the meaning (why do you do this?) is "in order to enhance the quality of people's lives."

From the description of the type of motivation felt—"devoted"—we can deduce that the Emotional Attitude of the teleotherapist is "Attraction"; and that the Meaning Motive's type is "Will."

---

196 Remember that in logoteleology, identities are generally nouns; purposes are action verbs; motivations are usually conveyed through adjectives, verbs, and adverbs; and meanings are usually expressed through adjectives and prepositional phrases.

For relevance's sake, how could this help with your and my daily reality? First, writing affirmations about our identities and purposes will remind us of

- who we are;
- what we commit to do with our lives;
- how it benefits others; and
- why we will have staying power.

A self-determined meaningful purpose can help us contrast our ideal aspirational state with our current state of affairs (e.g., work satisfaction). For instance, think for a moment about your level of satisfaction at work.

- What motivation type (Will, Drive, and Amotivate) would you use to describe the quality of your experience, productivity, and engagement at work?
- How intense is this motivation?
- If you are not very motivated by some or all the duties of your job or by the culture of your organization, why is that? Why are they meaningless?

If it is apparent that you are unhappy at work, your meaning set (why you do what you do) or purpose (what you do) could use an overhaul to improve the situation. On the other hand, if you are happy at work, your meaning set and purpose are probably aligned, accomplishing meaningful ends.[197]

> The effectiveness of an identity is determined by the attitudinal and motive influence of meaning sets on motivation.

To recap, *an identity is the sum of its purpose(s), motivation(s), and meaning*

197 The targets of our meanings are generally the self, other people, things, and ideals.

sets. The role of motivation in an identity is to provide the right Meaning Motive (energy level, and attitudinal or motive direction) to meet daily challenges, wants, and needs. Among other reasons, we use identity formulas and identity affirmations to help us understand the types of motivations (Meaning Motives) and their impact on performance and outcomes. Further, the formulas and affirmations can help us strengthen and improve our identity and its influence for good. In conclusion, the effectiveness of an identity is determined by the attitudinal and motive influence of meaning sets on motivation.

Now to the question, *how do people end up selecting one of the three motivation orientations?*

Selection of the Motivational Orientations and Their Consequence

Based on what we have covered so far, I believe it to be reasonable to propose that Will is the ideal motivational state to be in. But why? And how are Will and the two other options energized? Being more specific, how do people end up selecting one of the three motivation orientations?

We know meaning sets influence one of the three types of motivation. The logoteleological persistent person selects to be guided by her or his Will by answering the following questions in a meaningful way:

- What meaning will I give to this situation so that it is strong enough to energize and motivate me to persist and prevail against obstacles?
- How can I avoid being driven to do what I would prefer *not* to do?
- How can I evade being driven to do what is detrimental to me and others?

Fortunately, you do have the option to choose. Unfortunately, based on my experience, not enough people are asking these questions. This section will answer those three questions by exploring Will, Drive, and Amotivation in greater depth. Our starting point will be to review current motivational theories and their relationship to the Meaning Motives.

> ...consider that contemporary psychologists do recognize that the mind (the will) does think, plan, and form intentions that precede action.
>
> Johnmarshall Reeve, University of Iowa

What Is Intrinsic Motivation?

Intrinsic motivation is the innate desire to do what one enjoys doing. It is the expression of self-determined behavior with an absence of external regulation or introjected Drives. When intrinsically motivated, we are filled with curiosity, quest for challenge, and the desire to build competence.[198]

According to the self-determination theory,[199] intrinsic motivation fulfills three psychological human needs. The first is the *need for competence,* or the ability to produce favorable results and avoid undesired ones. The second is the *need for autonomy,* or the human desire to control one's behaviors. Third is *the need for relatedness* and involves the desire to feel connected to significant others through group membership and

198 Koestner, Richard, and Gaëtan, F. Losier. 2002. "Distinguishing Three Ways of Being Internally Motivated: A Closer Look at Introjection, Identification, and Intrinsic Motivation." Ryan, Richard M., and Edward L. Deci, Eds, 101.

199 Self-determination theory (SDT) embraces "the assumption that all individuals have natural, innate, and constructive tendencies to develop an ever more elaborate and unified sense of self." Further, "we characterize this tendency toward integration as involving both autonomy (tending toward an inner organization and holistic self-regulation) and homonomy (tending toward integration of oneself with others." Ryan, Richard M., and Edward L. Deci, Eds. 2002. "Overview of Self-Determination Theory: An Organismic Dialectical Perspective." 5.

association.[200] Hence, the intrinsically motivated individual is energized *to know*, *accomplish*, and *experience stimulation*.[201]

Research has shown that being intrinsically motivated brings a host of cognitive, affective, and behavioral benefits, including greater creativity, learning, smoking abstinence, general well-being, couples' happiness, persistence at a task, and other.[202], [203] But since humans are members of groups that place demands on other members, it is not possible to meet one's intrinsic needs all the time. The fact is that since birth most people are socialized to defer and to accommodate in order to respect others' needs as well as to accede for the greater social good. Such accommodation is known as *internalization*, or *the willingness to embrace and integrate oneself to sensible group norms*.[204] It is such internalization that makes it possible for people to allow, to cooperate, and to transcend through altruistic acts—in other words, to be civilized.

Learning to maintain the balance of satisfying individual innate intrinsic needs while supporting the greater good is one of the most important tasks facing humanity. It is perhaps, in my view, *the* most important task. Canada's McGill University's Richard Koestner and Université de Moncton's Gaëtan Losier explain that

Learning to maintain the balance of satisfying individual innate intrinsic needs while supporting the greater good is one of the most important tasks facing humanity. It is perhaps, in my view, the most important task.

---

200 Vallerand, Robert J., and Catherine F. Ratelle. 2002. *Intrinsic and Extrinsic Motivation: A Hierarchical Model*. 48.

201 Notice the similarities of these three with logoteleology's five strivings: to love, to be happy, to have peace of mind, to be challenged with interesting tasks and experiences, and to be prosperous.

202 Vallerand, Robert J., and Catherine F. Ratell, *Intrinsic and Extrinsic Motivation*, 38–63.

203 Reeve, Johnmarshall, *Understanding Motivation and Emotion*, 154–55.

204 "The process through which individuals take in and accept as their own an externally prescribed way of thinking, feeling, or behaving is referred to as internalization." Reeve, Johnmarshall, *Understanding Motivation and Emotion*, 282.

"understanding how to maintain or enhance intrinsic motivation and to facilitate successful internalization requires a consideration to the extent to which the social environment supports the satisfaction of the fundamental needs."[205]

In logoteleological terms, a healthy group makes two of its most important goals to

- encourage the expression of its members' intrinsic needs in support of the group task; and
- promote the development and integration of healthy, collaborative, meaningful norms.

For our purpose, intrinsic motivation and internalization express the Will. As I previously explained, *Will* is an energetic and enthused, "I want to!" A Willed-type motivation is intrinsic and self-determined. When something curious energizes our interest, we willingly do what it takes to discover and enjoy the experience.

Selecting Intrinsic Motivation

Self-determined individuals willingly engage in activities and relationships that innately have value and a positive consequence. When interacting with others, under self-directed (free-will) conditions, the group's tasks, norms, and roles are not experienced as imposed; rather, membership, activities, and goals are experienced as integrated with one's core person meanings.

> Healthy personalities are Willed, not Driven, and consequently Willed-motivated individuals model and foster the full expression of liberty and freedom. Keep in mind that Will is defined as the power or capacity of free, conscious choice.

People are willing to join a group when members share a common

205 Koestner, Richard, and Gaëtan F. Losier, *Distinguishing Three Ways of Being Internally Motivated,* 101.

meaning set. It is in this kind of positive and nurturing setting that we can expect people to enjoy encouraging and challenging experiences, as well as the ability to accomplish fulfilling goals. And such fertile conditions are where intrinsic motivation and thus the actively engage performer thrive.

Finally, healthy personalities are Willed, not Driven, and consequently Willed-motivated individuals model and foster the full expression of liberty and freedom. Keep in mind that Will is defined as *the power or capacity of free, conscious choice.* Any culture that is governed by leaders that are Driven carry in it the seed of oppression. Logoteleology promotes the development of cultures that are managed by citizens and leaders that are Willed to carry the seed of freedom of expression, growth, fulfillment, potential, and achievement through ACT and the five strivings.

What Is Extrinsic Motivation?

When people are extrinsically motivated, they act for an external reason rather than innately wanting or needing to. Not all extrinsic motivation is harmful, however, as we have seen in the case of internalization. Through internalization, members of a group are able to allow, cooperate, and transcend for the benefit of others because they embrace common and meaningful values. Effective internalization can generate and encourage conditions where others can fulfill their intrinsic needs of competence, autonomy, and interpersonal relations.

Selecting Extrinsic Motivation

There are four types of extrinsic motivations in a continuum of high to low control[206], [207] from which people can operate. The lower the internal control the stronger the anxiety and distress felt.

206 Baard, Paul. 2002. "Intrinsic Need Satisfaction in Organizations: A Motivational Basis for Success in For-Profit and Not-For-Profit Settings." Ryan, Richard M., and Edward L. Deci, Eds. 255—75.

207 Vallerand, Robert J., and Catherine F. Ratelle, *Intrinsic and Extrinsic Motivation,* 37–63.

Low Control			High Control
External Regulation	Introjected Regulation	Identified Regulation	Integrated Regulation

Table 8 Four Types of Extrinsic Motivation

- The first type of extrinsic motivation is *external regulation,* which is the least self-determined type of motivation. People follow external regulations to attain a positive end state or reward (e.g., to be promoted) or to avoid a negative consequence (e.g., being punished).

In external regulation, *the task*[208] is not to fulfill the external agent's demand but becomes either getting a reward or avoiding a negative consequence. For instance, a child might be enticed through external regulation to pick up her room for the reward of ice cream or being allowed to play with friends. Under these conditions, tidying the room is not done for the task of being organized and for the sake of cleanliness. Nor is it to please mom and dad. The task is to get the ice cream or to be able to leave the house in order to be with friends.[209]

> *An unbiased observation of what goes on in man when he is oriented toward meaning would reveal the fundamental difference between being driven to something on the one hand and striving for something in another.*
>
> Viktor Frankl

In a professional setting, for instance, an employee can be induced to produce a report. But if the task is performed in order to get the boss off his or her back (avoiding the negative consequence)—the task *is* to get the boss off one's back, not the writing and delivering of a quality report. The task is not to cooperate but to comply and submit. The meaning given to the situation (Why am I doing this?), as previously explained,

208 By *task,* it is meant the purpose being fulfilled.

209 In Gestalt terms, getting the ice cream is the figure and tidying the room is the background.

determines what type of meaning motive will be expressed (Will, Drive, and Amotivation). In this case, external regulation Drives behavior and offers the least locus of control for the individual.

Regardless of whether a person is extrinsically enticed or induced to do something, the consequences are still the same. Attention and effort are focused away from the ultimate meaningful benefit of doing something (e.g., willingly making sure my boss is well-informed so she can make a wise decision). Instead there is a distraction from the meaningful end by the fear of a negative consequence (e.g., driven by a meaningless reason for doing something).

- The second type of extrinsic motivation is *introjected regulation.* This kind of motivation is the first step toward the internalization process. There is some acknowledgment that there is some value in the behavior, but it is not yet fully internalized and hence not self-determined. An individual responding to introjected regulation does so out of obligation, and because it is what is expected. In the case of the child and the untidy room, she might choose to clean up her room to avoid feeling shame if her significant peers disapprove of messy environments. Because it is introjected, the task is to avoid shame, not to live in a clean and tidy environment.
- The third type of extrinsic motivation is *identified regulation*, where the task is perceived to be valued. Furthermore, the activity is carried out with a sense of choice given that the individual self-identifies with the cause or purpose of the situation. For instance, a young person will clean up her room in order to please her parents and fulfill a reasonable expectation that civil people live in organized and clean environments. In this case, identified regulation reveals a person who is being responsible for what is expected of her.

Further, the individual gives some sort of autonomous endorsement of the standard, behavior, and expected outcome (e.g., a clean and organized room). However, in the continuum, identified regulation might be limited to some types of activities. While performing the task does "make sense," it is not necessarily an expression of one's core values, beliefs and aims (i.e., meaning set). For instance, it would be a stretch to believe that the identified regulation of this young person will make her a full-time career cleaning lady.

To summarize, in identified regulation no imposition is being felt, and there is some level of autonomy in choosing to perform the activity. However, it is still extrinsic motivation because it does not meet the criteria of acting for the sake of an internal inherent interest and enjoyment.

- The fourth and last type is *integrated regulation,* which is the most autonomous form of extrinsic motivation in the continuum. It shares many of the attributes of intrinsic motivation; however, integrated regulation is still extrinsic for the same reasons as identified regulation—but to a lesser degree.

In terms of sharing common ground, the tasks of this fourth type are perceived to be aligned with and congruent to significant and self-determined meanings. What is different is the level of inherent interest and enjoyment (i.e., Emotional Attitude) when compared to activities or causes that are intrinsically motivating or meaningful.

For instance, following the example of the young person doing housework, the task of straightening the room could be habituated as an essential task of civilized people. Cleaning the room is done to fulfill a standard, and not because the activities related to tidying rooms are pleasurable. Moreover, in our example, the young woman has reached a point where she holds herself accountable to "do the right thing" in her role as a family member and is willing to cooperate to meet a family criterion as her own.

It should be apparent that any social setting that is formed by Drive-type motivations (particularly external regulation and introjected regulation) has the potential of being oppressive and despotic. Drive-type motivations foster self-censorship and groupthink. Further, the self-esteem of people under these conditions is generally fragile versus secure. I also believe that under these conditions, people run the risk of losing the ability for self-awareness and insight. Oppression is introjected into the personality and subsequently projected and imposed onto others.

Tim Kasser from Knox College reminds us that "it is perhaps (too frequently) the case that people's behavior arises not from the authentic strivings of the self but instead from feelings of coercion, control, and pressure."[210] Logoteleology is committed to help individuals, groups and organizations break oppressive cycles and nurture the expression of meaningful agendas that yield true and perfect freedom through the three pillars (ACT) and the five strivings.[211]

What Is Amotivation?

Amotivation can be the result of a state of helplessness, apathy or boredom, and rebellion. Amotivation has been related to a state of disengagement.[212] Amotivation is disaffection, which means a person withholds effort; gives up easily; does just enough to get by; feels burdened or pressured when she or he tries; and experiences anxiety, boredom, and even anger.[213] Following the example of the young person being required to tidy her room, under Amotivation she could either procrastinate or complain that she does not know where to start or where to put things.

---

210 Kasser, Tim. 2002. "Sketches for a Self-Determination Theory of Values." Deci, Edward L., and Richard M. Ryan, Eds. 127.

211 I will say more about types of cultures in a future volume on logoteleology and organization development.

212 Brockner, J., "Managing the Effects of Layoffs on Survivors." *California Management Review* 34 , no. 2 (1992): 9–28.

213 Reeve, Johnmarshall. 2002. "Self-Determination Theory Applied to Educational Settings." Deci, Edward L., and Richard M. Ryan, Eds. 194.

Selecting Amotivation

People end up following the Amotivation orientation when the affective quality and locus of control of the identity or person is at its lowest. People are at high risk of experiencing the existential vacuum when they are in a constant state of Amotivation. As explained by David G. Myers from Hope College, "Depressed or oppressed people, for example, become passive because they believe their efforts have no effect … depressed people … suffer paralysis of the will, passive resignation, even motionless apathy."[214]

Comparison of Models

Table 9 illustrates and compares how self-determination theory and teleotherapy theory fit their respective types of motivation. Will includes identified regulation, integrated regulation, and intrinsic motivation. Drive covers external regulation and introjected regulation, while Amotivation has no regulation. Self-determination theory and teleotherapy share in common Amotivation's concept of apathy and learned helplessness. However, different to self-determination theory, teleotherapy includes refusal or rebellion to a form of Amotivation.

> *Depressed or oppressed people, for example, become passive because they believe their efforts have no effect. …depressed people… suffer paralysis of the will, passive resignation, even motionless apathy.*
>
> David G. Myers
> Hope College

Table 9 below also includes the types of motivation, and their respective Emotional Attitudes. It too reveals the sources for the Types of Regulation, those being introjects, internalization, and self-determination. In the continuum, the affective quality, locus of control and degree of meaning increases as regulation is identified, integrated, and self-determined.

214 Myers, David G., *Social Psychology,* 60.

Type of Motivation SDT	Amotivation	Extrinsic Motivation				Intrinsic Motivation
Type of Regulation	No Regulation	External Regulation	Introjected Regulation	Identified Regulation	Integrated Regulation	Self-determined Regulation
Type of Motivation (Meaning Motives) Teleotherapy	AMOTIVATION	DRIVE		WILL		
Emotional Attitude Teleotherapy	AVOIDANCE	RESISTANCE		ATTRACTION		
Sources	INTROJECTS			INTERNALIZATION		SELF-DETERMINED
Affective Quality	Low					High
Locus of Control	Low					High
Degree of Meaning	Low					High

Adapted with permission from Figure 1.1, Edward I., Deci and Richard M. Ryan, eds., Handbook of Self-Determination Research Rochester: University of Rochester Press, 2002), 16.

Table 9 Motivational Types Continuum: A comparison of Self-Determination Theory and Logoteleology

The Power of Choice

The point of the table is to remind us that we have choices, and that we can ultimately select those options that best serve us as well as others.

Frankl makes the distinction "between being driven to something on the one hand and striving for something on the other." He further states, "It is one of the immediate data of life experience that man is pushed by drives but pulled by meaning, and this implies that it is always up to him to decide whether or not he wishes to fulfill the latter. Thus, meaning fulfillment always implies decision making."[215]

So there are three questions we all face:

- First, do I choose to be willed and pulled by strivings or to be compelled and pushed by Drives?
- Second, do I choose to create conditions that allow others to grow, to be self-determined and to collaborate or will I create conditions that stymie potential-expression?
- Third, do I choose to cooperate and transcend to fulfill meaningful ends through the five strivings, or will I resist others and/or be a social parasite?

To summarize, going back to the question *how do people end up following any of the three motivation orientations?* if the motivation type is extrinsic, as explained above, it is Driven or introjected. For all purposes the individual is conditioned to react rather than to act. Drives do not satisfy intrinsic needs and wants; rather, they are forces compelled to avoid

> It is one of the immediate data of life experience that man is pushed by drives but pulled by meaning, and this implies that it is always up to him to decide whether or not he wishes to fulfill the latter. Thus, meaning fulfillment always implies decision-making.
>
> Viktor Frankl

215 Frankl, Viktor E., *The Will to Meaning,* 43.

a negative consequence or to earn a reward. They could also be compulsions, impulses, and habits at the unaware level.

In contrast to Will, Drives' sources lie in their introjected past. Their primary task is to gain a reward or avoid a punishment. Will, however, is present-to-future-oriented, and its primary task is to learn, to relate, and to express autonomy.

People are Amotivated because of learned helplessness, apathy, and as an expression of rebellion or stubbornness.

Finally, these types of motivations are choices, and this implies that it is always up to us to decide whether or not we wish to thrive.

The next section will answer the question, *what are the best environmental conditions for meaning expression and fulfillment?*

Creating Meaningful Environments

What can you do to make sure you are Willed to live a meaningful life? What are the conditions where you and others can be intrinsically motivated to fulfill meaningful purposes?

There are five quick acts we can take to succeed in life:

1. Take responsibility to find the right answers to life's problems and act on them.
2. Dedicate your life to following the three pillars (allow, cooperate, and transcend [ACT]) and the Five Meaningful strivings (love, happiness, peace, challenge, and prosperity) for successful living.
3. Find the meaning of your life and then select a purpose to fulfill it using the three pillars and the five strivings as foundations.
4. Champion Group Identities (family, professional, political, religious, etc.) so that its members are motivated by a healthy

Will (versus Amotivate and Drive) to do meaningful things (through the Five Meaningful strivings).

5. Make sure your group and role identities remain aligned with your person identity.

Let's discuss each.

Take Responsibility

I started the book with the premise that there are answers to life's problems, and that people too often suffer needlessly despite those answers being available. I concluded on that premise after reading Viktor Frankl's view of what the meaning of life is: "Life ultimately means taking the responsibility to find the right answers to its problems and to fulfill the tasks which it constantly sets for each individual." [216]

The "right answers" of course are doing meaningful things and performing them *competently*. It is important to ask ourselves the right questions so we may solve the right problems.

- What must I know and be good at in order to solve this problem?
- What is required of me to be good at in order to succeed on this project or circumstance?
- What is the meaning of this situation, and how can I best respond by means of the three pillars of success (ACT) and the Five Meaningful strivings?

Life is about maximizing the joy of learning and improving oneself and situations. Learning is a means to achieving the Five Meaningful strivings. Both meaning and competence are important. Asking smart questions will trigger our problem-solving mental processes and help us find the best answers.

---

216 Viktor E. Frank, *Man's Search for Meaning* (Boston: Beacon Press, 2006), 77.

Dedicate Your Life to Succeed through Meaningful Acts

According to logoteleology theory, a person is successful when she is able to claim and fulfill her unique meaningful calling through the three pillars of success (ACT) and the Five Meaningful strivings. Again, when interacting with others, successful people allow, cooperate, and transcend. Further, people succeed when they dedicate their lives to helping others experience love, happiness, peace of mind, stimulating and interesting challenges, and prosperity. The evidence is overwhelmingly in favor of these as a meaningful style of life. I firmly believe that peace of mind and life fulfillment can only be achieved through the three pillars of success (ACT) and the Five Meaningful strivings.

Find and Fulfill the Meaning of Your Life

There is an answer to the question of the meaning and purpose of your existence. There is a role and task that no one can fulfill but you. Using as a foundation the three pillars of success (ACT) and the five strivings, find a meaningful purpose for your life. An effective way of discovering what is meaningful for you is to follow your passions. And if you have not yet found something you feel passionate about, make your preliminary meaningful life purpose to find your passion. It helps to study. Expose yourself to different types of situations, individuals, and groups with the goal of broadening your understanding and finding that meaningful urge to live for.

Once you find your meaningful passion, find a means to express it. For instance, my passion is to enhance the quality of life of the willing through meaningful purpose. I express it by writing papers and books, as well as through my coaching, training, facilitation, and consulting. Write your life purpose using the identity formula (I = P + W + Me). You can always improve it over time as you learn more about yourself, your potential, and your calling.

Champion Meaningful Environments

Your life *will be* meaningful if you are keen to commit yourself to fulfilling the previous three tasks and to make them part of an agenda that builds meaningful human environments. Such environments would be purposed to serve and to build people through the three pillars of success (ACT) and the five strivings. This is different from what too many people experience today—they are unfortunate victims of family circles, work environments, communities, and even countries that are meaningless and led by Driven-type people. The world needs great leaders with meaningful agendas at all levels of our global society. For instance, I encourage others to notice and follow the example of the CNN Heroes.

More people are needed to champion the cause of building meaningful organizations that serve people versus people serving organizations and leaders with meaningless agendas and work styles. We have an opportunity to learn how to build more humane or human-friendly environments that are cooperative, innovative, and profitable. This is tough work because the Driven-type leaders and organizations are more likely to be victims of self-censorship and hence low self-awareness. Under these conditions, leaders' judgment is limited, their options few, their scope myopic and narrow.

We are reminded by Richard Koestner and Gaëtan F. Losier, "The harshly evaluative and pressured character of an introjected self-regulatory style appears to compromise people's information processing and disrupt their emotional experiences in this domain."[217]

As a result, experiencing the freedom, potential, and prosperity of a Will-type environment remains elusive to many. This is in part because of ignorance on the options I have explained here and their respective consequence.

However, while in the minority, those of us who are committed to the cause of building human friendly organizations find solace in Frankl's encouragement that "in spite of belief in the potential humanness of

---

217 Koestner, Richard, and Gaëtan F. Losier, *Distinguishing Three Ways of Being Internally Motivated,* 101.

man we must not close our eyes to the fact that *humane* humans are, and probably will always remain, a minority. But it is precisely for this reason that each of us is challenged to *join* the minority. Things are bad. But unless we do our best to improve them, everything will become worse."[218]

Maintain Group and Role Identities Alignment with Your Person Identity

I have stated previously that it is important to maintain congruence and consistency between your core person identity and your social and role identities. Assuming that you have clearly articulated your meaningful life purpose, select friendships and associations where you can best express and practice your goals and values. As much as possible, your roles in life should be aligned with who you are, to what is meaningful to you and to others, and with your innate talents. Being in roles and engaged in tasks that do not reflect who you are only brings sorrow and distress.

Summary

There are four actions we can take to select and follow the most successful approach. First, take responsibility for your life's problems. Second, follow the three pillars for success (ACT) and the Five Meaningful strivings. Third, find and fulfill the meaning of your life. Fourth, be a catalyst and sponsor of meaningful human organizations. Fifth, be a member of groups and engage in roles where you can best make a meaningful difference.

Application

"What are some simple steps I could take *to champion a meaningful environment?"* you may ask. I would propose that you take on one, but no more than two tasks to improve on at a time. A good place to start is at home.

---

218 Frankl, Viktor, *Man's Search for Ultimate Meaning*, 89.

For instance, if you are in a relationship or have a family, plan and judge your actions through the lenses of the three pillars for success (ACT) and the five strivings. Commit yourself to learn and practice how to love others and how to enrich others' lives with happiness and laughter. You will not be able to help but end up being loved back by others, as well as laughing your way through a fun-filled life. Leverage your relationship with your significant other to jointly experience the full potential and power of love between two people. Also, foster the shared goal of learning, discussing, and practicing acts of peace in your interactions, as well as doing things that bring about peace of mind. You will have to study peace, conflict resolution, effective communication, managing finances, etc., but it will be useful and meaningful. In turn, the learning process will bring to you and your partner, as well as family members, an interesting challenge to live up to. Also, with your partner and family members, study and discuss what prosperity is and how to attain wealth. Then jointly commit to being prosperous and follow through on your commitments. These meaningful acts are the core to a rich and worthwhile life.

Learning from My Journey

Researching, learning, and applying the concepts on this chapter have allowed me to be more cognizant of my motivational options and to know when and why I am energized or not. I am more keen to remember that the only viable option to succeed in life is to Will myself to do meaningful things. To be Driven and Amotivated are no longer options for me. Thus it is easier for me to correct my course when I deviate. And when I do deviate, I know there is some adjustment required on my meaning set pertaining to the subject I am engaged in. I can identify the disruptive meaning and know how to set a plan to either fix or replace it with a more meaningful option.

Another interesting phenomenon during this phase of my research has been experiencing a roller coaster of emotions from extreme exuberance and joy to sadness and self-pity. Through the process of researching and writing this book, self-reflection and self-evaluation were unavoidable. In chapter 1 I wrote, "Books, besides imparting knowledge, can also be wonderful mirrors to build self-awareness, self-knowledge, strengthen one's conscience, and make life better. I plan to build a compendium of mirrors."

In my case, this omen has turned out to be true. In the spirit of being my own subject of study, I have embraced and explored the feelings and their origins in order to find their meaning. Specifically I followed the advice from chapter 3 on the subject of Meaning:

"Included in decoding meanings is the understanding of the emotions that emerge in the transaction. Gestalt practitioners Joseph Melnick and Sonia March Nevis claim that "Labeling of a sensation is one way to define 'meaning.'"[219] This means that when people face a situation their emotional reaction means something worth understanding. Thus, in this sense, meaning is the labeling of a sensation. It answers, 'What does this feeling mean?'"

I have also experienced feelings of exuberance and pride. This knowledge has also validated the way I have been practicing organization and leadership development, as well as coaching since the eighties; particularly aligning organization's cultures and leadership approaches to give equal weight to factors such as business, process and people, where people is first among equals. I too felt feelings of appreciation for my teachers, for instance, toward my mentor, the late Dr. Harold Bridger from the Tavistock Institute, for teaching me about psychological tasks and their impact on motivation.

I thus can predict that others who learn and reflect on the meaning of this book could experience a similar emotional array of feelings. If and when that does happen, I will be a better empathic listener and coach.

---

219 Nevis, Edwin C., Ed., *Gestalt Therapy* (New York: Gardner Press, 1992), 69.

Chapter 6: What Is My Life Purpose?

To everything there is a season, and a time to every purpose under the heaven.—Ecclesiastes 3:1

According to logoteleology, the hallmark of successful people is the ability to clearly state their meaningful life purpose and to act in ways that help them get ahead. That might explain why our daily language is full of purpose-related statements. For instance, we use terms such as planning, goal setting, strategizing, overcoming an obstacle, moving toward the goal, winning, and hitting the target. We use these and similar terms because we are purpose-directed beings. For that reason, this chapter is fundamentally concerned with the function and relevance of purpose in identities. It answers the following questions:

1. What is purpose?
2. What is the teleological nature of humans?
3. How are teleology and logoteleology alike and different?
4. What is the role of purpose in the Identity Model?
5. How does an identity self-regulate?
6. Why purpose matters?
7. What is my life's purpose?

What Is Purpose?

There are a number of definitions for purpose that are fitting with logoteleology theory. One is that purpose is a problem to be solved. As such, purpose is a *process that solves problems.*[220] Another source defines purpose as "the internally represented *mental goal or aim* that is set by an individual and guides and directs his or her behavior.[221] Thus, in this definition, purpose is also a process, particularly operating as a *guidance system*. Logical learning theory describes it as "the aim of the meaning.... Purpose may be thought of as the reason a certain intention is enacted."[222] According to this definition, purpose is in the business of *fulfilling meanings*. One of McMillan Dictionary's definitions gives purpose an existential definition as "a goal or meaning in your life because there is something you want to achieve."[223] Consequently, purpose is *to accomplish a meaningful life mission*. This previous definition supports analytical psychology's claim that, as social beings our purpose includes making meaning.[224] Thus, purpose, in this sense, is *the act of making meaning* (as an output).

Using the Identity Model as reference, meaning answers "who do I want to be?" while purpose answers "what must I do to achieve and become my meaning?"

> Purpose is a guiding system that monitors behavior, solves problems, fulfills meanings, gives meaning to one's life, and creates meanings.

So in summary, *purpose can be defined as a guiding system that monitors behavior, solves*

220 Douglas L. Medin and Brian H. Ross, *Cognitive Psychology* (Orlando, FL: Harcourt Brace and Company, 1997), 437–68.

221 Athur S. Reber, Rhianon Allen, and Emily S. Reber, *Penguin Dictionary of Psychology* (Penguin Books: New York, 2009), 642.

222 Joseph F. Rychlack, *Logical Learning Theory,* 37.

223 Accessed March 22, 2013, http://www.macmillandictionary.com/dictionary/american/purpose.

224 Mathers, Dale, *Meaning and Purpose in Analytical Psychology,* 238.

problems, fulfills meanings, gives meaning to one's life, and creates meanings.

This summary is fitting because according to logoteleology theory, purpose can be

1. An existential statement of an identity (I = P + Mo + Me) that explains the meaning of one's life or actions. A purpose statement answers three questions:[225]

    a. What do I do?
    b. For whom?
    c. To what end or benefit?

    For instance, "I publish children's books in order to promote the love of learning." Hence, what I do is "publish books"; for whom is "children"; and the meaningful benefit is "to promote the love of learning."
2. As seen in figure 16 below, purpose is a subsystem of a comprehensive guidance system within an identity that

    a. interacts with the meaning and motivation subsystems;
    b. performs activities that meet and fulfill the criteria from the meaning and motivation subsystems;
    c. reports back on its progress after making contact with the external environment; and
    d. makes the appropriate adjustments when required.

    As we previously learned, once the meaning subsystem commits to a cause[226] within an identity system, directives make their way through the motivation subsystem to select a fitting purpose. For instance, in the statement "I teach so others might succeed," a teacher demonstrates her commitment to the meaning "so others might succeed" by the act of teaching. There is consistency

---

225 I credit Jeff Bouchard from Lake Mary, Florida with providing this definition.
226 Cause as in the Greek *aitiá,* which means "responsibility."

between what she stands for (the criteria—why?) and what she does (the performance—what?).

3. An intention in action. It answers, "What do I do?" For instance, using the previous example, "I teach."

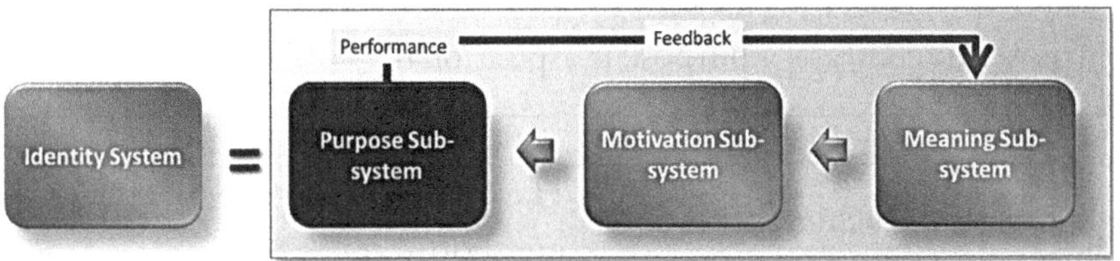

Figure 16 The Identity System and its sub-systems

Purposes can be directed (for whom?) to four types of subjects or targets:

- Self: as in when I meet my needs and/or shape my own identity and destiny
- Things: as in when I improve processes, objects, and nature
- Others: as in when I help others meet their needs
- Ideals: as in advocating for a cause

Purpose, Goals, and Performance

It is important to explain some semantic distinctions between purpose, goals, and behaviors. First, a purpose is not a goal. In addition to being a system, a purpose can be thought of as a mission that fulfills meanings through goals. Purpose precedes goals. Goals have beginnings and ends, while purposes

In addition to being a system, a purpose can be thought of as a mission that fulfills meanings through goals. Purpose precedes goals. Goals have beginnings and ends, while purposes are never fully achieved.

are never fully achieved.[227] Goals are intermediate targets that help us reach the final target or destination. As such, goals may change or be modified in order to adapt to changing situations; but the purpose has a more permanent presence. A purpose can have multiple goals. Goals are short-term and generally meet the SMART criteria (Specific, Measurable, Achievable, Relevant, and Timely) and directly link to the purpose. In contrast, a purpose is aspirational.

Purpose	Goals
Is never fully achieved	Have a beginning and an end; are short-term
Fulfill meanings through goals	Fulfill purposes
Precede goals	Are directly linked to a purpose
Can have one or more goals	Are intermediate targets
Is aspirational	Are SMART: Specific, Measurable, Achievable, Relevant, and Timely
Has a permanent presence	Can be modified and adapted

Table 10 Contrast of Purpose and Goals

To contrast purpose with goals, consider the previous example of the statement "I publish children's books in order to promote the love of learning" as a role identity purpose statement. A supportive and complementary goal would be expressed as, "Write and publish a book by March 10, 2020, that describes how a child became wise and wealthy as a result of studying." Or "Write one book a year that promotes the love of learning."

Once a purpose has been affirmed and goals have been planned, *performance* follows. Performance—as part of the purpose subsystem—occurs so goals can be attained.[228] *Performance is intention in action, behavior,* or *being on task.* Performance as *intention in action* is based

227 Mourkogiannis, Nikos, *Purpose: The Starting Point of Great Companies* (New York: Palgrave Macmillan, 2006), 145.

228 Weir, Michael, *Goal-Directed Behavior* (New York: Gordon and Breach, Science Publishers, 1984), 64.

on Immanuel Kant's concept of causality, where nothing can happen without being caused.[229] For instance, for a hungry hunter stalking game, aiming toward a target with a bow and arrow is not enough. At some point the hunter has to release the arrow.

Let us now understand how the brain actually fulfills purposes and what makes humans teleological.

The Teleological Nature of Humans

Now that we know what purpose is, let us explore what teleology is and what makes humans teleological.

Teleology comes from the Greek *telos*, which is described "as the purpose, the good, or the end of something."[230] A useful definition for teleology is *being goal-directed*. Rychlack defines it as, "The view that events are predicated according to plan, design, or assumption—that is, based on purposive meanings or reasons—and therefore directed to some intended end."[231] This definition fits with the previously discussed definitions for purpose.

Teleology gave origin to *cybernetics*, a term coined by the mathematician, engineer, and social philosopher Norbert Weiner, which denotes the study of teleological mechanisms. Cybernetics comes from the Greek word meaning "steersman." Cybernetics is concerned with principles of communication and control of regulatory feedback in goal-directed (teleological) systems. Because of its broad application to how subjects behave, cybernetics cuts across numerous disciplinary boundaries. However, we are limiting our explanation to how cybernetics is applicable to logoteleology's identity theory.

My intention is to explain the phenomena of self-determination, purpose

229 Kresge, Elijah Everett, *Kant's Doctrine of Teleology* (Allentown, PA: The Francis Printing Company, 1914), 26.

230 Miller, Frederic P., Agnes F. Vandome, and John McBrewster, Eds., *Four Causes* (Lexington, KY: Alphascript Publishing, 2009).

231 Rychlack, Joseph F., *Logical Learning Theory* ,322.

and goal setting, performance, and self-regulation in the Identity Model (I = P + Mo + Me). For the purposes of this book, teleology will be synonymous with cybernetics as it applies to individuals, groups, and organizations.

With the previous background information as context, let's return to the purpose of this section and answer the question, "What makes humans teleological?"

The Teleological Human

Teleology is an established concept in psychology. The psychology of action, Gestalt psychology, individual psychology, analytical psychology, cognitive psychology, Edward C. Tolman's purposive behaviorism, social psychology, and logical learning theory, as well as identity theory are examples of schools of thought and theories that make reference to cybernetic, self-directed, or teleological notions.

For instance, according to Gestalt's Mary Ann Huckabay, humans "display purposeful, teleological, or goal-oriented behavior."[232] Tulane University's Cognitive Studies Director Radu J. Bogdan, states, "People, possibly most social animals, are natural teleo-psychologists. They cannot help but see their conspecifics and themselves as being goal directed, and in particular, animated by beliefs and desires."[233], [234] Elsewhere he claims, "Organisms are

> A human teleology suggests that people behave for the sake of reasons, purposes, and intentions.
>
> Joseph F. Rychlack

232 Huckabay, Mary Ann. "An Overview of the Theory and Practice of Gestalt Group Process.", *Gestalt Therapy: Perspective and Applications (*New York: Gardner Press, Inc., 1992), 309.

233 Bogdan, Radu J., *Grounds for Cognition: How Goal-Guided Behavior Shapes the Mind* (Hillsdale, NJ: Lawrence Erlbaum Associates, Inc., 1994), 123.

234 Fitting with logoteleology, "beliefs and desires" are meanings (i.e., beliefs and aims).

teleosystems"[235] or goal-directed beings. MIT's physiologist Ragnar Granit adds that teleological operations allow living beings to adapt to their environment.[236] Finally, Rychlack offers, "A human teleology suggests people behave for the sake of reasons, purposes, and intentions."[237]

According to logoteleology theory, what makes humans teleological is their innate capacity to self-determine, to find purpose and set goals, to plan, to perform, and to self-regulate in support of a meaning set. These are not only cognitive operators, they are areas of competence and attitude that require strengthening and improvement over time. Hence, mental teleological processes can help us build knowledge and new meanings to improve self, things, others, and ideals.

So, from a practical point of view, why would teleological operations concern us? Because whatever meaning we hold as "truth," our teleological system is programmed to fulfill. Mental teleology affects much of our behavior and hence the quality of our lives.

Notice how Roy Baumeister explains the influence of teleological thinking on moods and behavior: "People will be most affected by the things they dwell on and think about for the longest times, and so by minimizing the amount of time spent attending to unpleasant events, a person can minimize any informational effects of such events."[238]

Being aware of how our thinking and view of situations influences behavior can help us better control our innate teleological mental operations.

---

235 Ibid., 43.

236 Granit, Ragnar, *The Purposive Brain* (Cambridge, MA and London, England: The MIT Press, 1981).

237 Rychlack, Joseph F., *Logical Learning Theory*, 8.

238 Baumeister, Roy F. "Self-Regulation and Ego Threat: Motivated Cognition, Self-Deception, and Destructive Goal Setting," *The Psychology of Action: Linking Cognition and Motivation to Behavior* (New York: The Guilford Press, 1996), 30.

Comparing Teleology with Logoteleology

Teleology and logoteleology are alike in that both can describe how a cybernetic (*Telos*) system operates in personality. Teleology is simply self-regulation. It is a goal-directed automatic operation that generally functions out of awareness. The evident contrast between the two is that logoteleology's theory includes—as its names suggests—the functions of meanings (*logo)* plus the Will (*thelos*) to explain goal-directed behavior. Hence the identity formula (I = P + Mo + Me) offers a more wide-ranging explanation of how humans can self-determine and self-regulate.

Figure 17 The Dynamics of a Logoteleological System

While simplistic, the general view of a dynamic logoteleological goal-directed system in personality is shown in figure 17. The illustration explains goal-directed systems, this time placing goals on the driver's seat. Performance follows goals. During performance there are moments for self-reflection to assess progress (i.e., feedback). Finally, the outcome of the insight (i.e., meaning) can confirm that things are going well or that goal adjustments are required in order to achieve the ultimate target. Once the meaning implications of the feedback are understood, energy is again reapplied in support of the goal.

I will explain below in greater detail the roles of the Meaning and Motivation systems in goal-directed behavior.

To summarize, both logoteleology and teleology provide explanations for goal-directed behavior in personality. Yet logoteleology's cybernetics is more comprehensive because it explicitly explains how the meaning and motivation systems contribute in guiding behavior. Each element of the identity formula (I = P + Mo + Me) plays a dynamic role in shaping direction.

Let's see the logoteleology system in detail.

The Logoteleology System

As seen in figure 17 above, the logoteleology system has five components: goals, performance, feedback, meaning, and motivation.

Purpose and Goals

I already provided evidence that humans are goal-directed. I also made the distinction between purpose and goals. Goal-directed or teleological behavior fundamentally deals with mental criteria from the meaning set. Remember that purpose and goals fulfill meanings. The meaning set establishes the criteria for

- the meaning motive type (direction);
- motivation strength;
- purpose, goal selection; and
- eventual performance.

Once action is committed (telosponse), the *purpose subsystem* plans goals and delineates processes to meet the criteria of the meaning's aims and targets.

Performance

Performance is movement and effort toward a target. It can be explained as carrying out the purpose and goals' plans. Successful performance requires knowledge, skills, and abilities. It uses motivation energy and type to carry out the instructions from the meaning system.

Feedback (for Self-Regulation)

To make sure performance is on track, the logoteleological system self-regulates actions, feelings, and thoughts through incoming feedback. Remember, there is no self-regulation or teleology without purpose, goals, processes, feedback, meanings, and motivation.

Self-regulation entails subset operations:

- **Self-observation** or being self-aware is the conscious capacity to have insight of one's performance within the context of the meaning set's criteria. In other words, self-observation allows the individual to know *what* he or she is doing (the action) and *why* (the meaning) he or she is doing it. The higher the degree of objective self-observation the greater the capacity for self-control or self-determination. In the same way, the greater the capacity to self-determine, the greater the willingness and capacity to self-observe. How well one self-observes impacts how well we self-reflect.

- **Self-reflection** follows self-observation. It is a feedback process that entails two sub-tasks:

- **Self-reference** is the act of evaluating *where* the agent is in relation to the goals and target. It answers the efficiency-based question: "Where am I in relation to my plan and final target?"

- **Self-evaluation** is the calculation of the accuracy of one's self-reference with the trajectory (path) and effort (self-determination) in relation to the goals and targets. It answers the effective-based question: "Am I on target?"

The Meaning

The incoming answers, as feedback from the self-regulation process, express a meaning. It answers the question, "What is the meaning of being or not being on target?" The meaning set considers the answer and sends instructions following the predetermined sequence which adheres to the Identity Model:

$$(I = P + Mo + Me) \text{ or } (P \leftarrow Mo \leftarrow Me)$$

These instructions sanction existing goals to stay the course or they might provide new instructions to make adjustments where and when appropriate in order to get to the target.

Meaning Motive Type and Motivation

Remember that the meaning motive type (Will, Drive, and Amotivation) dictates the degree of motivational autonomy or choice expressed in an identity. The selection of one of these three types determines telosponsivity[239] or how resolute and persistent performance will be, particularly when facing obstacles. If motivation is Willed, it is said that the selection of a choice is self-determined, conscious, voluntary, and intrinsic. The task of the Willed is to enthusiastically move on. If motivation is Driven, the choice is considered other-determined, external, imposed, and extrinsic. The task of the Driven is then to comply. If Amotivated, the choice is explained as a state of helplessness due to self-esteem or internal concerns over the lack of competence; a refusal due to its other-determined, external, imposed, and extrinsic nature, or a state of apathy. Briefly, in Amotivation the task is to retreat, resist, and ignore, respectively.

To review, the logoteleology system has five components: goals,

---

239 Taking a position and intending to act on it is known as a telosponse.

performance, feedback, meaning, and motivation. The interactions of these five components explain how the personality self-regulates to adapt to changing circumstances, to act resiliently, and to achieve goals and fulfill purposes.

Having explained the dynamic process of a logoteleological system, I will now give more detail about the role of purpose in the Identity Model.

The Role of Purpose in the Identity Model

In chapter 5, and below in figure 18, I explain that meaning antecedents form meanings. Moreover, individual meanings form and organize as a meaning set with instructions that are expressed through our person, social and role identities. Meaning sets have an emotional tone that prompts an emotional attitude. This emotional attitude is consequently expressed as one of three options: attraction, resistance and avoidance. The emotional attitude spawns a meaning motive type (i.e., Will, Drive, and Amotivate).

As seen in figure 18, once a meaning motive type has been selected, the meaning system officially commits the identity to act. Said differently, the meaning system gives instructions to the motivation system to put forth effort or energy plus direction. In turn, the motivation system—again, based on the assigned meaning motive type—selects the appropriate motivational channel (i.e., Will, Drive, or Amotivate) for action. The motor action forwards the information from the meaning system to *the purpose system*.

The purpose system selects an *action type* based on the meaning motive type criteria (Will, Drive, and Amotivate) and the intended meaning. An *action type* is a distinctive intention that is compatible with and supportive of the meaning motive type, the level of energy, direction, and intended meaning.

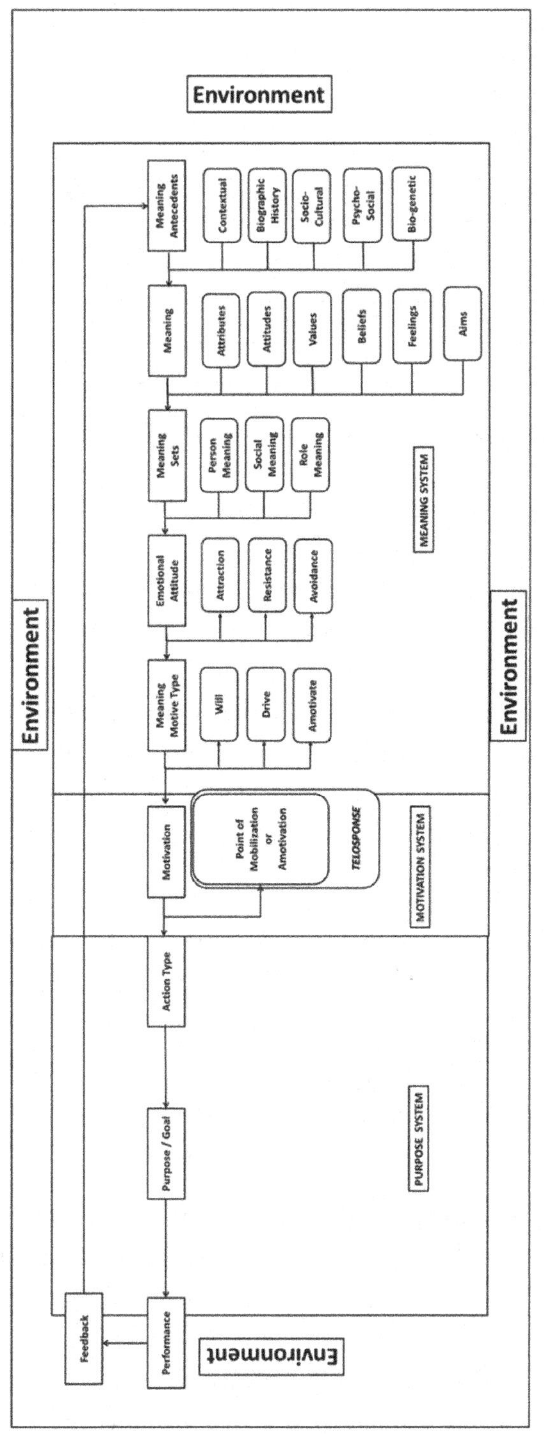

Figure 18 (from right to left): Logo, Thelos, and Telos in Identity

Examples of how meaning motive types prompt action types can be seen on table 11, below. Notice how the actions (verbs) are compatible with the meaning motive type.

	MEANING MOTIVE TYPE		
	WILL	**DRIVE**	**AMOTIVATE**
ACTION TYPE	Plan	Rush	Wait
	Engage	Command	Disengage
	Perform	Compel	Procrastinate
	Achieve	Finish	Excuse

Table 11 Meaning Motive Type and Action Type

Following the inner works of an identity as seen in figure 18 above, purpose and goals are expressed in conformance to the action type (table 11). Once purpose and goals have been committed, directed performance materializes. Contact and engagement with the environment generates feedback. And feedback makes self-regulation possible. The feedback becomes a meaning antecedent as a contextual learning (knowledge) and biographical history (experience). As illustrated on figure 18—assuming a psychologically healthy person—the identity cycle continues on its goal-oriented and adaptive tasks as it interacts with the surrounding environment.

Understanding the role of purpose in identity is particularly relevant because it explains why people behave the way they do. More specific, it clarifies how purpose is influenced by meanings and energized to act by a type of motivation.

Logoteleology also draws attention to its maxim that purpose is the realm of competence. Having a clear meaningful purpose does not guarantee success unless the individual is knowledgeable and competent, or at least has sources of knowledge

Logoteleology also draws attention to its maxim that purpose is the realm of competence.

Good intentions are not enough unless competent execution follows.

and competence in support of his goals. Good (meaningful) intentions are not enough unless Willed competent execution follows.

However, neither is competence a guarantor of a successful meaningful existence and results. Attempting to solve meaning-related problems (i.e., what is meaningless) through competence-building, in my experience, has limited positive impact and is not long-lasting. Competence is not enough unless its application is backed by a meaningful benefit. I will explain how I have applied logoteleology concepts when coaching others and consulting to organizations later and in future volumes. Sufficient for now is to understand that, according to logoteleology, psychological problems need to be solved at the meaning level.

To summarize, the role of purpose in an identity system is to fulfill the criteria from the meaning and motivation subsystems. Purpose requires skilled performance in order to meet the criteria exacted by the meaning system. A meaningful purpose performed competently increases the odds for success. Hence we can conclude that people are perfectly purposed for the results they achieve.

People are perfectly purposed for the results they achieve.

But what else does purpose do for the sake of one's identity? A very important contribution of purpose in an identity is to keep us predictable and true to ourselves. Purposes also restrict the range of choices in order to avoid distractions from the target. Let's see how.

How Does Identity Self-Regulate?

We self-regulate when we compare the results of our purposes and goals with the intended meanings. For instance, we are self-regulating when we ask questions such as:

- "Did I get the A on my test?"
- "Did I deliver the report on time?"

- "Was my behavior appropriate in light of my values?"

The answer to the question will ultimately

- confirm the value of the current approach and level of effort or
- propose making adjustments at the meaning, motivation, or purpose subsystems

Worth repeating, I stated the following in chapter 2:

> *Identities are self-regulating and self-fulfilling.* Identities steer behavior. Burke and Stets claim, "People act in ways such that the meanings of the behavior reflect the meanings they hold for themselves in their identities."[240] This supports Logoteleology's sixth basic proposition: *Humans are teleological or purpose driven.* We have a mental teleological mechanism employed to maintain environmental consistency with identity meanings. We cannot help but to act as we self-describe through our identities—consciously or involuntarily. We are wired to find ways to act according to our self-concept and to fulfill our self-image. Hence, person and role identities are inherently teleological.
>
> Role identities interact with other roles in order to achieve ends. I agree with Alfred Adler that, "A person would not know what to do with himself were he not oriented toward some goal. We cannot think, feel, will or act without the perception of some goal."[241] More recently Reeve affirmed that, "Defining or creating the self shows how *self-concept* energizes and directs behavior."[242] In short, we are goal-directed.

Let's dissect how identities are self-regulating and self-fulfilling, and understand the implications.

---

240 Burke and Stets, *Identity Theory,* 84.

241 Ansbacher, Heinz L., and Rowena R. Ansbacher, *The Individual Psychology of Alfred Adler,* 96.

242 Reeve, Johnmarshall, *Understanding Motivation and Emotion,* 261.

First, we all have a self-concept or a definition of who we are. Another way of referring to self-concept is self-identity, which could be a self-view that is different to how others might identify you. Some might not be aware of their self-concept—as when people struggle trying to figure out who they are, what is their purpose and what is the meaning of their life. But aware or not, everyone has a mental representation of who they are.

> *Thus, rather than dismissing the concept of a will to meaning as wishful thinking, one could more justifiably conceive it as a self-fulfilling prophesy.*
>
> Viktor Frankl

Second, as we have learned, our self-concept can be self-determined or scripted. This mental representation, you will recall, lies on the meaning set, which was shaped by meaning antecedents. The role of the purpose system is to keep you consistent with your self-concept. Our brain helps us maintain such consistency. Here is how:

The Reticular Activating System

Neurologically, one of the functions of the brain's Reticular Activating System (RAS) is to help us pay attention to and monitor what is happening in our surroundings. Moreover, the RAS gives access to what is relevant and blocks any information that is inconsistent with our self-concept or self-image. That is why I stated previously that purposes restrict the range of choices in order to avoid distractions from the target.

The RAS operates with electrical impulses that turn on and off attention switches. These switches of excitement and inhibition manage arousal and focus attention. Attention gets excited or is activated when incoming information is relevant. For instance, if you feel hungry, your RAS will be on the lookout for food until you satisfy the need to eat. These impulses can also prevent and block meaningless and irrelevant information. If you have no appetite and feel satisfied, you might perceive food, but the RAS will not excite your motivation. The inhibition switch will remain off until you feel hungry again. Actually, the RAS could be on the lookout for the next relevant input that will solve your next problem, want, or need. As such, the RAS is a gateway of information.

The RAS can inhibit sensing information from sight, smell, taste, hearing, or touch. This form of sensory inhibition is *scotoma*, or the inability to perceive stimuli, as in a blind spot. Scotomas can affect any of the five senses. A benefit of such inhibition is that the RAS prevent us from being bombarded and overwhelmed with information. The downside is that it can also prevent people from perceiving helpful information or from considering options that would go contrary to an erroneous belief. For instance, what sense does it make to save and invest money if one's belief is that being poor is a virtue? Or what reason would justify exercising and eating healthy if one's self-concept is being overweight? So the RAS, if not managed, can be a double-edged sword.

Hence, whatever you believe to be true and important, the RAS is designed to keep you performing and acting consistently with your self-view. Remember that what you believe is true about you—your self-concept or self-image—is a meaning.[243] Also, whatever you believe is true about others or whatever meaning you give to situations; your self-image system will bias you in favor of such a view. And again, as an incoming meaning the task of your purpose system is to leverage the assistance of the RAS to live up to its instructions.

But what evidence is there to sustain that your brain is designed to

243 Recall that meanings are attributes, attitudes, values, beliefs, feelings, and aims.

- inhibit information that goes contrary to your self-concept?
- allow access to information that meets your identity mental model?

Carl R. Rogers declared, "Psychological research has shown that if the evidence of our senses runs contrary to our picture of self, then the evidence is distorted. In other words, we cannot see all that our senses report, but only the things which fit the picture we have."[244] This was later confirmed by University of Texas at Austin's psychologists William B. Swan, Jr. and Stephen Read's research findings. They found that people do tend to discard information that is inconsistent with their self-image, even when they have a negative self-concept.[245, 246, 247] Citing research on self-fulfilling prophesy, Northwestern University's Douglas L. Medin and University of Illinois's Brian H. Ross indicated that "people may act on their beliefs in such a way that they bring about expected state of affairs." Further they professed that "expectations are not just predictions; they also influence our behavior in such a way as to confirm them."[248]

Further, in support to logoteleology's identity formula (I = P + Mo +Me), Medin and Ross's conclusions were clearly demonstrated by previously cited University of Stanford's Dr. Carol S. Dweck's research.[249] She reported that students' (a role identity) beliefs about their intelligence (i.e., meanings) influence (i.e., motivate) goal selection (purpose) and manage setbacks (i.e., feedback). Dr. Dweck and her colleague Elaine

---

244 Rogers, Carl, *On Becoming a Person: A Therapist's View of Psychotherapy* (Boston: Houghton Mifflin Company, 1989), 115.

245 Swan, W. B., and S. J. Read, "Self-Verification Processes: How We Sustain Our Self-Conceptions." *Journal of Experimental Psychology* 17 (1981): 351–72.

246 Swan, W. B., and S. J. Read, "Acquiring Self-Knowledge: The Search for Feedback That Fits." *Journal of Personality and Social Psychology* 41 (1981): 1119–28.

247 Swann, W. B. Jr., "Self-Verification Theory." Van Lang, P., A. Kruglanski, and E. T. Higgins, Eds. *Handbook of Theories of Social Psychology* (London: Sage, 2012), 23–42.

248 Medin, Douglas L. and Brian H. Ross, *Cognitive Psychology,* 15–16.

249 Dweck, Carol S., *Self-Theories*

Elliott proposed that students with a helpless orientation or low self-esteem (i.e., a low self-concept) are Driven to find extrinsic meaning by placing importance on looking smart and avoiding looking dumb. The orientation to look smart and avoid looking dumb she calls a "performance goal." In contrast, students with a mastery orientation find intrinsic meaning in learning new skills, mastering new tasks, and understanding new things. The mastery-oriented students are Willed to get smarter and pursue a "learning goal."

Another way of explaining Dweck and Elliot's conclusions in light of logoteleology theory is in the understanding that the task of the performance goal-oriented individual is to avoid shame. On the other hand, the task of the mastery-oriented individual is to build knowledge, competence, and eventually perform well. The task orientation is determined by the self-image or the logoteleological system's read of the operating belief in the meaning set. Hence these two task approaches to problem solving and learning yield results matching their respective meaning beliefs.

Dweck and Elliot's conclusions are another example of how the meaning set influences the type of motivation and goals chosen. Making reference to table 11 on page 176 (Meaning Motive Type/Action Type) above, the goals and tasks (action verbs) selected by the purpose system will differ between the meaning set of a performance goal-oriented individual and a mastery goal-oriented person. In the case of mastery oriented students some discernible action verb descriptors could be: plan, persist, learn, attempt, stimulate, strive, encourage, improve, enjoy, and discover. On the other hand, performance oriented students action verb descriptors could be: do well, avoid, lowball, underestimate, be careful, be perfect, endure, look smart, and give up.

In addition, as previously stated, logoteleology proposes that a meaning set's self-concept, as in the study cited (e.g., helpless or mastery oriented) chooses a fitting meaning motive type (Will, Drive, and Amotivate). The meaning motive type influences suitable goals and performance.

Self-concept beliefs are important because they guide the type of motivation, goals, and performance that people follow.

This understanding is relevant to individuals, groups, and organizations that wish to improve performance and results. The individual and collective self-concept is a self-fulfilling prophesy. The potential of limited awareness due to individual and collective beliefs will provoke the RAS to generate hindering scotomas to what could be important and relevant information. Information that if it remained outside the scope of awareness the individuals involved could suffer negative repercussions. Accepting the reality of scotomas should help us doubt the infallibility of our awareness and perception. Moreover, this reality should encourage us all to seek opinions and perceptions from others. Finally, it accentuates the importance of partnering and cooperating with others.

Self-concept beliefs are important because they guide the type of motivation, goals, and performance that people follow.

In conclusion, understanding the function of the RAS, and findings from recent research, helps explain how the purpose system keeps consistency with the self-concept. Humans cannot act contrary to the content of their meaning sets. The RAS manages awareness and attention based on the content of the meaning set. Thus, the quality of our meaning set will determine how much and what type of information we give access to. This can be a double-edged sword since it is always possible that meaningful data and opportunity are denied access.

Why Purpose Matters

In summary, this is why the role of purpose in the teleological system is relevant.

1. Purpose is a statement of what we believe in and stand for.

2. Through the actions of purpose, meaning intentions are fulfilled.

3. Purpose performs and solves problems.

4. Purpose is a mental aim that guides performance. Selecting a purpose can set boundaries from distractions by establishing and monitoring what is in and out of the meaningfulness scope.

5. Purpose is an important element of the logoteleological process that keeps us consistent and aligned with our self-concept or self-image.

6. Purpose fulfills our life calling. It can do so in a meaningful way and for meaningful ends when it is self-determined.

7. Purpose can be evaluated to help assess the quality of competence, meaning sets, and motivation.

What Is My Life Purpose?

Based on what we have covered up to this point, let's address how logoteleology answers, "What is my life purpose?"

Your life purpose is and has been to fulfill your meanings—whatever meaning you have given to your existence. As stated in chapter 4, I propose that psychologically, *the ultimate meaning and purpose of life for all humans is to master their abilities and attitudes in order to Allow, to Cooperate, and to be altruistic or Transcend.*

Logoteleology encourages us to deepen our self-awareness so that we can understand *how* we have been living, and what that says about the meaning we have given to our existence and our role in society. Further, the science also encourages us to self-determine by selecting a meaningful life purpose which, as mentioned, needs to be founded in ACT and the five strivings. Until proven otherwise, anything else is meaningless.

In summary, what we all—as a species—share as a common life purpose, is to master our abilities and attitudes so that we can do meaningful things for others through ACT and the five strivings.

Application

Reflect on the content of this chapter.

- What new things did you learn about purpose?
- Leveraging what you learned on previous chapters plus your own experience, what action verbs would best describe your current purpose? How would you answer the question, I have been living my life as if my purpose is (action verb[s])?
- What meanings (adjectives) influence your purpose?

My Journey

In light of my research on purpose, here are a few learning experiences and decisions I made along the way.

1. I pay attention to my actions to help me evaluate if I am walking my talk. In other words, I ask myself, "Is this behavior consistent with my life purpose and identity?" This allows me to validate my choices and self-correct when there is a deviation.
2. Given that I do have scotomas, I make it a point to get others' point of view and remain humble. I also give feedback to the willing in order to bring attention to what I observe. I am learning to remain more open minded to others' views, suggestions, and approaches. Knowing of scotomas, I am slower to judge others who "can't get me" or "can't get it."
3. I appreciate at a deeper level the role of purpose at the introjected and subconsciously scripted level, and how it can compete against one's aspirations. It allows me to test options and make choices that are congruent with whom I want to be. It also gives me the opportunity to coach and consult to those who want to close the breach between a current and ideal self.

4. As an organization development consultant and in-house professional, it validated the importance of

   a. remaining objectively aware of operating norms and assumptions in human systems;
   b. not colluding (being complicit) with what is meaningless; and
   c. maintaining an independent point of view.

Chapter 7: Logoteleology

You cannot teach a man anything, you can only help him to find it for himself.—Galileo

You will recall that the journey that led me to write this book started with a short but powerful quote by Viktor Frankl: "Life ultimately means taking the responsibility to find the right answers to its problems and to fulfill the tasks which it constantly sets for each individual." These words steered me to the conclusion that we humans do not suffer for lack of answers. Rather, the human race suffers despite the answers being available. I chose to take responsibility to find the right answers to my life's questions through psychology. I followed an approach, which I called the path to a meaningful life purpose. This path, you will remember, led me to answer four fundamental questions:

Who am I?

What matters in life?

Why am I here?

How do I go about fulfilling my life purpose?

I firmly believe that to take responsibility for finding the right answers to life's problems, we need to first answer the above questions. Moreover, as Frankl proposes, there is a second act of responsibility, which is to fulfill the tasks generated by our answers. For instance, Frankl was a proponent that there should be a monument parallel to the current Statue of Liberty in the American east coast. This new statue would be on the west coast and would be called the Statue of Responsibility. Liberty, he claimed, without action is not being responsible. Frankl, having lived through the horrors of Nazi death camps, recognized the importance of acting on what is meaningful.

With that understanding, let us review how the four existential questions have been addressed so far in this volume.

In chapter 2 I addressed the first question—"Who am I?" I explained that an *identity is the sum of its purpose(s), motivation(s), and meaning sets*. I also explained that there are three types of identities: person, social, and role. A *person identity* expresses the uniqueness of a core self in biological and psychological terms. *Social identities* explain our group memberships. A *role identity* explains duties, expectations, and responsibilities inherent on being a member of a group. It answers, "Who am I in relation to another?"

To explain the dynamics of an identity, we use this formula:

$$I = P + Mo + Me$$

(Where I = Identity; P = Purpose; Mo = Motivation; and Me = Meaning)

In chapters 2 and 3 I described that meanings are the expressed attributes, beliefs, attitudes, aims, feelings, and values in an identity. Further, that meanings stem from the conclusions and affirmations people make about themselves, others, and situations. A collection of organized meanings constitute a meaning set. I also shared that a meaning set contains the psychological instructions used in the development and functioning of a personality or identity, much like DNA has the genetic instructions of a person. Logoteleology studies meaning sets or strands to understand and improve behavior.

Further, I answered what matters in life. According to logoteleology, there are Five Meaningful strivings that make life fulfilling and meaningful. In order, these are (a) being in loving relationships; (b) fostering harmony and having peace of mind; (c) making others happy; (d) living, learning, working, and sharing a stimulating, productive, and interesting life with others; and (e) building and securing prosperity for oneself and others.

I also explained in chapter 4 that psychologically, *the ultimate meaning and purpose of life for all humans is to master their abilities and attitudes in order to Allow, to Cooperate, and to be altruistic or Transcend.* I proposed the acronym ACT (allow, cooperate, transcend) for the "pillars of success." The combined five strivings and ACT provide the foundation for successful living and psychological health. Logoteleology proposes that all life purpose should meet the criteria of the five strivings and ACT.

Logoteleology proposes that all life purpose should meet the criteria of the five strivings and ACT.

I described how a meaning set excites one of the three types of motivation: Will, Drive, and Amotivate. *Will* is a future-oriented intrinsic motivation energized toward meaningfulness. Its primary task is to be a positive force of influence for purpose and goal selection and development. I stated that *Drives* do not satisfy intrinsic needs and wants; rather, they are extrinsic forces compelled to avoid a negative consequence or to earn a reward. They could also be compulsions, impulses, routines, and habits at the unaware level. *Drives*, as *Amotivation*, are outcomes of introjects and psychological scripts. *Amotivation* is learned helplessness, apathy, and resistance. Helplessness is conveyed as discouragement while apathy is expressed as indifference. Resistance is articulated through a rebellious attitude and actions. Each of these motivational options helps determine the degree and type of energy employed.

Chapter 6 stated that *purpose* can be defined as *a guiding system that monitors behavior, solves problems, fulfills meanings, gives meaning to one's life, and creates meanings.* According to logoteleology theory, what makes humans teleological is their innate capacity to self-determine, to purpose and set goals, to plan, to perform, and to self-regulate in support of a meaning set. In addition to teleology *(telos)*, logoteleology's theory includes—as it names suggests—the functions of meanings (*logo)* plus the Will (*thelos*) to explain goal-directed behavior. Hence the identity formula (I = P + Mo + Me) and theory offers a wide-ranging explanation of how humans can self-determine and self-regulate.

So, to summarize, we can know who we are if we accept that we are the meaning we have given to our lives. And we also learned that the five strivings explain what is meaningful and worth living for. We know how to live with others through the three pillars of success (ACT). When we Will to do meaningful things we generally end up selecting healthy purposeful options to carry them out. And the stronger the positive meaning the stronger our motivational determination or willpower will be. The logoteleology approach uses human's teleology to advance self-determination and meaningful well-being. Logoteleology theory is a path to find and implement solutions to our innate aspirations and potential. It can also help us deal with our most pressing problems.

This chapter will expand on ways we can succeed in fulfilling our life purpose. It will answer the following:

1. What is logoteleology?
2. What is the Logoteleology Congruence Model?
3. How does the Congruence Model work?

What Is Logoteleology?

Logoteleology comes from the Greek words "logo," for meaning, "thelos," for will, and "telos," for purpose. *Logoteleology is a theory of personality that explains how meanings influence motivation and purpose; and a method that helps people live a meaningful purpose life.* Thus, logoteleology can be explained as a theory and as a method. Many of these explanations have been covered in previous chapters. I will expand on them below.

Logoteleology Theory

As a theory, I like to think of logoteleology as a branch of Viktor Frankl's logotherapy. In addition to embracing logotherapy theory, logoteleology gives special attention to how motivation and purpose give meaning to life. A tool for such explanations includes the previously covered logoteleology identity formula (I = P + Mo + Me). Like logotherapy, logoteleology is existential; but in addition, logoteleology embraces the self-directed or teleological nature of humans. Logoteleology explains self-regulation and how it can be used for authentic self-determination. Said differently, *logoteleology studies and explains the mind's ability to stay on course.*

While I encourage further studies to determine its value in treating meaning disorders, logoteleology is primarily a proactive striving to finding, committing, and fulfilling a meaningful purpose. In other words, it is biased to *prevent* meaning disorders over finding a post-mortem meaning to an event. Logoteleology is concerned with the questions

- "Why life?" in terms of defining why life has meaning.
- "What will I do?" in order to take a stand, and to commit or purpose to do what is meaningful.
- "How will I do it?" to follow through and persist on the fulfillment of the meaningful purpose.

> Logoteleology is a theory of personality that explains how meanings influence motivation and purpose; and a method that helps people live a meaningful purpose life. Thus, Logoteleology can be explained as a theory and as a method.

Logoteleology's thesis is that if people follow its methods then they will experience a life that is meaningful. It is a proactive psychological response and solution that builds the individual's capacity to experience all the meaningful things that life has to offer. As a remedial therapy, logoteleology has potential to treat disorders related to the human existential vacuum. Moreover, logoteleology is an attempt to give people a practical and proven method where love, peace and peace of mind, happiness, interest and prosperity are real daily experiences in their lives. Therefore, *logoteleology helps people find what is meaningful in order to define, will, and fulfill a purpose.*

Logoteleology's propositions are shared in the introductory part of this volume and will not be repeated here.

Logoteleology Method

As a method logoteleology is designed to help individuals, groups and organizations find and commit to a meaningful purpose, and to take actions worthy of a significant legacy. The fundamental models and concepts employed by the method include

- the identity formula;
- ACT and the five strivings; and
- the Congruence Model.

The identity formula has potential for individual, group, and organization development. It has demonstrated some preliminary promising results as a coaching tool. For instance, I have found the following to be true when the client understands personality through the lens of the identity formula:

- The dynamics of how meaning sets influence motivation and purpose "makes sense."
- She or he feels more confident that improvement is possible. The client is encouraged.
- Goals and priorities are easier to plan through the use of *identity* identification through nouns and pronouns; *meaning* adjectives and prepositional phrases; *Will* expressed in adverb, verb, and

adjective form; and *purpose* conveyed as verbs. The construct of its structure is simple, malleable, and powerful.

- Specific goals and metrics are easier to plan and implement. Working with the identity formula encourages action and traction.

The logoteleology method includes ACT and the five strivings. Combined, they are foundational to meaning goal setting and expression. ACT and the five strivings provide the standard for meaning selection and implementation. The teleotherapist encourages the client to test how well her or his meanings, purpose, and goals meet ACT and the five striving criteria.

> Logoteleology is a proactive psychological response and solution that builds the individual's capacity to experience all the meaningful things that life has to offer. As a remedial therapy, logoteleology has potential to treat disorders related to the human existential vacuum.

The Congruence Model, the subject of the next section, was influenced by principles of holism, self-determination psychology, logical learning theory, cognitive psychology, logotherapy, positive psychology, psychology of action, Transactional Analysis, and humanistic psychology, among others. As a tool it responds to my belief that people can be and should be involved in shaping and living their lives to fulfill meaningful ends. Actually, as I will explain, the tool came to being in great measure by my clients' reflections. Let's take a look to learn how it happened and to explain how the Congruence Model works.

Logoteleology's Congruence Model

The Congruence Model had its origins with client work. During my work sessions with individuals I noticed a recurring pattern about how people described situations, particularly how they went about formulating their hypothesis to explain intrapersonal dynamics, and how these internal dynamics influenced their ability to succeed in their environments. Over time I took interest on the emerging themes because they would tell a story that revealed intra-psychic causal relations. I started to draw "if-then" inferences using the labels voiced by clients. For instance, clients would use labels that had to do with positive and negative evaluations of their identity ("I am …" and "I would like to be …"), competence ("I am good at …"); motivation ("I will …"), and others. Ultimately, I ended up with a construct of nine client-centric variables or themes.

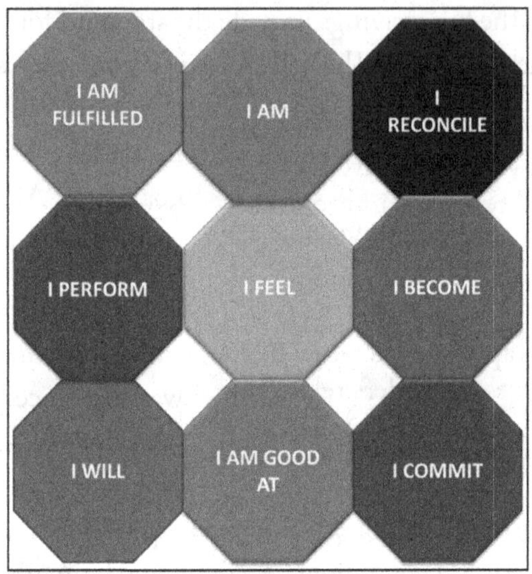

Figure 19 Logoteleology Congruence Model

Further, I concluded that these themes and their dynamics played a function in helping the client make sense of their person and their actions. The client, I concluded, was following an innate cognitive-affective problem-solving approach. I built on the clients' inherent approach in order to understand and help them with and on their own terms.

> The Logoteleology Congruence Model is a cognitive and affective map that describes how humans solve identity-related problems.

Simply stated, the Logoteleology Congruence Model is a cognitive and affective map that describes how humans solve identity-related problems.

The themes can be seen in figure 19. They are expressed as causal, interdependent, holistic, teleological, and dynamic.

> *Causal* in terms that one variable affected another.
>
> *Interdependent* because success or failure in one was dependent or caused by one or more variables.
>
> *Holistic* because the nine variables make up a system that helps the individual interact with the greater environment. Thus the Congruence Model assumes and operates in an open system.
>
> The combined variables working together are *teleological* because the system self-regulates.
>
> As a model or system it is *dynamic* because it solves problems.

I embarked on a study of these variables individually and as a system that included building psychometric tools to measure and help me understand their dynamic forces. Early testing found that a disturbance or problem in one of the functions affects the others in some way. For instance, incompetence affected mood, self-esteem, and motivation. Also, lacking a clear commitment affected motivation. Thus the general well-being of the person could be impacted if any of these variables showed either a positive or negative tendency. The general well-being of the client could be enhanced if any of the variables improved. I also found ample evidence in professional journals and textbooks to affirm the causal relationships inherent on these psychological dynamics. Many of those have been quoted throughout this book.

> It can be said that as a construct the logoteleology congruence model is a set of organized functions that accomplish goals.

The Logoteleology Congruence Model begins with some basic assumptions:

1. The elements in the model are distinct from one another, each performing a function.
2. The elements interact with and influence other elements.
3. The model is not a personality representation; rather, it represents the dynamics of self-identification and teleological self-regulation.
4. The model is not a representation of a healthy identity; rather, it provides the tools to diagnose and improve it.
5. A healthy identity preserves equilibrium between the elements.

These simple assumptions provide insight into how people can plan and experience a life of meaning and purpose. It also explains the mechanics to meaning and purpose creation. Each element can play a creative role in the process of building and fulfilling a meaningful purpose. It also explains where a maladaptation occurs.

> The elements of the congruence model accomplish three motives: to store information; to fulfill a function; and to meet a need. It can be said that each element has a store of meaning (attributes, beliefs, attitudes, aims, feelings and values).

It can be said that as a construct, the Logoteleology Congruence Model is a set of organized functions that accomplish goals. My attempt has been to understand and explain such organization, how it occurs, and how it both maintains and changes performance and results over time.

The Goal and Elements of the Congruence Model

Illustrated in figure 19 above, the goal of the model is to help the individual achieve identity integration and coherence among the functions for her or his well-being—thus why it is called the *Logoteleology Congruence Model.* The model has shown preliminary promising results building the client's self-determination over her or his life. However, more research is encouraged. The optimal aim is to maintain the appropriate equilibrium among the elements.

The elements of the Congruence Model accomplish three motives: to store information; to fulfill a function; and to meet a need. It can be said that each element has a store of meaning (attributes, beliefs, attitudes, aims, feelings, and values). Each element also has a role or function to fulfill in relation to the others. For instance, "I will" provides energy to "I perform." And finally, each element helps fill a life yearning in the identity. For instance, "I am good at" fills the yearning of being competent which in turn leads to being proud of doing something worthwhile ("I feel" enjoyment).

The nine elements of the Logoteleology Congruence Model (LCM) are described below.

Element	Stored Information	Function	Life Task	Label	Questions
I am	Self-description	The motive for self-understanding and self-reference	Know yourself	being or self (Be)	Who am I?
I become	Vision of the future self	The motive for the ideal.	Be yourself	aspiration (Idealize)	Who will I become?
I reconcile	Gap information (I am versus I become)	The motive to remain self-aware in order to improve	Free yourself	identity awareness (Reflect)	Am I closing the gap between my current and ideal selves?
I commit	Purpose and goals	The motive to be and stand for something	Determine yourself	commitment (Commit)	What is my life purpose?
I am good at	Knowledge, skills and attributes	The motive to learn and to be competent	Build yourself	competence (Develop)	What will I excel in?
I will	Why doing what I do matters	The motive to meaning	Will yourself	willingness and motivation (Will)	Do I have the attitude and self-confidence to accomplish this?
I perform	Habits, routines, and processes (i.e., work habits)	The motive to act and implement	Direct yourself	performance (Perform)	Am I taking action on my commitments?

Element	Stored Information	Function	Life Task	Label	Questions
I achieve (I feel)	Awareness of task movement and progress	The motive to value short-term progress and relish the moment	Measure, validate, correct, and enjoy yourself	achievement and delight (Feel)	Am I monitoring, valuing, celebrating, and enjoying my work-in-progress (i.e., closing the immediate gap)?
I am fulfilled	Historical legacy and general life mood	The motive to reflect on one's long-term impact, to celebrate and renew	Celebrate and reenergize yourself	fulfillment (Fulfill)	Am I fulfilling my life purpose?

Table 12 Elements of the Logoteleology Congruence Model

I Am

This element expresses our core identity. As covered in chapter 2, anytime we self-refer through the statement "I am," we are saying something about who we are or think we are in the present tense. In the Congruence Model, "I am" is the primary point of reference of a personality. Thus the content of this element is our self-description and self-definition. And when desiring to make changes in one's life, "I am" is the target of transformation. "I am" is our foundational starting point that points to our strengths as well as our unrealized potential. The element "I am" reflects who we are at the moment, including describing the self as it continues to mature and progress. The self does not remain static, it either progresses or digresses. Progress is achieved through the assistance of the other elements of the Congruence Model.

The "I am" element is a repository of archaic and validated data in the form of meanings about the meaning of our life. It also has the function to keep us grounded on and true to what we believe is our accurate and predominant identity and person. At any moment we cannot help but to be the person that we believe we are.

As has been covered, an identity that has a meaningful set, and a Willing disposition that does meaningful things, is symptomatic of a healthy personality. The individual knows who he or she is and has a clear meaningful purpose to live for. He or she is the author of his or her life. On the other hand, a meaningful set with meaningless content will most probably be Driven or Amotivated and will exhibit unhealthy symptoms. Healthy identities produce forward movement toward potential.

I Become

"I become" is our aspirational self. Desires are future-oriented. The function creates a tension between the person we are today (I am) and the person we wish to become or be.[250] A child daydreaming about becoming an astronaut is expressing an ambition, as is an aspiring university student of law who is aiming to become a successful lawyer. The child and the adult on the previous examples do not yet have the identity to which they aspire, but they have the ambition to do so. Hence, "I become" represent our meaningful dreams, aims, goals, hopes, aspirations, and ambitions. While "I am" is articulated in the present tense, the aspirational "I become" is always verbalized in the future tense. "I become" crystallizes and labels the ideal identity. In a healthy identity, it aims to describe our potential and what is possible. Our aspirations become the target for identity transformation and potential fulfillment.

Healthy and clear identities are inspired and willed by meaningful ambitions. Becoming is never realized because our potential for learning, accomplishments, and growth is unlimited. Realizing this great truth can be liberating because it assures us of a life with never-ending opportunities to experience awe and deep meaning.

The logoteleology method helps the client express aspirations, which include building a meaning set that is resilient and ready to courageously take on life's obstacles, failures, and disappointments. Being resilient (Willed) builds the character, integrity, and strength of the identity. To meet such a standard, the individual who aspires to have a strong identity must embrace universal standards of civility, ethics, and morality. In other words, at minimum, "do no harm" will be part of her or his modus operandi. Simply stated, obstacles are tackled without hurting self and others. This includes embracing and passing the test of ACT and the five strivings.

---

250 It must be emphasized that the wish to become or be is intrinsic and self-determined. As such, the wish is free of introjects. Hence the individual is not pursuing an identity of what "should be" but what she or he genuinely wants it to be.

I Reconcile

This element is tasked with three fundamental functions:

1. Help form the ideal self ("I become")
2. Maintain awareness and tension between the person one claims to be ("I am") and the person one wants to become ("I become")
3. Orchestrate the gap closure between the current and ideal selves

These three functions are accomplished through the other elements in the Congruence Model. To accomplish the above three functions "I reconcile" help form the

- definition of the ideal *meaning* of the identity; and
- *purpose* to fulfill it.

It also makes sure we are true to the ideal visions about our future and our self-image. It does so primarily by highlighting disparities between who we are and who we aspire to be. With the assistance of the previously discussed Reticular Activating System (RAS), the reconciliation function maintains gap awareness and attention on what matters to us. Consider the law student in the previous example where his or her current role identity is "student" and the aspirational role identity is to become a "lawyer." The transformation from the "I am a student" to the "I am a lawyer" is the charge of the "I reconcile" element. Gap awareness activates other functions to ensure congruence between the current and ideal states.

> *The unexamined life is not worth living.*
>
> Socrates

To close gaps, the reconciliation element leads the process that studies and reconstructs meaning sets. As such, "I reconcile" is also in the identity formation business. As explained in the example of the aspiring student who wants to become a lawyer, "I reconcile" replaces old identities with new ones.

"I reconcile" can help us maintain congruence and alignment in person, group and role identities. In other words, assuming a logoteleological approach, the individual would select membership in groups and assume roles where meaningful practices can be conveyed and meaningful ends fulfilled. For instance, being an author on a psychological subject allows me to share my passions with individuals that share my interests, and to make a positive difference in people's lives. Because doing meaningful things for others is part of my life's agenda there is alignment between who I am (person identity), my relationships (group identities), and what I do as an author, coach, and consultant (role identities).

Finally, *the act of reconciliation helps with the management of identity dilemma and ambiguity.* A well-functioning and objective reconciliation process tackles and resolves confusion and uncertainty head on. For instance, if I find myself asking, "Am I being realistic in wanting to become a doctor?" it is the "I reconcile" function that is asking such a question. Also, can you think of a time when you made a very dumb mistake and found yourself asking, "Why did I do that? It was so stupid!" That internal dialogue is another example of our reconciliation function trying to come to terms with a behavioral anomaly between what the embarrassing actions says about us and how we see our ideal selves behaving. In a way, *the reconciliation element is tasked with being a conscience.* It makes value judgments.[251]

The quality of the related elements in the Congruence Model determines how well the reconciliation process functions. In other words, the reconciliation function's contribution is at the mercy of what the other functions have to offer. It is ineffective if one or more of the model's elements are weak or disturbed. For instance, the "I reconcile" function cannot

251 It should be apparent that the reconciliation function also has a dark side that could be overly critical. Its quality will depend on the content of its own meaning set.

do its job if the individual lacks a vision for him or herself (I become). In that case there is no gap to close and thus no need to reconcile. On the other hand, if the other elements of the Congruence Model meet minimum criteria the reconciliation process will perform as expected. For instance,

- when the gaps between the current and ideal identities are clear and
- the ideal identity is credible and inspiring,
- we can expect the Will to invest the right level and type of motivation to commit the individual to a meaningful purpose.

When weak and incapable, the reconciliation function can be helped and strengthened through the assistance of an effective teleotherapist or coach.

A helpful "I reconcile" element supports growth, self-determination and congruence with the real self.

I Commit

Becoming the person we envision requires commitment. To commit[252] is the first active step to close the gap between who we are and what we want to become. Commitment reveals the power of our word to say what we mean and mean what we say. "I commit" is a pledge a person makes to himself or herself as well as to others. It is about taking a position to stand, dedicate, and live for a cause.

A person commits in the present to live up to his or her potential self in the future. In a healthy identity this element defines one's meaningful life purpose and supportive goals using the identity formula (I = P +

252 Commitment is a form of telosponse, as discussed in the chapter related to motivation.

W + Me),[253] as well as ACT and the five strivings. Again, it is worth repeating that committing to live meaningfully means that the selected life purpose must meet the criteria of ACT and the five strivings. It is a hollow and empty promise if it is not moved by a willing motivation.

A person fully committed to a worthwhile life purpose would answer in the affirmative to the following. Does my life purpose

- actively support others' inherent right to achieve their individuality and potential?
- include the practice of shared dependence or mutual aid toward a common purpose?
- embrace selfless concern for others?
- include being empathic, respectful, and considerate toward others?
- foster harmony by building meaningful bridges of communication and shared understanding? Does its agenda contain actions that bring peace of mind to me and others? Does the approach prevent offensive distractions?
- commit me to make others happy?
- encourage me to live, work, and share an intrinsically stimulating, productive and interesting life with others?
- compel me to build and secure prosperity for me and others?

In a healthy identity, once an aspiration (I become) becomes a commitment (I commit), the other elements in the Congruence Model assist to ensure the undertaken aspiration is achieved.

Again, an effective commitment meets the criteria of ACT and the five strivings. When the "I commit" is not self-regulated, the "I am" scripts and introjects Drive direction.

253 Identity = Purpose + Will + Meaning.

I Am Good At

When a person commits to a purpose, assuming the path followed is meaningful, she or he is encouraged to determine whether he or she has the required knowledge, skills, and abilities to succeed. Building one's potential entails developing and sustaining the right competence for the right purpose and goals.

"I am good at" as a function asks, "Do I have the competencies to accomplish this purpose and its tasks?" The "I am good at" and the "I achieve" functions cooperate to determine what competence is available and required. They also cooperate to close knowledge and skill gaps. Thus, following the example of the student lawyer above, earning a law degree will require getting the right knowledge and meeting the standards set by the university, the licensing body, and the state.

As we learned, our potential for learning, accomplishments, and growth is unlimited. Referring to the example of the law student, after becoming a licensed lawyer the individual will most probably be "good enough" compared with a more senior and experienced counsel. Thus, after the aim of becoming a lawyer is fulfilled, the new attorney will have another bar to reach, this one being "to become an *experienced* lawyer who wins cases," as it is in many situations in an area of specialty. That is why the new lawyer will have to practice for many years before she or he can confidently claim "I am good at" practicing law. The point is that there is always room to improve. Life can be enjoyable when we are being stretched to acquire and put into effect new knowledge and experiences.

Furthermore, competence is important because it helps us do and achieve meaningful things. It helps us succeed, to have a positive impact on others, to have a positive self-image, and to be more self-reliant, autonomous, and interdependent.

To summarize, "I am good at" is about achieving mastery toward meaningful ends.

I Will

I have explained how a meaning set powers motivation. "I will" in the Congruence Model has the same role as motivation in the identity formula (I = P + Mo + Me). "I will" provides a degree of energy and a type of motivation (Will, Drive, and Amotivate) in an identity. The energy or telosponse is directed to the purpose system, you will recall, which in turn fulfills and creates new meanings. A strong-willed and intrinsic motivation reveals a healthy meaning set. On the other hand, if the level of motivation is low and/or the type is extrinsically driven, it points to a poor and unhealthy meaning set in the identity. It has been corroborated by research "that when goals are regulated by forces experienced as external rather than internal to the self (the "why" of goal pursuit), the quality of goal-regulated action and its impact on personality and mental health are more negative."[254]

Fortunately, through the use of the Congruence Model we can be reminded to pay attention and notice how willingly we conduct ourselves. We can tell when, if, and how we are motivated by our meaning set, in order to achieve our purpose and supportive goals and tasks. Among others, low energy can mean

1. life or the task has no meaning;
2. life or the task has meaning, but we do not have a purpose to express it;
3. life or the task has meaning and there is a purpose; however, the individual does not have the tools to express her or his purpose and goals (for instance, due to a lack of competence, our efforts are not supported and encouraged by others or circumstances), and the obstacles are insurmountable; and

---

254 Ryan, Richard M., Kennon M. Sheldon, Tim Kasser, and Edward L. Deci, "All Goals Are Not Created Equal: An Organistic Perspective of Goals and Regulation." *The Psychology of Action: Linking Cognition and Motivation to Behavior* (New York: The Guilford Press, 1996), 20.

4. we are actively doing things but without appropriately connecting them to meaningful priorities and a well-directed purpose.

Let's see each in greater detail.

Lack of meaning: A life or tasks without meaning—what Frankl called the existential vacuum[255]—makes it difficult for anyone to be energized. People with no life meaning are generally sad, dispirited, and even depressed. We frequently experience this in industry. For instance, people with this problem are labeled as disengaged and actively disengaged from work. They are not as productive as they can be because they consider that what they do is meaningless. And if there is meaningfulness to what they do, the employees are many times not aware of it. Thus, motivation is felt as low and extrinsic (Amotivated and Driven).

Lack of purpose: There are times when an individual *does know* what is meaningful but has difficulty finding a goal and channel to act it out. For instance, an individual might love music yet struggles finding a practical channel to make it meaningful enough for others to pay him a living wage. As a result, his meaningful passion remains unfulfilled.

Lack of tools: There are situations when a person has a clear meaning and a well-defined purpose yet does not know how to proceed. This can be due to a lack of competence or an obstructive script that makes it difficult for the individual in question to move forward. For instance, let's say our lover of music believes that becoming a producer could be the way to go. Yet he or she is plagued by doubts about her or his ability to succeed. Lack of competence could be a concern, as well as a history of false starts and failures that plague the person's confidence.

Lack of a supportive environment: This is seen in situations where individuals have committed to improve themselves and achieve their aspirations, but they meet with the unfortunate resistance and

---

255 In logoteleology, the existential vacuum is known as *hypologo*, a type of meaning disorder.

discouragement from people and circumstances. We can see this in countries that practice intolerance against women and minorities—for instance, where women are not given equal access to education and entrepreneurship. This unfortunate circumstance is also found in many organizations that are steered by poor and meaningless leadership practices.

Lack of prioritization: This is usually a reflection of poor work habits, such as trying to do too many things at the same time. It is also symptomatic of a person who is a victim of the previously discussed "activity trap." You will remember that this happens when an individual remains stuck in meaningless activities. It can also happen when there is little to no connection between what one does and one's self-determined life's purpose. In other words, the individual's life aim (I become) and the purpose (I commit) are not clear and robust enough to bring focus and discipline to goal selection and achievement (I perform). Thus, as we say in the vernacular, when lacking clear direction, "Anything goes."

> *What we are is nothing; what matters is where we are going.*
>
> Hölderlin

The quality and strength of our current self-image (I am), our life's aspiration (I become), and the pledge we express about the person we aim to be (I commit) will ultimately determine the type of motivation and effort we invest. When behavior is amotivated and driven, we are influenced by introjects and scripts by the "I am" element in order to stop us from progressing. I believe that when behavior is willed, we increase the probability that our dreams will come true.

I Perform

This element is purpose in action. As explained by the identity formula, purpose (I commit) in action (I perform) follows the instructions of the dominant meaning set[256] (I become) and is fueled by motivation (I will). Thus, assuming a healthy meaning set,

Identity = Purpose in action + a strong and energized Will + a meaningful set

"I perform" sets short-term goals and designs an approach to remain aligned to one's overall life purpose. In other words, "I perform" answers "what" we are going to do to fulfill our meaning set. "I perform" is directed action and grammatically rich in action verb usage.

> Performance is action toward and engagement with the outside environment. In ideal conditions our actions and the quality of our interactions are meaningful when they are in compliance with ACT and the five strivings standards.

Performance is action toward and engagement with the outside environment. In ideal conditions our actions and the quality of our interactions are meaningful when they are in compliance with ACT and the five strivings standards.

To do well the individual requires a clear end game (I commit), competence (I am good at), a robust sense of self (I am), and a strong aspiration (I become) that energizes the will (I will) to take action (I perform). The next element will explain a mental process that allows us to keep track of our progress.

I Achieve (I Feel)

The achievement element monitors and mirrors the degree to which short-term tasks and commitments are being fulfilled. It answers, "As the result of my actions (I perform), am I on track? Am I successful?" While the reconciliation function is concerned with gaps between the current and desired identity, the achievement function is concerned

256 By "dominant" I mean the higher-order meanings that hold our attention and focus. It is possible to have competing meanings and priorities.

with the degree in which one's short-term goals and actions (I perform) are bringing one closer to fulfilling one's commitment (I commit). For instance, continuing the example of the law student, the reconciliation function wants to change the role identity state from "student" to "licensed lawyer." On the other hand, the achievement function wants to know if the student passed the Constitutional studies class requirements with an A. The aim of the latter is short-term and it is seeking a gratification for its (I perform) efforts.

This function is expressed many times by my clients as "I feel successful." When they are not doing so well, they say, "I am not feeling successful." Hence, a trigger for me to understand how successful people believe they are is generally through "I feel" type wording, which is the reason it is included as another name for the element.[257]

It is worth repeating that the "I achieve" function has a short- to mid-term attention span. It is concerned with monitoring progress in the here and now and feeding information and commands to other functions to ensure congruence. A recurring sense of achievement, progress, and positive confirmation over time builds positive self-esteem and the sense that one has a worthwhile legacy to be proud of (I am fulfilled). A healthy and robust sense of achievement also means "I perform" is doing its job and that there is a sense that one is achieving one's commitments. In other words, "I commit" equals or is steadily progressing toward "I achieve."

A healthy sense of achievement requires patience. The persistent individual remains grounded in the reality that things do take time. Each individual success is appreciated and valued by the "I achieve" function because it perceives movement toward the final goal. Also, there is the realization that the perceived results are supporting the broader life purpose (I commit) and aspiring identity (I become).

A person acting and performing in an anxious and impatient way could indicate that there are motivational *drives* influencing behavior.

257 More logical types could use "I think." That label is also acceptable.

Impatience comes across as restless, compulsive, neurotic, and narcissistic behavior. The anxiety reveals unhealthy meanings in a disturbed sense of self (I am). For instance, when action toward a new self (I become) is being resisted (Amotivation or Drive) by the current self-image (I am)—the individual would say or think something like, "I can't see myself becoming that type of an ideal person and acting like that." Hence, in this situation the task of the anxiety expressed in the "I achieve" element is to keep the identity sound and true to its self-image (I am) or how it perceives itself to be.

If you pit the current sense of self (I am) against the desired sense of self (I become), the stronger identity will ultimately win. By "win" I mean the leading self-image gets to determine the type (Will, Drive, and Amotivate) and strength of motivation that will be invested.

Impatience and its symptoms describe an identity with a low sense of self-determination. It displays a personality that feels she or he has little to no control over what is happening and what can be done. A confident and healthy achievement function, on the other hand, is realistic, patient, pragmatic, well-adapted, optimistic, positive, and appreciative of its progress. The "I achieve" element is what allow us to "smell the roses" when in the path of goal and task achievement. It does not have to wait to experience satisfaction until the final result is achieved because the journey itself is meaningful. The task is meaningful because

- the aim is the right one (I become);
- the commitment is strong (I commit);
- the inclination is robust and resilient (I will); and
- there is forward movement (I perform).

For instance, I have enjoyed researching and writing this book. I have also found meaning and learned from the emotional roller coaster I have gone through as a result of new understanding and awareness. At the moment I am fully aware that I am not done with the book yet. However, I feel no anxiety or push to meet a deadline. Rather, I am enjoying the process of seeing weekly progress. The fact that I am now working on chapter 7 gives me great satisfaction. I am also pleased that my contributors and editors have so far found meaning and value in the content of this volume. Learning and growing are some of the great benefits of writing this book. I celebrate and enjoy each thought. The book will be done when it is done, and according to the standards I have set for myself.

The point I wish to make by sharing my own experience is that a healthy achievement function monitors *and* celebrates the here and now. In logoteleological terms, the achievement function is there to remind us that being appreciative and happy of the positive things we are doing—however small—is very important. It should also remind us to give appreciation to others who share our lives in some way.

Finally, a healthy "I achieve" element is also realistic and reasonable when facing failures. Failures and setbacks in a healthy identity are used as learning opportunities rather than negative judgments of our potential and being. In a positive personality early symptoms of discouragement are silenced with affective encouraging affirmations, aims, and a willed determination to persist. It is helped when our aspirations (I become) and our pledges (I commit) include self-sustaining and resilient meanings.

Our achievements influence how we feel about our long-term impact (I am fulfilled). Remaining realistic and constructive when judging our failures and successes can motivate us to succeed. After all, the negative option is unacceptable and meaningless, so why even consider it?

How well the "I achieve" element functions depend on the strengths of other elements—for instance, those related to the strength of one's sense of self, aspirations, commitments, and competence.

I Am Fulfilled

This function reveals the general, long-term, and sustained mood of the identity. A healthy affective element describes a loving, serene, happy, and purposeful person. It reveals vitality and an encouraging and optimistic outlook toward life. Fulfillment is felt as the result of recurring successes over time. Thus, while the previously discussed "I achieve" operates in the present tense, fulfillment in this sense looks to the cumulative results of past performance (I perform) to assess its long-term benefit and impact.

A general positive mood and disposition toward life is indicative of a fulfilling and meaning-rich emotional state. Again, the sustained successful accomplishment of goals (I achieve) produces a sense of fulfillment, particularly when the achievements are aligned with one's aspirations (I become) and purpose (I commit).

Experiencing fulfillment energizes the Will to persist.[258] It makes us more resilient because it gives us the necessary positive emotional reserves to sustain us during trying times. On the other hand, individuals with a general negative disposition toward life feel emotionally depleted and defeated. Hence, a lack of fulfillment has a discouraging effect.

Fulfillment is experienced when all the elements of the Congruence Model are positively aligned. This happens because we are becoming the person we wish to be as a result of the collaboration of all the elements. The functions are doing precisely all the right things to maintain momentum in identity formation and self-actualization. This includes the role of the "I am fulfilled" element since it remains aware of and positively responsive to the effects of the long-term buildup of incoming feedback related to our successes. The feedback can come from our own sense of progress, others' insights, and additional information coming from our surroundings.

On the other hand, consistent lack of fulfillment suggests that one or more elements in the Congruence Model are misaligned, that our actions are not well received by others, or that our aims and efforts are not congruent with the demands and expectations of the external environment. In a healthy identity, when an individual experiences lack

258 Rychlack, Joseph F., *Logical Learning Theory,* 197.

of fulfillment, other functions in the teleological Congruence Model are activated to self-correct in order to ensure internal and external harmony.[259]

In conclusion, the general life mood (I am fulfilled) embodies the individual's growing legacy as a result of the meaning given to his or her actions. It also describes how the self and others label the meaning of one's life. Since people label us by our actions, the achievement function records and describes the established reputation of our identities. Fulfilled individuals self-describe as successful and are generally inclined to declare that their life is meaningful and worthwhile. It looks backward to judge the meaning of one's life. I have found that fulfillment is important because it is an effective barometer of our psychological health.

The Whole Person

True to logoteleology theory, the Congruence Model reminds us that each of us is unique and extraordinary. We study the different cognitive and affective elements of the model to understand, value, and nurture our whole identity. It can be said that the elements of the Logoteleology Congruence Model help us differentiate ourselves in order to integrate us in a meaningful way within ourselves and with others.

To differentiate, the elements of the Congruence Model are in fact demarcations of psychological operations in personality. The elements use operators and rules: if/then; and/or; either/or, etc., where a change in one element impacts one or more of its other inner functions. With a clear understanding of how the Congruence Model works, these operations can

259 Individuals who show strong resilience (i.e., Will) to self-correct when encountering failure are defined by Sanford University's Dr. Carol Dweck as "incremental theorists." Those inclined to be less resilient in the face of failure she calls "entity theorists." See Dweck, Carol S., "Implicit Theories as Organizers of Goals and Behaviors," Gollwitzer, Peter M., and John A. Bargh, Eds. *The Psychology of Action* (New York: The Guilford Press, 1996), 69–90.

- bring awareness about our person and behavior;
- help us generate helpful and conscious questions and targeted choices for our betterment; and
- encourage us to find our answers to life's questions. Remember Frankl's challenge: "Life ultimately means taking the responsibility to find the right answers to its problems and to fulfill the tasks it constantly sets for each individual." [260]

That includes answering fundamental questions as the ones I have covered in this book:

- Who am I?
- What matters in life?
- What is my life purpose?
- How do I achieve my life purpose?

There are also the more specific questions we need to ask ourselves to make sure we are aligned and on track with the above questions, such as

- Do I stand for something worthwhile?
- Am I committed to a worthy cause?
- Do I have the right skills?
- Am I inspired and motivated by my cause, as well as its goals and tasks?
- Do I have the determination and resolve to deal with obstacles and to succeed?

Knowing ourselves and valuing our uniqueness is important if we are going to be psychologically congruent and healthy, interact in positive ways with others, and enjoy all life has to offer. On the other hand, a

260 Viktor E. Frankl, *Man's Search for Meaning,* 77.

lack of congruence inhibits our ability to create solutions, to intent, and to invest energy toward our desired goal. We all face the choice between the latter and the former. Unfortunately, too many people suffer, drift, and are prevented from reaching their potential, which is why I believe humanity suffers from an identity crisis. And as stated previously, I also believe humans suffer despite answers being available. The prominent psychiatrist Erik Erikson lamented, "our civilization does not really harbor a concept of the whole life."[261] Yet I am optimistic that logoteleology's models can make a positive difference helping people find the path to a life well lived with meaning and purpose. I believe the Congruence Model provides the cognitive and affective map to understand problem-solving processes and to improve self-determination.

Our civilization does not really harbor a concept of the whole life.

Erik Erikson

The Dynamic Nature of the Congruence Model

I previously indicated that the elements within the Congruence Model interact with one another. There is a cause and effect relationship among the elements. A change in one causes changes in others. Let's see two examples based on work with two clients[262] to understand the dynamics among the elements.

The Case of Joe

Joe came to terms with the reality that his career as a nurse was not fulfilling him (I am fulfilled), nor did it pay as much as he would like to earn (I achieve). Going to work was becoming increasingly de-motivating and thus difficult (I will). He was quite unhappy being on

261 Robert Coles, ed., *The Eric Erikson Reader,* (New Yrk: W. W. Norton Company, Inc., 2000), page 205

262 The names and specific details of the two cases have been altered to protect confidentiality.

what he considered "the low end of the hospital's totem pole" (I achieve), taking orders from others (I perform), and not being able to exert control over his life (I will). Joe had higher aspirations and ambitions (I become) and wanted to do something (I perform) he could feel proud of in his later years (I am fulfilled). Joe was ready to make a positive difference in others' lives (I commit).

After attending a few coaching sessions to think about and address his predicament (I reconcile), he decided to register at the local university to pursue a degree in medical sciences (I commit) and become a doctor (I become). Joe was a persistent and faithful student (I will and I perform) who eventually graduates[263] as a doctor (I am good at and I am). He now works in the same hospital, with more pay, and in an area of specialty that he enjoys (I achieve). Over time Joe built a reputation as a fine surgeon (I am good at) and feels upbeat about the long-term prospects of his career (I am fulfilled).

Notice how in the case of Joe there are causal relations among the different functions.

Below are Joe's Logoteleology Congruence Model (LCM) pre- and post-psychometric results based on a scale where 1 = strongly agree and 7 = strongly disagree.

Low scores point to a positive satisfaction tendency while higher scores point to a negative satisfaction tendency. Specifically, the scoring is interpreted as follows:

1 to 2 = You are generally in agreement.

3 to 5 = For the most part you are not really sure.

6 to 7 = You disagree.

On this version of the LCM survey, the "I reconcile" and "I perform" functions are not measured.

---

263 Once an aspiration is achieved, it becomes present-tense reality.

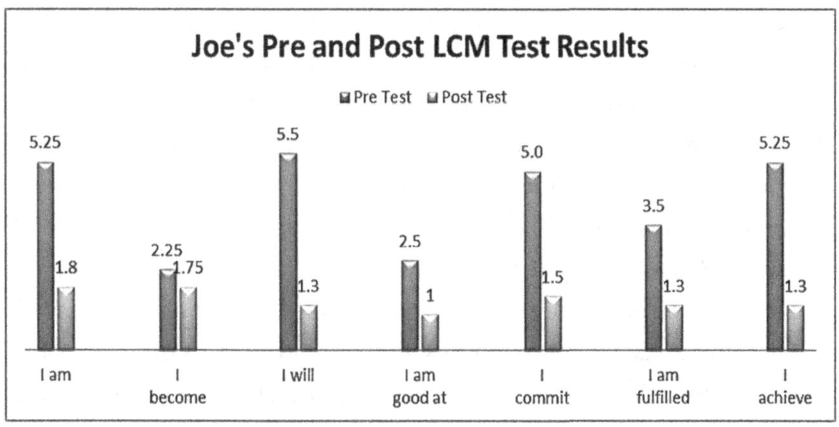

Chart 1 Example of Pre- and Post-LCM Test Results

Interpreting Joe's Results

As can be seen from the "I am" scores, Joe has deepened his self-awareness. He has a better appreciation of who he is and of his potential. The positive low scores in the other elements corroborate that assumption. Moreover, the alignment of his "I am" and "I become" scores are a positive indication that there is congruence between who he is and who he wants to be. When these two scores are compared to the positive score of "I commit" we can also conclude that Joe is acting on his commitments to become and remain being the person he wishes to be.

Joe's "I will" score tells us he is excited to fulfill his commitments and purpose (I commit). The "I achieve" positive score informs us he is getting feedback that his efforts are having a positive impact. Notice that the cumulative positive feedback and deep satisfaction from doing his work is fulfilling to Joe (I am fulfilled). He is optimistic about his future legacy.

The Case of Emily

Now consider the case of forty-five-year-old Emily. For years she has struggled with bouts of depression and loneliness (I am fulfilled). She does not have a purpose in life (I commit) or know why she is here (I am). As she self-describes, "I go through the movements in a predictable and boring routine." She has worked the bulk of her professional career as a bookkeeping clerk for a small accounting firm. She is competent in her craft (I am good at) but would rather do something else (I become). However, she does not know what (I become), nor can she find the motivation to do something different (I will). Her house is full of self-help books, videos, and CDs which she studies (I am good at) in her search for self-understanding and meaning (I reconcile). However, while she finds the content of these self-help tools of great interest and revealing, for some reason (I will) Emily does not commit to a purpose (I commit), nor does she take action to help herself (I perform). She seeks help from a professional coach. But she quits after attending her first coaching session.

Interpreting Emily's Results

Chart 2 below describes Emily's pre-test results based on a scale where 1 = strongly agree and 7 = strongly disagree. As in the previous case, low scores point to a positive satisfaction tendency while higher scores point to a negative satisfaction tendency. The scoring is interpreted as follows:

1 to 2 = You are generally in agreement.

3 to 5 = For the most part you are not really sure.

6 to 7 = You disagree.

Again, on this version of the LCM survey, the "I reconcile" and "I perform" functions are not measured.

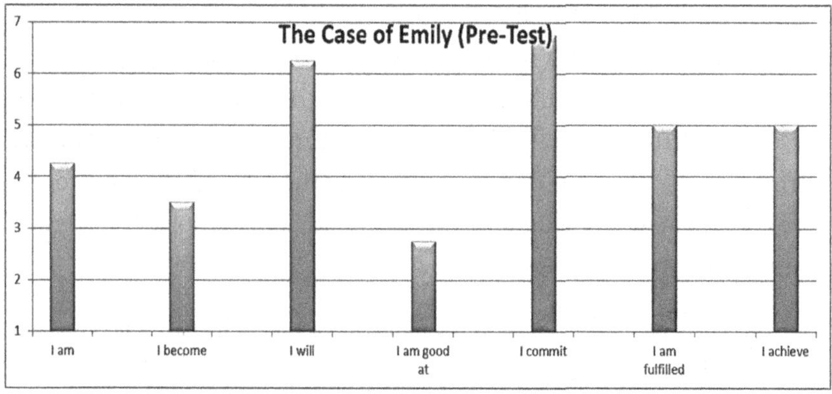

Chart 2 Example of Pre-Test Results

As can be seen from the chart, Emily is having some difficulty defining who she is (I am) and coming to grips with what she wants to do with her life. She is challenged conveying her aspirations (I become). As a result she doesn't know where (I commit) to invest her energies (I will). Hence, she is not happy (I achieve) and has concerns about her long-term prospects (I am fulfilled). However, there is a silver lining in her results. Emily believes her current competencies (I am good at) as a bookkeeper meet her immediate needs.

Key Learning from Case Studies

For coaching purposes, while further work is required, these and other findings are favorable indicators of a promising method. The preliminary results indicate that when the client understands the (cognitive and affective) problem-solving approach of the model, he or she is more inclined to use its labels, definitions, and causal dynamics to make sense of self. For instance, in the case of Joe, he was helped by seeing the outcomes of a pre-assessment that included a four-hour interview and the use of revealing psychometrics, which included the Logoteleology Congruence Model. The cumulative data deepened self-understanding, provided a foundational point of departure toward the future, and allowed Joe to self-select the best approach to meet his needs.

The case of Emily is also shared as a recognition that as with any other method, logoteleology is not a cure-all. While conditions for the most part were similar to Joe's, Emily never got to see the results of her assessment. After the preliminary session, Emily moved on to a more promising job. One can only speculate whether she might have found hope that the new role would be fulfilling and help her solve her original predicament.

Moving forward in chapter 8, I would like to address with greater specificity how the Congruence Model helps develop and strengthen identity formation and performance. I will also explain the propositions that influence the teleotherapy approach.

Application

What new things did you learn about meaningful purpose? If you were to reflect on your own life and build your own Congruence Model chart, what would be the strengths of the bars as measured by the proposed metrics? What would be your story? Why?

My Journey

In light of my research on purpose, here are a few ways I have applied them to my life.

1. I can better get to root causes for my successes and setbacks. I can thus understand myself with greater clarity and meaning.
2. I appreciate the value of remaining positive when facing roadblocks, difficulties, and setbacks. I am helped by my adherence to ACT and the Five Meaningful strivings.
3. I ask myself more intelligent questions. Frankl's challenge, "Life ultimately means taking the responsibility to find the right answers to its problems and to fulfill the tasks which it constantly sets for each individual" continues to inspire and

motivate me to stay in the here and now, to be responsible and accountable for my results and future, and to stay on course.

4. I have built stronger coaching competence and deliver greater value for my clients.

Chapter 8: Teleotherapy

First learn the meaning of what you say, and then speak.—Epictetus

According to the logoteleology theory, individuals cannot succeed and proceed to new experiences as long as elements of the Congruence Model have unfinished business standing in the way. A disturbance at one of the functions affects the others. Solutions can ultimately be implemented by intervening at the source of the disturbance. To treat disturbances, I felt compelled to develop an effective and responsible method, which I call *teleotherapy,* [264] or the therapy for meaningful purpose.

Congruence in an identity is experienced to the degree that the nine functions are harmonious and are capable of producing synergy. When all functions are working and interacting harmoniously, the person

- can clearly explain who she or he is;
- discerns what matters (the individual fundamentally follows ACT[265] and the five strivings[266]);

264 The name *logoteleotherapy* is considered an alternate label, but for practical reasons related to its length the shorter version (teleotherapy) is preferred and most often used.
265 ACT is the acronym for Allow, Cooperate, and Transcend.
266 The five strivings for meaningful purpose are the capacity to love, to be at peace, and to experience joy, stimulate challenge, and bring prosperity to others.

- has a meaningful purpose and goals to live for;
- knows what she or he stands for. The individual consciously means exactly what she or he says;
- has feelings and motivations that match what he or she expresses and how she or he acts; and
- builds a positive and meaningful legacy over time.

In this chapter I will delve further into the Logoteleology Congruence Model, since an understanding of the tool is required to diagnose a personality as well as plan, carry out, and measure the impact of a coaching strategy. The chapter will answer the following:

1. What is teleotherapy?
2. How do the Identity and the Logoteleology Congruence Models complement one another?
3. What methods does teleotherapy offer to help with identity formation, reformation, and development?

What Is Teleotherapy?

Literally, teleotherapy means therapy *for meaningful purpose.* It is a client-centric therapy, a coaching and organization development method aimed at helping people, groups, and organizations enjoy a meaningful life through identity formation, development, and reformation.

As a coaching and consulting method it is a proactive, preventive, formative, and developmental approach designed to clarify, build, and strengthen identities.

> Teleotherapy means therapy *for meaningful purpose.*

As a therapy it is a reformation approach that aims to help people, groups, and organizations with meaning and purpose crises, which manifest themselves in a feeling of aimlessness. It also remedies problems people face daily but are not yet necessarily grave.

As it pertains to organization development, teleotherapy is a creative, developmental as well as remedial tool designed to help organizations equally meet their business, technical, and human needs in a balanced and responsible way.

In the case of people, **identity formation** is about helping the client self-determine and self-identify. The coaching and therapy process models follow self-determination approaches. This means that the process adopts the belief that the answers pertaining to existential questions lie in and are determined *by the client*. The client is capable of discovering and inventing solutions. The teleotherapist's task is to ask questions to bring insight (versus giving insight) so the client can come up with his or her own answers. It is an exercise that helps the individual answer the four existential questions:

- Who am I?
- What matters in life?
- What is the purpose of my life?
- How do I fulfill my life purpose?

The demarcation between *corrective therapy* and *developmental coaching* is one of degree. A therapeutic remedy would deal with dysfunctional symptoms such as depression, while a developmental approach is directed to strengthen an identity, such as a couple who, in the context of their family identity, want to define the meaning and purpose for having a child.

Identity formation is about helping the client self-determine and self-identify.

While teleotherapy has applications at the individual, group, and organization levels, this volume is primarily concerned with its application at the person identity level. However, where appropriate, examples pertaining to groups and organizations will be provided. Future volumes will build on the foundation of this book to introduce remedies for individuals in particular roles—such as that of a leader—as well as solutions for groups and organizations.

The Complementary Nature of the Identity and Logoteleology Congruence Models

This section will answer how the Identity Model[267] and the Congruence Model work together. This is relevant because the Logoteleology Congruence Model plays a key role in identity formation, development, and reformation. Worth repeating, the model follows these basic propositions:

1. The elements in the model are distinct from one another, each performing a function.
2. The elements interact with and influence other elements.
3. The model is not a personality representation; rather, it represents the dynamics of self-identification and teleological self-regulation.
4. The model is not a representation of a healthy identity; rather, it provides the tools to diagnose and improve it.
5. A healthy identity preserves equilibrium between the elements.

> What is common between the Congruence and Identity models is that they both explain the dynamics of identities.

What is common between the Congruence and Identity Models is that they both explain the dynamics of identities. They both can be

267 The Identity Model is expressed through the formula I = P + Mo + Me, where P = Purpose, Mo = Motivation, and Me = Meaning. Purpose, Motivation, and Meaning are also subsystems in an identity.

used for identity formation, development, and reformation, usually in combination. The Identity Model explains how the meaning set is formed and how it powers a type of motivation to take actions. *The Congruence Model is a more detailed, client-centric, and cognitive-affective problem-solving method used in coaching and therapy.* When used in combination with the Identity Model, the Congruence Model has shown preliminary promising results as a coaching and therapeutic tool to form, develop, and reform identities.

Identity Formation

Identity formation *is a method that builds a healthy identity through a strong and positive meaning set, which in turn willingly motivates the person to select fitting purposes and goals.* Identity formation has application in many settings such as family dynamics, child rearing, education, career and vocational planning, community building, and in organizational strategy and culture work.

Identity formation happens when the individual person is in the process of claiming her or his life's meaningful purpose. The method is also valuable when forming group and role identities, such as when forming the new identity of a couple and family-to-be, as well as what it means for members to be in roles of husband, wife, parents, and children. *Identity formation adopts ACT and the five strivings as conditions for meaningfulness.*

The approach for identity formation has been referred to previously, it is where the individual

1. embraces ACT and the five strivings;
2. explores the content of her or his meaning set;
3. identifies areas to improve;
4. improves the quality of the meaning set so it triggers the right type of motivation;

5. defines purposes and goals that best support the meaning set; and

6. monitors progress and makes adjustments.

Identity Development

Identity development is what happens after the identity has been formed through the selection of and commitment to a meaningful purpose—for instance, when a duly constituted group decides to build team members' competence on problem solving, or when parents teach their child proper table manners. Identity development sustains ACT and the five strivings as fundamental ground rules and operating principles in personality. As a result, identity development includes embracing standards and building knowledge, competencies, and those attitudes that allow the individual to be a contributing and responsible member of society.

Once the meaningful purpose has been defined, the whole person needs to be built up and nurtured through identity development in order to help the individual

- achieve goals;
- adapt to the demands of the environment;
- meet its person, group, and role identities obligations; and
- master ACT and the five strivings.

Identity Reformation

Identity reformation is an intervention that guides a person to self-correct a disturbance or a personality disorder. It can be self-directed or coached by a qualified professional, such as a teleotherapist. Identity reformation reinforces the use of ACT and the five strivings.

In logoteleology, there are two categories of personality and social disturbance that require identity reformation, each with two types of disorders.

Category	Type
Meaning (logos)	hyperlogo and hypologo
Purpose (telos)	hypertelos and hypotelos

Table 13 Categories of Personality Disturbance

Ultimately, all disturbances originate from the meaning sub-system in the identity. However, each category (meaning and purpose disorders) is distinctively classified according to the observed symptoms.

Simply stated, **a meaning disturbance** *is observed when a person*

- *is unable or unwilling to implement or act on its intended meanings; and*
- *finds attempts to remedy the situation fruitless and meaningless.*

On the other hand, **a purpose disturbance** *is observed when a person is*

- *unable to understand the meaning of her or his actions; and*
- *frustrated by the inability to find a purposeful way to implement the desired meanings.*

There are degrees of severity with any of the above disorders. They serve to help the coach determine potential root causes and hence the most appropriate coaching approach.

The Four Types of Disorders

In the following descriptions, the identity formula is included to help explain the discernible force of each of its elements in the disturbance.

- A high case means the particular identity subsystem is active to very active.

- A low case means that the particular identity subsystem is moderately active to inactive.

Thus, (I = p + A + Me) denotes that a busy meaning set has content that is unable to motivate action, where I = Identity, p = inactive purpose, A = Amotivation, Me = Active Meaning Set.

Meaning Disorders[268]

Hyperlogo[269] is defined as *meaning inflation or an overactive meaning set.* Some of the observed symptoms include constant confusion; being overwhelmed; feeling anxiety, despair, anger, phobias, stress, and helplessness; as well as the inability to focus. The individual is unable or unwilling to act or resolve problems. The person thinks but does not act, and when he or she does, effort is timid and ineffective. The individual has some level of awareness that there is something wrong and generally desires to improve her or his condition. She or he faces difficulty dealing with ambiguity and paradox. On some level she or he has some hope that a way out is possible, but deep down there is the belief that she or he lacks what it takes to resolve it.

The identity formula describes hyperlogo as (I = p + A + Me), where there is agitated activity in the meaning set, but the individual remains amotivated to act. Hence the external witness can perceive the internal struggle of the observed, with no coherent or meaningful action to resolve the problem.

Hypologo [270]is defined *as meaning implosion or an underactive meaning*

---

268 These types of disturbances are also known in logotherapy as hyper-reflection, a form of excessive attention paid to oneself. Hyper-reflection undermines a person's ability to achieve his or her goal because his or her attention is focused on the self, thus making any desired outcome less likely to achieve.

269 Hyperlogo must not be confused with *hyperlogia* or morbid verbosity or loquacity. However, hyperlogia could be classified as a type of hyperlogo or hypertelos disturbance.

270 Hypologo must not be confused with *hypologia* or the lack of ability for speech.

set. This is a type of what Frankl called the "existential vacuum."[271] Simply stated, the existential vacuum is when a person cannot clearly articulate what is meaningful in her or his life; and when she or he does act, it is without being able to plainly express why.

> A mind is healthy when it has achieved a sufficient store of meaning.
>
> Viktor Frankl, *Psychotherapy and Existentialism*

Some of the observed symptoms include Amotivation; low self-control and self-determination; apathy; excessive sleep; and feelings of helplessness, depression, and substance abuse. Energy is directed toward the self through internal dialogue (self-talk) and is generally expressed in a negative, self-deprecating, and self-defeating fashion. The individual does not spend much time thinking (why) or acting (what) on the meaningful. Problem solving is ineffective and unable to trigger a positive and rational response. While the person who suffers symptoms of hyperlogo believes there is or should be a solution yet not found, for the individual who displays hypologo symptoms, there is generally no way out. Effort is futile.

The identity formula explains hypologo as (I = p + A + me), where the meaning subsystem in the identity remains underactive and depressed, the individual lacks motivation, and hence the individual's activities are passive and meaningless.

Purpose Disorders[272]

Hypertelos is defined as *an overactive and misdirected purpose subsystem in an identity.* Motivation is Driven and can be unbalanced and misapplied (e.g., bull in the china shop). People displaying the hypertelos symptom

271 The four disturbances are types of existential vacuums, but each has different symptoms.

272 Purpose disorders are not the same as logotherapy's hyper-intention (a matter of trying too hard), which itself prevents you from succeeding at something. However, hyper-intention can be a symptom of a purpose disorder.

self-describe or are observed as multitasking, over-committing, talking too much, and feeling anxious; they have difficulty letting go, can be excessively competitive and ambitious, and can have high control needs. Further, they spend little time reflecting, and when they do they are generally not able to discern and learn. Decision making can be based on routines and habits, leveraging past experience and knowledge. This does not mean the individual displaying these symptoms is not smart. Actually, he or she can be an intelligent and talented quick thinker who has a particular expertise. The problem generally lies in how he or she handle their life priorities, where they tend to place more value on activity and self-gratification than on intimacy. They also have a fixed view of how things should be, and as a result come across as insensitive and abrasive.

The identity formula describes hypertelos as (I = P + D + me), where the individual is highly active and driven by meaningless or misguided meanings.

Many times the individual with hypertelos symptoms is not aware of her or his drives. It is difficult for the person to clearly articulate why she or he is driven and hyperactive. At times it is challenging to free the self from the drives, as in the case of compulsions and addictions. This person's definition of the "meaningful" does not meet the criteria of logoteleology's ACT and the five strivings; and generally one or two of the strivings are overused, generally the most impersonal (e.g., interest and prosperity).

Hypotelos is defined as *an underactive, underperforming, and misdirected purpose subsystem in an identity.* Simply stated, in hypotelos the individual gets little satisfaction and pleasure from current goals, relationships, and activities. She or he is generally active doing things of little interest or meaning. There is awareness that there is more to life than the actual experience, yet the individual cannot find a suitable solution to make life more meaningful. At work, for instance, she or he performs enough to get by, to meet basic needs such as food, transportation, and shelter, and to buy pleasures that are not present in the existing role. Going to work is something "one must do" (hence, a Drive) versus a fulfillment of one's meaningful life purpose. Relationships with others can be designed to meet a convenient or pragmatic need rather than a true partnership based on ACT and the five strivings.

The identity formula describes hypotelos as (I = p + d + me). It describes a person who has not thought through what is meaningful, has an undefined and compelling life purpose, and functions to meet basic obligations and responsibilities. This type of individual is described in the vernacular as "just cruising through life," "existing," and "hanging in there."[273]

The examples that follow describe individuals with mild, moderate, and severe symptoms for each of the disturbances.[274]

Examples of Disturbances

Hyperlogo (I = p + A + Me)

Mild: Within four months, Joe will graduate from high school. He has no idea what he is going to do with the rest of his life. His parents want him to "move on" and become independent. He is overwhelmed with the amount of options. He stands still in the hopes of eventually sorting his dilemma. However, his constant thinking about his predicament does not allow him to sleep well at night.

Severe: Forty-six year old Albert has lived all his life with his now seventy-year-old mother, a widow. His mother has helped him as he struggles to do something productive with his life. He tried college but did not finish, he has held odd jobs, and his efforts are in vain. Joe places great

273 Individuals showing symptoms of hypomania, for instance, display hypologo-type behaviors. Hypomania is characterized by a persistent euphoric and irritable mood, and behaviors that are consistent with such a mood state. Hypomania is most associated with the bipolar (II) spectrum.

274 Tables have been added in the Addendum to explain in greater detail Identity Formation, Development, and Reformation for readers who might be interested in these approaches.

emphasis on his external appearance to hide his sense of failure. He is a socially active talker with grandiose ideas but does not act on them.

Hypologo (I = p + A + me)

Mild: Sue just lost her job after twenty years as a result of her company moving offshore. She not only lost her job, she lost her friends and her sense of self since Sue proudly defined herself by what she did. Sue is in a state of shock and suffers from disbelief, deep sadness, and utter confusion.

Severe: Jack is a high-level executive who succeeded in making money but failed in keeping his family together. His problems at home are having an adverse impact at work. People are complaining about his inability to perform and to get along with people. After being confronted by his manager, Jack becomes clinically depressed. For Jack, his life and all he has done are now meaningless. He tries to find solace in alcohol and is defined by others as a functional alcoholic.

Hypertelos (I = P + D + me)

Moderate: Carla is considered a successful engineer and performer at a car manufacturer. But it has come at a cost. Because of her want to please others and her inability to say no to unrealistic requests, Carla now finds herself in the emergency room with a severe migraine due to hypertension.

Severe: Mike is a hardworking and ambitious project manager who piles on sixty to seventy work hours a week in his refinery. Mike delivers results, so given the culture of the organization, management puts a blind eye to his bullying of others and willingness to cut corners—or as he would say, "Cutting through the red tape." Turnover is high and costly due to his work approach. For Mike, the ends justify the means. To keep costs down he bypasses routine maintenance work. There is an explosion in the refinery that claims the life of five subcontractors.

Hypotelos (I = p + d + me)

Mild: Sandra is bored and feels that she is under-employed. What she is doing at work as a manufacturing technician is totally unrelated to her education as an entomologist. She found studying insects interesting, but never thought through how to translate her interest into a meaningful purpose and career. Unable to find a job in her field, she had to take a manufacturing job to support herself.

Severe: Richard inherited great wealth from his father. His father passed away and left him fortune and the role of CEO of his company, Steel Products. As a young boy, after his mother passed away, the widowed father sent him to an all-boys' school in Switzerland. He returned to his country of origin for his university degree. Growing up, he occasionally saw his father. Despite all he has, Richard finds life meaningless and entertains thoughts of suicide.

Treatment for Disturbances

As previously explained, all disturbances with observable meaning or purpose symptoms are ultimately disorders in the identity's meaning subsystem. One can distinguish meaning disorders from purpose disorders in these ways:

- Meaning disorders remain in the meaning subsystem, or "in the head." There is no action because there is no meaningful reason to do so.
- With purpose disorders, the individual performs, yet without a full awareness of the meaning of his or her actions. If she or he does have the awareness, for some reason the individual is unable to improve her or his condition.

To treat the four disturbances, teleotherapy uses the Congruence Model, ACT, and the five strivings to help the individual answer to her or his satisfaction the four questions:

- Who am I?
- What matters in my life?

- What is the purpose of my life?
- How do I achieve my life purpose?

To solve these four existential disturbances, the teleotherapist uses the results of the Logoteleology Congruence Model psychometric plus his or her own trained judgment to plan the treatment approach. The goal is to guide and encourage the client to answer the four existential questions to her or his satisfaction. Each question, by design, is best addressed by some of the elements of the Logoteleology Congruence Model, as shared below. For instance, as a rule, to treat symptoms of meaning disorders, it is best to help the individual define who she or he is and who she or he wishes to be and achieve in life. While it might vary from client to client, to treat the disorders of purpose, it is best to start solving meaning disorders and then help the client find suitable purposes and goals while building the will to follow through.

In the second column labeled "Congruence Model Elements", the element that plays a leading role is bolded.

Question	Congruence Model Elements	Disturbance Being Treated
Who am I?	**I am** I reconcile I become I am fulfilled	hyperlogo and hypologo
What matters in my life?	**I become** I commit	hyperlogo and hypologo
What is the purpose of my life?	**I commit**	all four
How do I achieve my life purpose?	**I will** I am good at I perform I achieve	hypertelos and hypotelos

Table 14 Existential Questions and Disturbances

It is the bias of logoteleology that ACT and the five strivings are important elements in identity formation, development, and reformation. The goal is to help the individual succeed through ACT and the five strivings.

Regarding ACT:

- Is the individual capable of allowing others be while encouraging their self-determination and ability to cooperate?
- Is the person cooperating and fostering interdependence?
- Is she or he caring, giving, and altruistic with fellow humans and with nature?

Regarding the five strivings:

- Love
    - o Is the person in caring and loving relationships?
    - o Can the individual be kind, considerate, and respectful toward others?
    - o Can the person treat people as subjects of their attention and consideration or does he treat others as objects?
    - o Does he or she believe to be deserving of affection, love, and respect?
- Happiness
    - o Is life meaningful, enjoyable, and worth living?
- Peace
    - o Does the individual experience peace of mind and contentment?
- Challenge
    - o Is life interesting and fulfilling?

- Prosperity
    - o Is the person making financial headway and thriving?

The teleotherapy method is still being researched, and findings will be printed in a future publication. Others are encouraged to build upon this foundation to test its validity and to bring about improvements. For now it has been my intent to provide some highlights on the methodology, particularly to explain how the Congruence Model, ACT, the five strivings, and the Identity Model are used synergistically in favor of remedies for identity formation, development, and reformation remedies.

The PASCAS Method™

One of the core goals of the teleotherapy method is to build the person's capacity and confidence to self-determine. It is founded on Frankl's lesson, "Life ultimately means taking the responsibility to find the right answers to its problems and to fulfill the tasks which it constantly sets for each individual."

Individuals are encouraged to pay attention to their needs and wants as a way to

1. **p**repare a problem statement;
2. **a**sk the right questions;
3. **s**et goals;
4. **c**ommit;
5. **a**ct; and
6. **s**olve.

I call those six steps by their acronym, the PASCAS Method™.

The essence of the method is to remind clients that they are surrounded by answers. When facing challenges we need to slow our pace and pay attention to the question life is asking. Hence, the method helps clients turn "why" into "how to." For instance, let's say the problem is that the person is not performing well at work and wishes to meet the expectations of his or her management. The individual can transform, "Why can't I perform better at work?"[275] into a "how to" question, such as "How can I perform better at work?" The goal is strongly suggested by the question, which is to *find ways to improve performance.* The person is also encouraged to answer why setting such a goal is meaningful in order to ensure a willing motivation to act. Once a goal has been decided, the next steps are to commit to following through and to take the appropriate action steps until the problem is resolved.

Sean's Case

Let's take Sean as an example of a person with hyperlogo symptoms. Notice how the teleotherapist coaches Sean.

Sean does not know what his talents are. He claims that in part, it is because people do not offer him honest feedback. He also claims he does not know how to find out what his talents are. He has taken no action, finds excuses why he cannot solve his situation, and thus remains "stuck" in a constant dilemma. He meets with his teleotherapist. A condensed version of the dialogue follows:

Sean: I don't know what my talents are.

Teleotherapist: What is it you want?

Sean: I want to know what my talents are.

Teleotherapist: So you want to find out what you're good at. Let me capture in my own words how you are describing the situation. Please let me know it if fits and helps.

275 This question, of course, can be appropriate to get to the root cause of the poor performance. However, it is inappropriate when the question is intended to self-blame or self-degrade.

(Writes on a whiteboard)

My problem: I do not know what my talents are.

My question: How do I discover what my talents are?

My goal: I will discover what my talents are.

Sean: Yes. That's it …

Teleotherapist: Why is discovering your talents meaningful to you?

Sean: If I knew what my talents are, I could prepare and work in a career that would leverage my strengths.

Teleotherapist: It would be meaningful for you to discover what your talents are in order to have a satisfying career, right?

Sean: Yes.

Teleotherapist: So, Sean (pointing to the third bullet on the whiteboard), I offer that the task before you is to discover your innate talents. Is that correct? And if so, can you commit to that?

Sean: Yes. But I do not know how to go about it.

Teleotherapist: Let's assume for a minute you did know. What one or two things could you do? Take your time to think about it.

Sean: You could tell me … (smiles).

Teleotherapist: Good answer (smiles affirmingly). Asking other people is a wonderful way to find out. And I will later suggest a couple of ideas. But first, what else could you do to find out how one goes about learning about one's talents? Take your time.

Sean: Ask my school counselor?

Teleotherapist: Sounds like a great idea. You can also check on the Internet, and also by taking vocational tests through your school counselor.

Sean: Oh! So obvious! Why didn't I think of that?

Teleotherapist: Remember what I shared with you earlier: most answers to questions are available. But you need to ask the right question. And then, of course, take the initiative to pursue the answer and solve the problem.

So far you have a few options: first, asking others—for instance me and your school counselor. I mentioned taking vocational tests, and I also offered checking the Internet.

Can you commit to follow those leads?

Sean: Definitely!

Teleotherapist: Set a goal. What are you going to do and by when?

Sean: I will set an appointment with my school counselor tomorrow to get his advice and to check on the vocational tests. Also, I will check the Internet for additional ideas.

Teleotherapist: (Smiles approvingly) Sounds like a great plan!

Now, how would you know you are done? That you have successfully met your goal?

Sean: When I know what my talents are?

Teleotherapist: What was the meaningful reason you would bother to discover your talents?

Sean: I see where you are going. I would be done when I have chosen the right professional career, right?

Teleotherapist: (With an approving and affirming tone) That is what I heard you say before. Is that still okay?

Sean: Definitely!

Teleotherapist: Will you tell me next time we meet how you are progressing on your actions?

Sean: Of course!

Teleotherapist: On our next time together I will explain the PASCAS Method™ so you can use it to help you solve similar situations. Is that okay?

Sean: It sure is! This is helpful.

End of coaching session.

The PASCAS Method™ is an additional tool that can be a positive force to help form, transform, and develop identities, particularly when used in combination with ACT, the five strivings, and the Identity and Congruence Models. It encourages the client to pay attention to her or his needs and ask the right questions required by the situation.

Summary

To summarize, teleotherapy is a coaching and remedial tool that assists in identity formation, development, and reformation.

Identity formation is a creative process where a person self-discovers and self-determines. Through a successful identity formation exercise the person would be able to

- understand and describe herself or himself in a satisfactory way;
- describe his or her life's meaningful purpose;
- articulate the difference between what is meaningful and meaningless;
- make decisions to achieve meaningful ends;
- avoid meaningless distractions;

- work toward and accomplish his or her life purpose and goals; and
- achieve a positive and meaningful legacy.

Identity development is an iterative and continuous improvement process that builds competence and character over an established and self-determined identity.

In logoteleology, there are two broad personality and social disturbance categories that require identity reformation, each with two types of disorders. These four disturbances are

- **Hyperlogo** (I = p + A + Me): A meaning inflation or an overactive meaning set that to some degree incapacitates the person from solving her or his problems. Sometimes the person is able to think rationally, even acknowledging the absurdity of the condition, yet finds himself or herself unable to take action (e.g., as a result of an underlying fear).
- **Hypologo** (I = p + A + me): A meaning implosion or an underactive meaning set. As in hyperlogo, people who display hypologo symptoms are unable to take action in order to solve their problems. The difference is that a person suffering of hypologo cannot think coherently or take action. Hypologo symptoms are comparable to the nihilists', particularly holding the belief that life is pointless.
- **Hypertelos** (I = P + D + me): An overactive and misdirected purpose system that operates without the conscious awareness of the meanings influencing behavior. It can be said that the person is on autopilot and going through the motions without fully comprehending what is happening and what the potential consequences of the behavioral trend could be. The individual acts but is not fully aware, nor can he or she explain why. Type-A personalities and the narcissist fit this description.
- **Hypotelos** (I = p + d + me): Describes an underactive,

underperforming, or misdirected purpose. A person with an underactive purpose, as with hypertelos, has difficulty attaching meaning to behaviors. Characteristically, this underactive type lacks energy and resolve due to misplaced potential, a lack of commitment, and incompetence. He or she lacks meaningful, actionable, and pragmatic purpose, goals, and answers. Finally, people displaying hypotelos symptoms have misaligned person, group, and role identities. This is in great measure because the person lacks a robust, meaningful purpose to guide such alignment. The individual acts, but timidly and poorly. He or she shows up but is not able to make strong meaning connections to energize the Will to do something worthwhile.

The PASCAS Method™ is a coaching tool that helps the client build self-determination to form, transform, and develop his or her identity. PASCAS is an acronym.

1. **P**repare a problem statement
2. **A**sk the right questions
3. **S**et goals
4. **C**ommit
5. **A**ct
6. **S**olve

The client is encouraged to find the meaning for improvement and change and to ask action-oriented questions to make things better.

Application

I stated in this chapter that congruence in an identity is experienced to the degree that the nine functions are harmonious and capable of producing synergy. What about you? Can you answer the following statements in the affirmative?

- I know who I am.
- I know what matters in life. My actions follow ACT and the five strivings.
- I have a meaningful purpose and goals to live for.
- I know what I stand for (I consciously mean exactly what I say).
- My feelings and motivations match what I say and how I act.
- I am not distracted by the meaningless.
- Through my actions I am building a positive and meaningful legacy.

If there is room for self-improvement, which of the following approaches do you believe would be most helpful to you, and why?

- identity formation
- identity development
- identity reformation

My Journey

In light of my research on teleotherapy, I am able to

1. identify and categorize strengths and disturbances through observation and application of the Identity and Congruence Models, both mine and others;
2. better contract with clients to determine the type of help they need, and to assess if I am the right resource for their needs (I coach when I can help and opt out when I am not the right person);
3. self-assess and better solve my developmental needs and life

challenges (I can be more precise and targeted on tactics to self-improve);

4. adapt my approach when interacting with others who display any of the disorders; and

5. strengthen my identity and meaningful purpose.

The Synergy of the Logoteleology Models Chart

The following chart describes the goal and role of the Congruence Model for identity formation. It also explains how the teleotherapist relates and leverages the Congruence Model with the identity formula, ACT, and the five strivings when working with clients.

I have found this chart helpful when analyzing Logoteleology Congruence Model psychometrics.

In the second column labeled "Leverage Elements of the Congruence Model in Identity Formation," the element that plays the leading role is bolded.

Goal	Leveraged Elements of the Congruence Model in Identity Formation	Role of Identity Formula in Identity Formation (I = P + Mo + Me)	Role of ACT in Identity Formation	Role of the Five Strivings in Identity Formation
Define who you are and where you are in your life.	**I am**	Assess your ability to answer with certainty and clarity the question "Who am I?" following all the elements of the identity formula. Affirm your unconditional regard to yours and others' lives. Test the strengths and synergy of the elements of the Identity Model.	Assess what the current operating norms are *vis-à-vis* ACT.	Assess how well you are experiencing and fulfilling the five strivings.

Goal	Leveraged Elements of the Congruence Model in Identity Formation	Role of Identity Formula in Identity Formation (I = P + Mo + Me)	Role of ACT in Identity Formation	Role of the Five Strivings in Identity Formation
Highlight what meanings about your identity are sources of satisfaction and pride. Describe how the meanings benefit you and others.	**I am** I achieve I am fulfilled	Bring attention to the positive content of the meaning set. Highlight how the meanings Will and produce the right actions; and how it reveals your positive attributes. Value and celebrate the meaning of the positive outcomes. Answer life's question: What needs to be continued and sustained? Why has this been important to me to this day? Why is it important and meaningful to continue this path?	Determine the degree that these successes and sources of pride relate to ACT (e.g., what does it say about your ability and willingness to allow, cooperate, and transcend when interacting with others?).	Determine if the sources of satisfaction and pride are due to your ability and willingness to apply one or more of the five strivings. Pinpoint the particular striving(s) that produces this satisfaction. Encourage further expression.

Goal	Leveraged Elements of the Congruence Model in Identity Formation	Role of Identity Formula in Identity Formation (I = P + Mo + Me)	Role of ACT in Identity Formation	Role of the Five Strivings in Identity Formation
Determine current meaning dissatisfaction themes and consequences.	**I am** I achieve I am fulfilled	How can I leverage and build on these strengths for an even more determined and satisfactory future? Assess what the sources of dissatisfaction are and their implications. Get life's answers to life's questions: What needs to change? Why does it need to change? (For what meaningful reason?)	Assess how the sources of dissatisfaction related to each part of ACT (for instance, your inability to allow others). Determine their consequence; and consider the possibility of embracing them as operating norms.	Pinpoint how the sources of dissatisfaction relate to the five strivings. Determine their consequence; and consider the possibility of embracing them as operating norms.

Goal	Leveraged Elements of the Congruence Model in Identity Formation	Role of Identity Formula in Identity Formation (I = P + Mo + Me)	Role of ACT in Identity Formation	Role of the Five Strivings in Identity Formation
Study and embrace the benefits of ACT and the five strivings.	**I reconcile** I become	Understand how the quality of the meaning set is strengthened when one embraces ACT and the five strivings. For instance, understanding their effect on the type and strength of motivation when applied to life's tasks.	Consider the merits of embracing ACT as a guide to influencing your choices.	Ponder the benefits and your readiness to embrace and use the five strivings as a behavioral and problem-solving guiding compass.

Goal	Leveraged Elements of the Congruence Model in Identity Formation	Role of Identity Formula in Identity Formation (I = P + Mo + Me)	Role of ACT in Identity Formation	Role of the Five Strivings in Identity Formation
Determine who you wish to be and become. In other words, answer to your satisfaction: What is the meaning *of* life? What is the meaning *of* my life? How will my life be meaningful to me and others?	**I become** I am I reconcile	Bring clarity and strength to the meaning set through developmental and reformation (improvement) strategies.	ACT will remind you that the meaning of life and the meaning of your life are intertwined. All life, yours and others', deserve reverence.	Decide if you will chose to do those things that will bring meaning to your and others' lives through the five strivings.

Goal	Leveraged Elements of the Congruence Model in Identity Formation	Role of Identity Formula in Identity Formation (I = P + Mo + Me)	Role of ACT in Identity Formation	Role of the Five Strivings in Identity Formation
Once you have decided on the meaning of your life, commit to a purpose in order to fulfill your meaningful aims. Make sure your purpose leverages your strengths and maximizes your potential. Use your commitment to guide you when making choices. Be clear as to when to engage and when not to so that you are not derailed from your purpose.	**I commit** I become	Select a purpose, and then determine the role of the purpose system in helping you fulfill your meaning set's aspirations and standards. For instance, think of goals that can help fulfill your purpose (e.g., for a purpose to save lives, the goal could be to become a rescue worker). Your purpose should keep you from being distracted with the meaningless. Pick your battles, tasks and associations, and thoughts carefully. Remain focused and effective!	Assess alignment of purpose and supportive goals with the expectations set by ACT.	Determine how the purpose will fulfill each one of the meaningful strivings. How will your purpose bring you and others love and affection? peace of mind? happiness? stimulating, interesting, and challenging experiences? prosperity?

Goal	Leveraged Elements of the Congruence Model in Identity Formation	Role of Identity Formula in Identity Formation (I = P + Mo + Me)	Role of ACT in Identity Formation	Role of the Five Strivings in Identity Formation
Identify what excites and concerns you about making this commitment. The target is to help you make the most of your life's quest (i.e., purpose) and find ways to deal with obstacles.	**I will** I am **I reconcile** I become	Determine what the meaning set's *emotional attitude* and *meaning motive type* are. How strong are the motivational forces? Which meaning motive type is dominant: Will, Drive, or Amotivate?	For your exciting cause, determine how ACT can be part of your implementation strategy. If you have concerns about achieving your goal, use ACT to find root causes (for instance by assessing your ability to find people who will gladly support and cooperate with you).	Use the strivings to determine which applies. For example, figuring out how what excites or concerns you is related to one or more of the five strivings. If exciting, how can you relate and leverage the striving(s) to build your resilience? If concerned, how can one or more of the strivings help you overcome the problem?

Goal	Leveraged Elements of the Congruence Model in Identity Formation	Role of Identity Formula in Identity Formation (I = P + Mo + Me)	Role of ACT in Identity Formation	Role of the Five Strivings in Identity Formation
Determine which competencies and emotional attitudes are required to accomplish your purpose and goals.	**I am good at** I become I commit	In light of the actions you need to implement, what meanings and competencies will you need to succeed? For instance: Do you have meanings to help you be resilient and determined? Do you have the skills and emotional attitudes to build collaborative relationships with others? Are you an expert in your role and craft? During execution, are there new, emerging demands that require additional skills and different meanings?	Leverage ACT to strengthen relationships, to build goodwill, and to broaden your ability to influence. Determine what you need to learn in order to successfully leverage ACT.	Determine the degree to which your commitment supports the five strivings and how well they benefit you as well as others. Assess your skills and willingness to master the five strivings. Identify opportunities and plan your development.

Goal	Leveraged Elements of the Congruence Model in Identity Formation	Role of Identity Formula in Identity Formation (I = P + Mo + Me)	Role of ACT in Identity Formation	Role of the Five Strivings in Identity Formation
Take action. Put a plan in place and implement it. Gain and sustain momentum. Remember that a body in motion stays in motion.	**I perform** I will I achieve	All cylinders of the identity formula should be working in synergy. Determine if the operating identity is a source of pride and of a meaningful purpose. Ensure alignment between person, group, and role identities.	Faithfully follow and apply ACT.	Make a positive difference and add value to others through the Five Meaningful strivings.
Put metrics in place to determine how successful you are in meeting your purpose and short-term goals. Track your progress.	**I achieve** I commit I perform	Clear and self-determined identities are capable of remaining self-aware, monitoring impact, and making the right adjustments in order to meet meanings through purpose and goals. Monitor alignment between person, group, and role identities.	Observe the degree to which you are applying ACT, and its impact. Test your commitment to ACT. Adjust and improve where required.	Assess to what degree you are adding value to others through the Five Meaningful strivings.

Goal	Leveraged Elements of the Congruence Model in Identity Formation	Role of Identity Formula in Identity Formation (I = P + Mo + Me)	Role of ACT in Identity Formation	Role of the Five Strivings in Identity Formation
Monitor, reflect on, and celebrate the emerging and established meaningful legacy. Your goal is to answer the following questions in the affirmative: Am I becoming the person I wish to be? Am I having a meaningful impact on the lives of others? Am I a model and a source of inspiration and hope for others?	**I am fulfilled** I become I commit I am	The identity formula is a self-regulating system that includes a feedback loop between the action one takes, the outside environment, and the meaning response from the environment. Use metrics to help you make the most of your teleological system! To self, in thankful humility, celebrate your ability to achieve successful outcomes through an identity that sustained alignment between what is meant, what is done, and what has been achieved.	Assess how ACT helped you succeed, and convey its value to others for their benefit.	Test your commitment to the Five Meaningful strivings. Adjust and improve where required. Assess how the five strivings helped you succeed, and convey its value to others for their benefit.

Chart 3 Identity Formation

Identity Development Chart

The following chart describes the goal and role of the Congruence Model for identity development, and explains how it relates and leverages the identity formula, ACT, and the five strivings. The elements that are highlighted in bold in the second column play the primary key role in support of the goal.

Goal	**Leveraged Elements of the Congruence Model**	**Role of Identity Formula (I = P + Mo + Me)**	**Role of ACT**	**Role of the Five Strivings**
Identity development strengthens a defined identity. It is an iterative process. Frequently monitor your knowledge, talents, limits, inclinations, motivations, strengths, weaknesses, and aspirations. The "I am good at" function asks, "Using all the elements of the Logoteleology	**I am good at** (All other elements as dependent variables)	Discern your capabilities in the following areas: ability to relate with others ability to get things done Continue to explore what is meaningful and meaningless to you, and why. Determine if what you consider meaningless is based on a false assumption that could obstruct your potential. For instance,	Determine the degree to which you have followed ACT in order to identify competence and attitude gaps and to plan your development.	Determine the degree to which you have followed the Five Meaningful strivings to identify competence and attitude gaps and to plan your development.

Chart 4 Identity Development

Goal	Leveraged Elements of the Congruence Model	Role of Identity Formula (I = P + Mo + Me)	Role of ACT	Role of the Five Strivings
Congruence Model, what is it that I need to believe, know, feel, and do in order to solve this problem, prevent it from happening again, and thrive?" Prioritize, sequence, and plan your development accordingly.		you might find math irrelevant and difficult, but it could be due to past poor teaching methods that were not aligned with your learning style. Continue to assess how you can make the most of and build on your strengths and talents		

Identity Reformation Chart

A brief explanation of each disturbance is introduced below as it applies to individuals.[276] As explained previously, the identity formula is included to help explain the discernible force and activity of each of the elements in the disturbance.

- A high case means the particular identity subsystem is active to very active.
- A low case means that the particular identity sub-system is moderately active to inactive.

Thus, (I = p + A + Me) denotes that a busy meaning set has content that is unable to motivate action; where I = Identity, p = inactive purpose, A = Amotivation, and Me = Active Meaning Set.

276 These disturbances have applications to groups and organizations, but their full explanation will be left to a future volume.

Meaning Disturbances

Disturbance	Definition	Symptoms	Description
Hyperlogo **I = p + A + Me**	Meaning inflation or an overactive meaning set.	constant confusion anxiety self-doubt anger cynicism inability to focus, discern, concentrate, and decide overwhelmed with information can be rational about her or his state, but unable to solve the dilemma feelings of incompetence helplessness feelings of being a fake	Energy remains at the meaning level (why) and is not able to motivate internal resources to come up with and implement a meaningful response (what). The individual is unable or unwilling to act and to resolve problems. The person thinks but does not act or action is weak and ineffective. Unwillingness to act can be due to a rebellious anger and cynicism that leads to amotivation. The situation creating the anger consumes mental energy in a negative way. The individual is unable to effectively apply ACT and the five strivings to the situation.

Chart 5 Identity Reformation for Meaning Disturbances

Disturbance	Definition	Symptoms	Description
Hypologo **I = p + A + me**	Meaning implosion or an underactive meaning set (e.g., existential vacuum).	amotivation low self-control and self-determination apathy feelings of helplessness depression can lead to substance abuse and other nihilistic tendencies.	As in hypologo the person with the hyperlogo disturbance can also experience feelings of helplessness. Different to hypologo the person with the hyperlogo disturbance is more aware of—and to a degree—tormented or disturbed by the inability to solve his or her dilemma. At some level the person showing symptoms of hyperlogo has some hope that a way out is possible, but she or he lacks what it takes to resolve it. Also, if and when there are actions, they are perceived as meaningless, fake, and unfitting.

Disturbance	Definition	Symptoms	Description
Hypologo (continued)			Energy is directed toward the self through internal dialogue (self-talk), usually in a negative, self-deprecating, and self-defeating fashion. Life has no meaning for the individual. For this nihilist action is futile. In terms of applied energy, it can be said that the individual does not spend much time thinking (why) or acting (what) on the meaningful. Thinking is ineffective and unable to trigger a positive response.

Disturbance	Definition	Symptoms	Description
Hypologo (continuted)			The person who suffers symptoms of hyperlogo believes there is or should be a solution yet not found; while the individual who displays hypologo symptoms sees no way out of his or her condition.

Purpose Disturbances

Disturbance	Definition	Symptoms	Description
Hypertelos **I = P + D + me**	An overactive and misdirected purpose system.	multitasking over-committing anxiety in constant movement taking on too much compulsive behavior; unable to control senseless routines and actions obsessed with accomplishing tasks quickly narcissisism high control needs overestimates self self-centered spends little time reflecting excessively competitive and ambitious	The meaning set's motivational energy is outward but driven, unbalanced, and misapplied (e.g., bull in the china shop). Colloquially it would be said the individual acts but does not think. The person is not aware of the meaning (why) behind his behaviors (what). Hypertelos includes Type-A and narcissist behavior. Symptoms can be the result of poor self-esteem and feelings of inadequacy. The individual could be operating from childhood directives where the emphasis is on the actions divorced from the meanings, such as do what I say and let me do the thinking; you are paid to do and follow, not to think; and don't question my decisions.

Disturbance	Definition	Symptoms	Description
Hypotelos **I = p + d + me**	An underactive, underperforming, and misdirected purpose system.	*Underactive* difficulty finding ways to channel meaningful aspirations unable to understand the hidden motives behind behaviors failing to commit to a cause or person poor follow-through lack of resolve *Underperforming*: lack of competence repeat mistakes problems prioritizing misplaced potential *Misdirected*: lack an overarching life purpose to implement meanings and guide behavior disconnect between person	The faulty meaning set can experience feelings of self-doubt. Energy in this case is driven by "have tos" rather than willed by a well-thought, meaningful aim. As in hypertelos, it is possible that the person is not aware of the meaning (why) behind his behaviors (what). While there is action and movement, energy is outward but weak, timid, and lacking focus. The individual could lack a clearly defined meaningful identity that would embolden the Will to act more forcefully.

Chart 6 Identity Reformation for Purpose Disturbaces

Disturbance	Definition	Symptoms	Description
Hypotelos[5] (continued)		identity and group identities Driven by habits, routines, and others versus self-directed intentions. The individual is on autopilot. cannot find relevancy and meaning in activities and situations invests energy on the familiar can lack a moral compass to influence decision making	Hypotelos is also symptomatic of a person who is active doing things of little interest or meaning. Energy can be described as driven, aloof, apathetic, slow, routine, and self-centered.

Afterword

Viktor Frankl stated that "the future of logotherapy is dependent on all logotherapists." Further he stated that he wished "that the cause of logotherapy be taken over and carried out by independent and inventive, innovative and creative spirits."[277] I would like to think I have made a humble effort to be such a creative spirit and contribute something significant toward existential psychology.

This book was written with four questions in mind:

- Who am I?
- What matters in life?
- Why am I here?
- How do I go about fulfilling my life purpose?

Relying on the best psychology I could find plus my own experience and contributions, I hope the reader will find solace in the proposed methods to answer these fundamental questions. As a pragmatist, my goal has been to help you increase your ability to experience what is meaningful in life and to avoid the futility of the meaningless.

Ultimately, you are the meaning you have given to your life. Logoteleology provides you with the tools to form, develop, and reform your identity.

277 Frankl, Viktor E., *The Will to Meaning*, 158.

I too hope the therapists and coaches who read this book will find the proposed tools enlightening.

The thesis of the book rests on the belief that *mankind does not suffer from a lack of answers. Rather, it suffers despite the answers being available.* I concluded on this thesis after taking Frankl's admonition that "Life ultimately means taking the responsibility to find the right answers to its problems and to fulfill the tasks which it constantly sets for each individual." I believe asking intelligent questions through a helpful concept such as logoteleology can be helpful. The task of life is to discover or invent meaningful solutions. You should now be better equipped to take on this task.

And pertaining to what matters in life? I hope to have impressed upon my audience that the five strivings (love, peace of mind, happiness, interest, and prosperity) are foundational to a meaningful life experience. The options—their antonyms—are unbearable. Such antonyms have a proven historical track record of being disastrous alternatives.

Logoteleology's answer to why we are here rests on the three pillars of success. We are here to succeed in our pursuit of the worthwhile or meaningful (the five strivings). And we create conditions for success when we allow, cooperate, and transcend when interacting with others. Alfred Adler stated, "The only individuals who can really meet and master the problems of life, however, are those that show in their strivings a tendency to enrich all others, who go ahead in such a way that others benefit also. All human judgments of value and success are founded, in the end, upon cooperation; this is the great commonplace of the human race."[278]

Related to fulfilling one's life purpose, I also have faith in the promising results of the Identity Model, the Logoteleology Congruence Model, and the PASCAS Method™, among others. It is my goal to continue researching and refining them to make a positive difference. These tools have so far shown promising and encouraging results. For instance,

278 Ansbacher, Heinz L. and Rowena R. Ansbacher. 1956. 255.

understanding what is an identity and how behavior develops and flows from meanings through motivation and purpose has had an empowering effect on people. It allows them to understand "what is happening" and to take conscious charge of meanings and eventual actions that yield meaningful results.

This book is the first of an anthology on logoteleology. Over time I will be returning to this original volume and make improvements based on learning and discovery. It is my desire to publish updated versions over time. Logoteleology has a meaningful agenda to fulfill. I look forward to working with those that have shown an interest in the theory and who are willingly committed to continue refining it in the service of others.

I also welcome questions, comments, and suggestions. I would particularly value learning from others' experiences as they use the tools and methods proposed here. In addition, for further information on logoteleology-related services, I can be reached at teleotherapy@aol.com.

Now that you have read *The Path to a Meaningful Purpose*, what is life asking of you?

Bibliography

Abbott, D. 2000. *Symbiosis.* http://www.ms-starship.com/sciencenew/symbiosis.htm.

Adler, Alfred. *What Life Could Mean to You.* Center City, MN: Hazeldn, 1998.

Adler, A. *What Life Should Mean to You.* CT: Martino, 2010.

Anda, R., et al. "Depressed Affect, Hopelessness, and the Risk of Ischemic Heart Disease in a Cohort of US Adults." *Epidemiology* 4 (1993).

Anderson, C. A., et al. "Behavioral and Characterological Attributional Styles as Predictors of Depression and Loneliness: Review, Refinement, and Test." *Journal of Personality and Social Psychology* 66 (1994): 549–58.

Ansbacher, Heinz L., and Rowena R. Ansbacher, Eds. *The Individual Psychology of Alfred Adler.* New York: Harper and Row, 1956.

Arnold, M. B. *Emotion and Personality* (Vols. 1 and 2). New York: Columbia University Press, 1960.

Arnold, M. B. "Perennial Problems in the Field of Emotion." *Feelings and Emotions.* New York: Academic Press (1970), 169–85.

Baard, Paul. "Intrinsic Need Satisfaction in Organizations: A Motivational Basis for Success in For-Profit and Not-For-Profit Settings." 2002.

Bains, G., et al. *Meaning Inc.* Glasgow: Profile Books, 2007.

Bandura, A. "Self-Referent Thought: A Developmental Analysis of Self-Efficacy." *Social Cognitive Development: Frontiers and Possible Futures.* Cambridge, UK: Cambridge University Press, 1981. 200–239.

Bankruptcy statistics. n.d. United States Courts. http://www.uscourts.gov/Statistics/BankruptcyStatistics.aspx.

Baumeister, Roy F. "Self-Regulation and Ego Threat: Motivated Cognition, Self-Deception, and Destructive Goal Setting." Gollwitzer, Peter M., and John A. Bargh, Eds. *The Psychology of Action: Linking Cognition and Motivation to Behavior.* New York: The Guilford Press, 1996. 30.

Baumeister, R., and M. R. Leary. "The Need to Belong: Desire for Interpersonal Attachments as a Fundamental Human Motivation." *Psychological Bulletin* 117 (1995): 479–529.

Blacksmith, N., and J. Harter. October 28, 2011. "Majority of American Workers Not Engaged in Their Jobs." http://www.gallup.com/poll/150383/majority-american-workers-not-engaged-jobs.aspx.

Bogdan, Radu J. *Grounds for Cognition: How Goal-Guided Behavior Shapes the Mind.* Hillsdale, NJ: Lawrence Erlbaum Associates, Inc. Publishers, 1994.

Bowlby, John. *Loss, Sadness, and Depression. Vol. III of Attachment and Loss.* London: Basic Books, 1980.

Brockner, J. "Managing the Effects of Layoffs on Survivors." *California Management Review* 34 no. 2 (1992): 9–28.

Burke, Peter J., and Jan E. Stets. *Identity Theory.* New York: Oxford University Press, 2009.

Carton, J. S., and S. Nowicki. "Antecedents of Individual Differences in Locus of Control of Reinforcement: A Critical Review." *Genetic, Social, and General Psychology Monographs* 120: (1994)31–81.

Causes of Divorce. December 21, 2009. http://www.divorceline.org/blog/causes-of-divorce/.

Cohen, I. S., Ed. "The G. Stanley Hall Lecture Series (Vol. 9, 39–73). Washington, DC: American Psychological Association.

Cohen, S., D. R. Sherrod, and M. S. Clark. "Social Skills and the Stress-

Protective Role of Social Support." *Journal of Personality and Social Psychology* 50 (1986): 963–973.

Robert Coles, ed., *The Eric Erikson Reader,* (New York: W. W. Norton Company, Inc., 2000)

Costa, P. T., and R. R. McCrae. "Influence of Extraversion and Neuroticism on Subjective Well-Being: Happy and Unhappy People." *Journal of Personality and Social Psychology* 38 (1980): 668–78.

Costello, Stephen J. "An Existential Analysis of Anxiety: Frankl, Kierkegaard, Voegelin." *Journal of Search for Meaning* 34, no. 2.

Davidson, R. J. "On Emotion, Mood, and Related Affective Constructs." Ekman, P., and R. J. Davidson, Eds., *The Nature of Emotion: Fundamental Questions.* New York: Oxford University Press, 1994. 51–55.

Davis, C. G., S. Nolen-Hoeksema, and J. Larsen. "Making Sense of Loss and Benefiting from the Experience: Two Construals of Meaning." *Journal of Personality and Social Psychology* 75 (1998): 561–74.

Deci, E. L., and R. M. Ryan. "The Support of Autonomy and the Control of Behavior." *Journal of Personality and Social Psychology* 53 (1987): 1024–37.

Deci, E. L., and R. M. Ryan. *Intrinsic Motivation and Self-Determination in Human Behavior.* New York: Plenum, 1985.

Deci, E. L., and R. M. Ryan, Eds. *Handbook of Self-Determination Research.* New York: The University of Rochester Press, 2002.

Depue, R. A., and P. F. Collins. "Neurobiology of the Structure of Personality: Dopamine Facilitation of Incentive Motivation and Extraversion." *Behavioral and Brain Sciences* 22 (1999): 491–569.

Diener, E., E. Sandvik, W. Pavot, and F. Fujita. "Extraversion and Subjective Well-Being in a US National Probability Sample." *Journal of Research in Personality* 26 (1998): 205–15.

Dweck, Carol S. *Self-Theories: Their Role in Motivation, Personality, and Development.* Philadelphia: Psychology Press, 2000.

Dykman, B. M. "Integrating Cognitive and Motivational Factors in Depression: Initial Tests of a Goal-Orientation Approach." *Journal of Personality and Social Psychology* 74 (1998): 139–58.

Ekman, P. "All Emotions Are Basic." Ekman, P., and R. J. Davidson, Eds. *The Nature of Emotion: Fundamental Questions.* New York: Oxford University Press, 1994. 15–19.

Elliot, A. J., and T. M. Trash. "Approach-Avoidance Motivation in Personality: Approach and Avoidance Temperament and Goals." *Journal of Personality and Social Psychology* 82 (2002): 804–18.

Erikson, E. *The Life Cycle Completed.* New York: W. W. Norton and Company, 1997.

Etzioni, A. "The Kennedy Experiment." *The Western Political Quarterly* 20 (1967): 361–80.

Feldman, D.B., and C.R. Snyder. "Hope and the Meaningful Life: Theoretical and Empirical Associations between Goal-Directed Thinking and Life Meaning." *Journal of Social and Clinical Psychology* 24, no. 3 (2005): 401–21.

Findley, M. J., and H. M. Cooper. "Locus of Control and Academic Achievement: A Literature Review." *Journal of Personality and Social Psychology* 44 (1983): 419–27.

Frankl, Viktor E. *The Will to Meaning: Foundations and Applications of Logotherapy.* New York: Meridian, 1998.

Frankl, V. E. *Man's Search for Ultimate Meaning.* New York, NY: Basic Books, 2000.

Frankl, Viktor, *Man's Search for Ultimate Meaning.* Boston: Beacon Press, 2006.

Frankl, Viktor. *Psychoanalysis and Existentialism.* New York: Pocket Books, 1967.

Frankl, Viktor E., *The Doctor and the Soul: From Psychotherapy to Logotherapy.* New York: Vintage Books, 1983.

Frankl, Viktor E., *The Unheard Cry for Meaning.* New York: Touchstone, 1978.

Frankl, Viktor E., *The Will to Meaning.* New York: Meridian, 1988.

Freasure-Smith, et al., "Gender, Depression, and One-Year Prognosis after Myocardial Infarction." *Psychosomatic Medicine* 61 (1999): 26–37.

Granit, Ragnar. *The Purposive Brain.* Cambridge, MA, and London, England: The MIT Press, 1981.

Gunnar, M. R. "Contingent Stimulation: A Review of Its Role in Early Development." Levine, S., and H. Ursin, Eds. *Coping and Health.* New York: Plenum, 1980. 101–19.

Heckhausen, H., *Motivation and Handeln.* New York: Springer-Verlag, 1980.

Hogg, Michael A., "Social Identity Theory." *Contemporary Social Psychological Theories.* Burke, P. J., Ed. Stanford: Stanford University Press, 2006. 111–36.

Hoholik, S. October 9, 2011. "Psychiatric Patients Overcrowd Hospitals." *The Columbus Dispatch.* http://www.dispatch.com/content/stories/local/2011/10/09/psychiatric-patients-overcrowd-hospitals.html.

Huckabay, Mary Ann, "An Overview of the Theory and Practice of Gestalt Group Process." Nevis, Edwin C., Ed. *Gestalt Therapy: Perspective and Applications.* New York: Gardner Press, Inc. 1992.

Inamori, Kazuo, *For People and for Profit.* Tokyo: Kodansha International Ltd, 1997.

Izard, C. E., "The Structure and Functions of Emotions: Implications for Cognition, Motivation, and Personality." *The G. Stanley Hall Lecture* Series (Vol. 9, 39–73). Washington, DC: American Psychological Association, 1989.

Izard, C. E., and C. Z. Malatesta, "Perspectives in Emotional Development: I. Differential Emotions Theory or Early Emotional Development." *Handbook of Infant Development* (2nd ed., 494–554). New York: Wiley-Interscience, 1987.

Izard, C. E., *The Psychology of Emotions.* New York: Plenum, 1991.

Izard, C. E., "Basic Emotions, Relations among Emotions, and Emotion-Cognition Relations." *Psychological Review* 99 (1992): 561–65.

Izard, C. E., "Four Systems for Emotion Activation: Cognitive and Noncognitive Development." *Psychological Review* 100 (1993): 68–90

Janis, Irving L., *Victims of Groupthink.* New York: Houghton Mifflin, 1972.

John F. Kennedy on May 25, 1961, before a Joint Session of Congress.

Jung, Carl. Summary. n.d. http://www.sonoma.edu/users/d/daniels/Jungsum.html.

Kasser, T., "Two Versions of the American Dream: Which Goals and Values Make for a High Quality of Life?" Diener, E., and D. Rahtz, Eds. *Advances in Quality of Life: Theory and Research.* Dordrecht, Netherlands: Kluwer, 2000.

Kasser, T., *The High Price of Materialism.* Cambridge, MA: MIT Press, 2002.

Kasser, Tim, "Sketches for a Self-Determination Theory of Values.", 2002

Khan, R., and N. M. Richhariya. n.d., "2010 Annual Global Corporate Default Study and Rating Transitions." http://www.standardandpoors.com. Retrieved from http://www.standardandpoors.com/ratings/articles/en/us/?assetID=1245302234237.

Koestner, Richard, and Gaëtan F. Losier, "Distinguishing Three Ways of Being Internally Motivated: A Closer Look at Introjection, Identification, and Intrinsic Motivation.", 2002.

Kresge, Elijah Everett, *Kant's Doctrine of Teleology.* Allentown, PA: The Francis Printing Company, 1914.

Lefcourt, H. M., *Locus of Control: Current Trends in Theory and Research.* Hillsdale, NJ: Erlbaum, 1982.

Lepore, S. J., "Social Conflict, Social Support, and Psychological Distress: Evidence of Cross-Domain Buffering Effects." *Journal of Personality and Social Psychology* 63 (1992): 857–67.

Lewin, Kurt, *A Dynamic Theory of Personality: Selected Papers.* Adams, D. E., and K. E. Zener, Trans. New York: McGraw Hill, 1935.

Lewin, K., "Action Research and Minority Problems." *Journal of Social Issues* 2, no. 4 (1946): 34–36.

Lubin, G. n.d. "Fifteen Mind-Blowing Facts about Wealth and Inequality in America." *Business Insider*. http://www.businessinsider.com/15-charts-about-wealth-and-inequality-in-america-2010-4.

Lucas, R. E., and F. Fujita, "Factors Influencing the Relation between Extraversion and Pleasant Affect." *Journal of Personality and Social Psychology* 79 (2000): 1039–56.

Maddux, J. E., and J. T. Gosselin, "Self-Efficacy." Leary, M. R., and J. P. Tangney, Eds. *Handbook of Self and Identity*. New York: Guilford, 2003.

Markus, H., and E. Wurf, "The Dynamic Self-Concept: A Social Psychological Perspective." *Annual Review of Psychology* 38 (1987): 299–337.

Mathers, Dale. *Meaning and Purpose in Analytical Psychology*. Philadelphia: Taylor and Francis Inc, 2001.

McAdams, D. P., "A Thematic Coding System for the Intimacy Motive." *Journal of Research in Personality* 14 (1980): 413–32.

Medin, Douglas L., and Brian H. Ross, *Cognitive Psychology*. Orlando, FL: Harcourt Brace and Company, 1997.

Medin, Douglas L., and Brian H. Ross, *Cognitive Psychology*. Fort Worth, TX: Harcourt Brace College Publishers, 1996.

Mental health statistics. n.d. http://www.mentalhealth.org.uk/help-information/mental-health-statistics/.

Mental Health Statistics: UK and Worldwide. n.d. http://www.mentalhealth.org.uk/help-information/mental-health-statistics/UK-worldwide/?view=Standard.

Miller, Frederic P., Agnes F. Vandome, and John McBrewster, Eds., *Four Causes*. Lexington, KY: Alphascript Publishing, 2009.

Miller, K. I., and P. R. Monge, "Participation, Satisfaction, and Productivity: A Meta-Analytic Review." *Academy of Management Journal* 29 (1986): 727–53.

Milller, P. C., et al., "Marital Locus of Control and Marital Problem Solving." *Journal of Personality and Social Psychology* 51 (1986): 161–69.

Mourkogiannis, Nikos, *Purpose: The Starting Point of Great Companies.* New York: Palgrave Macmillan, 2006.

Myers, D. G., *Social Psychology.* New York, NY: McGraw-Hill, 2005.

Nevis, Edwin C., Ed., *Gestalt Therapy.* New York: Gardner Press, 1992.

Novellino, Michele, "On Closer Analysis: Unconscious Communication in the Adult Ego State and a Revision of the Rules of Communication within the Framework of Transactional Psychoanalysis." New York: Grove Press, 2003.

Osgood, C. E., *An Alternative to War or Surrender.* Urbana, IL: University of Illinois Press, 1962.

Osgood, C. E., "GRIT: A Strategy for Survival in Mankind's Nuclear Age?" Paper Presented at the Pugwash Conference on New Directions in Disarmament, Racine, WI, 1980.

Park, C. L., and S. Folkman, "Meaning in the Context of Stress and Coping." *Review of General Psychology* 1 (1997): 115–44.

Pederson, N. C., et al., "Neuroticism, Extraversion, and Related Traits in Adult Twins Reared Apart and Reared Together." *Journal of Personality and Social Psychology* 55 (1988): 950–57.

Pierce, G. R., B. R. Sarason, and I. G. Sarason, "General and Relationship-Based Perceptions of Social Support: Are Two Constructs Better Than One?" *Journal of Personality and Social Psychology* 61 (1991): 1028–39.

Pierce, G. R., B. R. Sarason, and I. G. Sarason, Eds., *Handbook of Social Support and the Family.* New York: Plenum Press, 1996.

Purpose (n.d.). http://www.macmillandictionary.com/dictionary/american/purpose.

Reber, Arthur S., Rhianon Allen, and Emily S. Reber, *Penguin Dictionary of Psychology.* New York: Penguin Books, 2009.

Reeve, Johnmarshall. *Understanding Motivation and Emotion.* New Jersey: John Wiley and Sons, Inc., 2005.

Reeve, Johnmarshall. "Self-Determination Theory Applied to Educational Settings." *Handbook of Self-Determination Research.* Rochester: The University of Rochester Press, 2002.

Reis, H. T., and P. Franks, "The Role of Intimacy and Social Support in Health Outcomes: Two Processes Or One?" *Personal Relationships* 1 (1994): 185–97.

Rogers, Carl. *On Becoming a Person: A Therapist's View of Psychotherapy.* Boston: Houghton Mifflin Company, 1989.

Ruvolo, A., and H. Markus. "Possible Selves and Performance: The Power of Self-Relevant Imagery." *Social Cognition* 9 (1992): 95–124.

Ryan, Richard M., et al., "All Goals Are Not Created Equal: An Organistic Perspective of Goals and Regulation." *The Psychology of Action: Linking Cognition and Motivation to Behavior.* New York: The Guilford Press, 1996. 7–26.

Ryan, Richard M., et al., Eds., "Overview of Self-Determination Theory: An Organismic Dialectical Perspective." Ryan, Richard M., and Edward L. Deci, Eds. *Handbook of Self-Determination Research.* Rochester: The University of Rochester Press, 2002.

Ryan, R. M., "Psychological Needs and the Facilitation of Integrative Processes." *Journal of Personality* 63 (1995): 397–427.

Rychlack, Joseph F., *Logical Learning Theory: A Human Teleology and Its Empirical Support.* Lincoln: University of Nebraska Press, 1994.

Sarason, B. R., et al., "Perceived Social Support and Working Models of Self and Actual Others." *Journal of Personality and Social Psychology* 60 (1991): 273–87.

Schneewind, K. A.,"Impact of Family Processes on Control Beliefs." Bandura, A., Ed. *Self-Efficacy in Changing Societies.* New York: Cambridge University Press, 1995. 114–48.

Schultz, D.P., and S. E. Schultz, *A History of Modern Psychology.* Belmont, CA: Wadsworth, Cengage Learning, 2012.

Seligman, Martin E. P., *Flourish.* New York: Free Press, 2011.

Senge, Peter, et al., *Presence: Human Purpose and the Field of the Future.* New York: Currency, 2004.

Sills, Charlotte, and Helena Hargaden, Eds. *Ego States: Key Concepts in Transactional Analysis: Contemporary Views.* London, UK: Worth Publishing.

Sisodia, Rajendr S., David B. Wolfe, and Jagdish N. Sheth, *Firms of Endearment.* New Jersey: Wharton School Publishing, 2007.

Skinner, Ellen, and Kath Edge, "Self-Determination, Coping, and Development," *Handbook of Self-Determination Research.* New York: The University of Rochester Press, 2002.

Skinner, E. A., J. Zimmer-Gembeck, and J. P. Connell, "Individual Differences and Development of Perceived Control." *Monographs of the Society for Research in Child Development,* whole no. 204, 1998.

Stets, Jan E., and Peter J. Burke. Sociological Perspectives 38: 129–50. 1994. And "Inconsistent Self-Views in the Control Identity Model." *Social Science Research* 23: 236–62.

Steger, Michael F., and Joo Yeon Shin, "The Relevance of Meaning in Life Questionnaire to Therapeutic Practice: A Look at the Initial Evidence." The International Forum of Logotherapy: *Journal of Search for Meaning* 33, no. 2 (2010): 95–104.

Steiner, Claude, *Scripts People Live.* New York: Grover Press, 1974.

Stets, Jan E., and Peter J. Burke, "Identity Theory and Social Identity Theory." *Social Psychology Quarterly* 63 (2000): 224–37.

Suicide Awareness Voices and Education (n.d.). SAVE. http://www.save.org/.

Suomi, S. J., "Contingency, Perception, and Social Development." Sherrod, L. R., and M. E. Lamb, Eds. *Infant Social Cognition: Empirical and Theoretical Considerations.* Hillsdale, NJ: Erlbaum, 1980.

Swan, W. B., and S. J. Read, "Self-Verification Processes: How We Sustain Our Self-Conceptions." *Journal of Experimental Psychology* 17 (1981): 351–72.

Swan, W. B., and S. J. Read, "Acquiring Self-Knowledge: The Search for Feedback That Fits." *Journal of Personality and Social Psychology* 41 (1981): 1119–28.

Swann, W. B. Jr., "Self-Verification Theory." Van Lang, P., A. Kruglanski, and E. T. Higgins, Eds. *Handbook of Theories of Social Psychology.* London (2012): Sage, 23–42.

Tangney, J. P., R. F. Bauemeister, and A. L. Boone, "High Self-Control Predicts Good Adjustment, Less Pathology, Better Grades, and Interpersonal Success." *Journal of Personality* 72 (2004): 271–324.

Taylor, S. E., "Adjustment to Threatening Events: A Theory of Cognitive Adaptation." *American Psychologist* 38 (1983): 1161–73.

Tesser, A., L. Martin, and D. Cornell, "On the Substitutability of Self-Protective Mechanisms." *The Psychology of Action.* New York: Guilford Press, 1996. 51.

Thoits, Peggy A., "Multiple Identities and Psychological Well-Being: A Reformulation and Test of the Social Isolation Hypothesis." *American Sociological Review* 49: 174–87. Also: 1986. "Multiple dentities: Examining Gender and Marital Status Differences in Distress." *American Sociological Review* 51 (1983): 259–72.

"Top Ten Reasons For Divorce and Marriage Breakdowns: American Stats" (n.d.). http://www.top10stop.com/lifestyle/top-10-reasons-for-divorce-and-marriage-breakdowns-stats-from-the-us.

Vallerand, Robert J., and Catherine F. Ratelle, "Intrinsic and Extrinsic Motivation: A Hierarchical Model.", 2002.

Valliant, G. E., Report on Distress and Longevity. Paper presented to the American Psychiatric Association convention, 1997.

Watson D., and L. A. Clark, "Extraversion and Its Positive Emotional Core." *Handbook of Personality Psychology*. San Diego, CA: Academic Press, 1997. 767–93.

Whitney, M. October 2, 2009. "Exclusive: New Poll Shows Clear Majorities Distrust Big Corporations, Favor Unions." http://workinprogress.firedoglake.com/2009/10/02/exclusive-new-poll-shows-clear-majorities-distrust-big-corporations-favor-unions/.

Weir, Michael, *Goal-Directed Behavior.* New York: Gordon and Breach Science Publishers, 1984.

Zajonc, R. B. "Feeling and Thinking: Preferences Need No Inferences." *American Psychologist* 35 (1980): 159.

Zajonc, Robert B., "Social Facilitation." *Science* 149 (1965): 296–274.